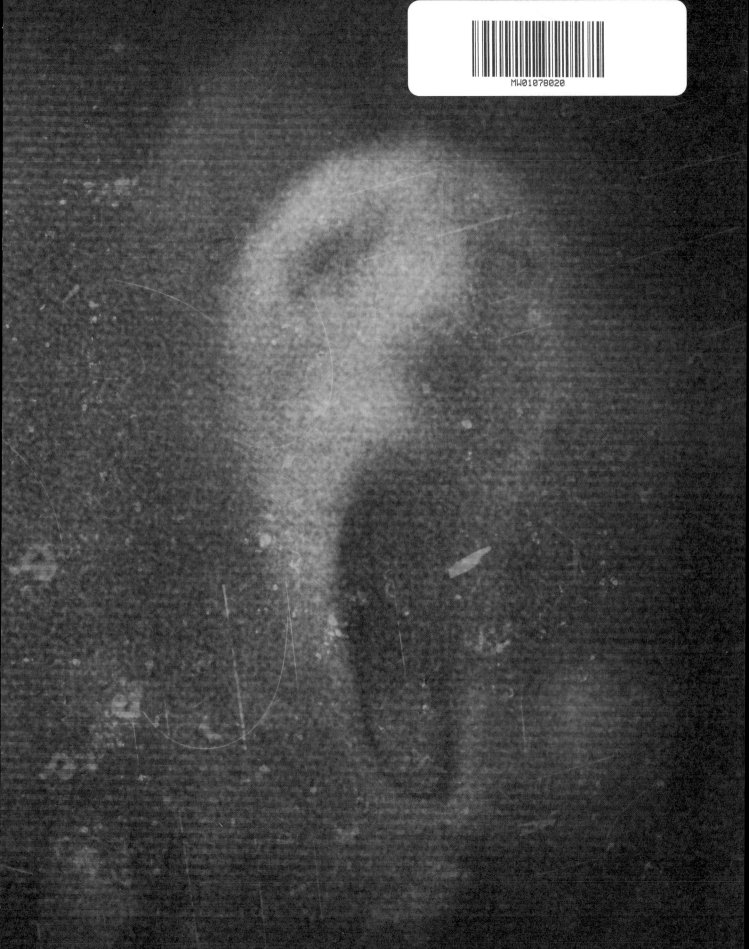

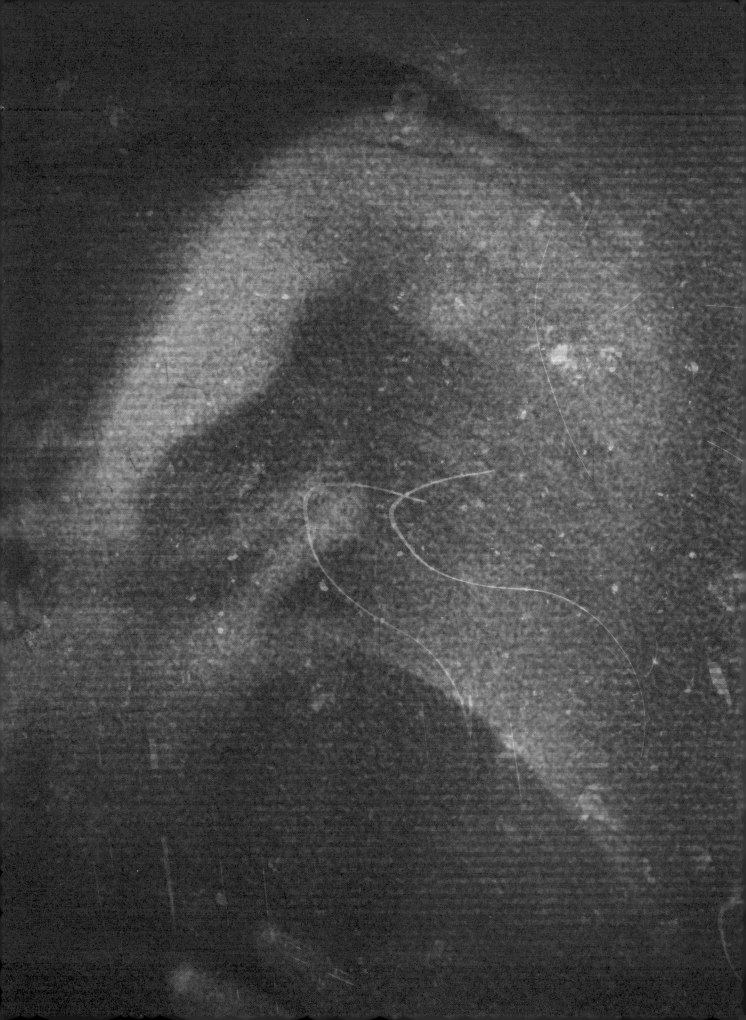

HORROR
UNMASKED

"The best horror films are adult fairy tales, no more, no less."

—Terence Fisher, veteran British horror director

The Ring (2002)

HORROR
UNMASKED

A HISTORY OF TERROR
FROM
NOSFERATU TO *NOPE*

BRAD WEISMANN

EPIC INK

First published in 2023 by Epic Ink,
an imprint of The Quarto Group,
142 West 36th Street, 4th Floor,
New York, NY 10018, USA
T (212) 779-4972 F (212) 779-6058
www.Quarto.com

Published by agreement with University Press of
Mississippi, 3825 Ridgewood Road, Jackson, MS 39211.
Website: www.upress.state.ms.us

Epic Ink titles are also available at discount for
retail, wholesale, promotional, and bulk purchase.
For details, contact the Special Sales Manager by
email at specialsales@quarto.com or by mail at The
Quarto Group, Attn: Special Sales Manager, 100
Cummings Center Suite 265D, Beverly, MA 01915 USA.

10 9 8 7 6 5 4 3 2 1

ISBN: 978-0-7603-7679-9

Library of Congress Cataloging-in-Publication Data

Names: Weismann, Brad, author.
Title: Horror unmasked : a history of terror from
    Nosferatu to Nope / Brad Weismann.
Description: New York, NY : Epic Ink, 2023. | Includes
    bibliographical references and index. | Summary:
    "Horror Unmasked offers a general introduction to
    the popular film genre, serves as a guidebook to its
    film highlights, and celebrates its practitioners,
    trends, and stories"—Provided by publisher.
Identifiers: LCCN 2022060119 (print) | LCCN
    2022060120 (ebook) | ISBN 9780760376799
    (hardcover) | ISBN 9780760376805 (ebook)
Subjects: LCSH: Horror films—History and criticism.
    | LCGFT: Film criticism.
Classification: LCC PN1995.9.H6 W419 2023 (print)
    | LCC PN1995.9.H6 (ebook) | DDC 791.43/6164—
    dc23/eng/20230120
LC record available at https://lccn.loc.gov/2022060119
LC ebook record available at https://lccn.loc.gov/
    2022060120

Group Publisher: Rage Kindelsperger
Creative Director: Laura Drew
Managing Editor: Cara Donaldson
Editor: Katie McGuire
Cover Design: Laura Drew
Interior Design: Brad Norr Design

Printed in China

To Bonnie,
who ain't 'fraid of no ghost.

It Came from
Outer Space
(1953)

CONTENTS

Nosferatu (1922)

WORLD MAP

**PSYCHO
(USA)**

**HALLOWEEN
(USA)**

**GET OUT
(USA)**

**CANDYMAN
(USA)**

**DRACULA
(1958)
(UK)**

**EL VAMPIRO
(MEXICO)**

**SANTO
CONTRA
LOS ZOMBIES
(MEXICO)**

This map highlights just a small sampling of the world's best known, most loved, and impactful horror films. There are far too many incredible films to cover here, so please read on for many more titles to add to your watch list.

# of HORROR

THE CABINET OF DR. CALIGARI (GERMANY)

GODZILLA (JAPAN)

NOSFERATU (GERMANY)

THE HOST (SOUTH KOREA)

RINGU (JAPAN)

BLACK SUNDAY (ITALY)

DUST DEVIL (NAMIBIA)

THE BABADOOK (AUSTRALIA)

INTRODUCTION

Horror film is bigger than ever. It's both wildly popular and critically esteemed. It is universal; it leaps over cultural barriers.

We need to be scared. We need to test ourselves; to blanch, scream, and clutch. We need to get through the fear and come out on the other side, blinking, but still in one piece.

Horror is rebellion. Horror is subversion. It questions our most casual and fundamental assumptions. It asserts that there is no safe hiding place. Using fear as a focal point, it bends reality into a misshapen but illuminating mass.

Horror is a universal guilty pleasure. As an experiment over the past year, at every social occasion and public interaction, I decided to bring up horror movies, casually, as quickly as I could, in conversations. In every situation, it took only a moment for people's eyes to light up as they began debating horror-film favorites and giving me recommendations. It's in moviegoers' blood.

When I was very young, I found myself curled up on the basement floor in front of the TV every Saturday night watching *Creature Features*. This was the local incarnation of *Shock Theater*—the legendary syndicated package of fifty-two classic (and not-so-classic) horror films that my generation grew up on. My favorite reading material? Forrest J. Ackerman's lovingly garish monthly magazine *Famous Monsters of Filmland*.

Later on, horror films helped me squirm closer to my dates in darkened theaters. When I reached what I laughingly refer to as adulthood, my interest in horror films, like that in comic books, model airplanes, and tetherball, waned.

But, to my surprise, as I continued to age I found that my steady diet of grown-up culture stalled. I yearned for simpler, more visceral thrills. And, wouldn't you know, the horror films, comics, and fanzines our parents despised and forced us to smuggle like forbidden Soviet *samizdat* were now deemed high art themselves, and the formerly suspect delights of fright flicks drew me back.

My working definition of horror is pretty straightforward. For me, it's anything that deals with our darker impulses—whether fear, hate, dread, despair, bloodlust, or evil. Underneath our civilized veneers, there are howling, terrified animals that, under the right circumstances, can feel as though they're in the grip of something that is going to kill them. And eat them. The live-or-die thrill that results is the adrenaline rush the horror junkie is after.

The ancient mythoi of all cultures contain horrors. Fairy and folk tales in all countries bear horrific elements—Celtic, Norse, Arabian, and the sometimes brutal collectings of the Grimm brothers and their like. Even the fabulist Hans Christian Andersen, translated precisely, dishes up some grim and bloody stories.

All the archetypes are there at the beginning of mankind's cultural history: visions of the man-made monster, the vengeful ghost, the unworldly predator, the insatiable killer, the persistent undead, the evil twin, the shape-shifting seducer. These creatures are embodiments of the dangers that lurk outside the borders of everyday experience. They are aberrations, manifestations of evil, the punishment of the gods.

Horror has two essential elements—it deals with factors outside "normal" experience (within us and/or outside of us), and it is threatening. This makes horror a kind of perverse anti-faith. THERE'S SOMETHING THERE, AND IT'S AFTER US! Take away the supernatural element and you have the crime film, the thriller, the dark psychological drama. Take away the malevolent element, and you have the fantasy film.

The best horror films want to rip off the tops of our heads and make us peer within at the suppressed impulses we harbor. They want us to contemplate a universe in which death, decay, and corruption have a role. The horror genre, despite limitations and clichés, allows us to say things about life we think or believe and that we rarely articulate: that innocence is doomed, that retribution is sure, that death is nigh. Sometimes we need to inundate ourselves with the abnormal in order to reconceive what constitutes normality. Through horror, we can safely ponder chaos and dissolution. Through it, we integrate our darknesses into ourselves. We need the catharsis.

In that horror film tells us that everything is not perfect, it is an enemy of repressive societies, political tyrants, and bourgeois authorities. Consequently, it is frequently censored and/or banned. But societies need horror films, too. Through them, together we can look at the monsters and ghosts that populate our collective consciousness. Different eras and cultures produce horror cinema that is unique

Best Movies for Those New to Horror

Looking to begin your journey into horror history? Start with the classics, work your way through "best-of" lists, and familiarize yourself with the many subgenres out there!

These five are a good place to start:

Dracula (1931)

Frankenstein (1931)

The Wolf Man (1941)

Invasion of the Body Snatchers (1956)

Psycho (1960)

Forrest J. Ackerman, magazine editor and sci-fi/horror expert, poses in his "Son of Ackermansion" in Los Angeles, CA, in 1995.

LEFT: An issue of *Famous Monsters of Filmland.*

and appropriate to their psychic needs. This text examines the major facets of this ongoing worldwide phenomenon.

Sometimes horror films offer us redemption, and sometimes the gate clangs shut at the end, trapping us in madness and doom. We challenge ourselves with horror films, lost in the dark for a time. Through them we face the unfaceable and live through it, blinking, happy, and alive again, outside the theater.

OPPOSITE: Bela Lugosi in *Dracula* (1931).

SHADOWY SILENCE

HORROR BEFORE SOUND

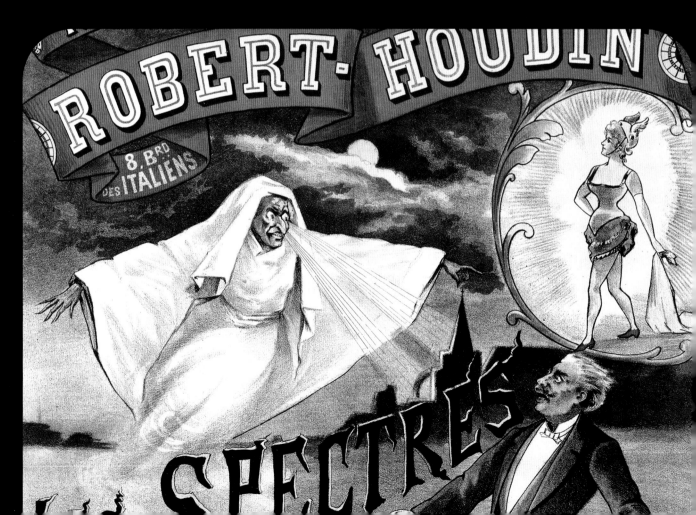

F ilm is a spectral medium. It casts moving shadows that tell stories, and someone from the pre-film era might mistake a movie for a convention of ghosts.

The first film with identifiable "horror" content was Georges Melies's *The Haunted Castle*, aka *The House of the Devil*, made in 1896. Melies was the first great director, progressing from stage magician to cinematic wizard with classic efforts such as *A Trip to the Moon* (1902). *The Haunted Castle* is typical of the shorts of the time. It uses a stage-bound, single-camera setup that features a lot of stop-motion trickery. A bat turns into Mephistopheles, who torments two gentlemen in period garb. There are witches, a skeleton, and pokes in the behind with a pitchfork from a dwarfish henchman. The Devil is eventually repelled by a wielded crucifix.

A careful examination of the development of silent horror film, such as that essayed by Roy Kinnard,[1] reveals that the feature horror film was built component by component. Of the 1,100-plus silent horror films he lists as made between 1896 and 1929, the majority are shorts. (And most of them are lost films, including gems such as 1915's *A Cry in the Night*, which features "a winged gorilla under the control of a mad scientist." This screams for a remake, does it not?)

Nearly every horror theme and twist of plot is prefigured in these one-reel, seven- to eight-minute experiments of early filmmakers. Here are the seeds of feature-length horror subjects to come—murder, madness, curses, black magic, vampires, ghosts, mummies, werewolves, monsters, giant insects, demons, telepathy, time travel, waxworks, chambers of horrors, and even the perils of hypnosis and mind control (George du Maurier's 1894 novel *Trilby*, featuring the evil mesmerist Svengali, was a bestseller, and was adapted many times for film).

Until 1912, most movies were being made in Europe, with France, England, Germany, Italy, and Denmark leading the way. In 1905, groundbreaking woman filmmaker Alice

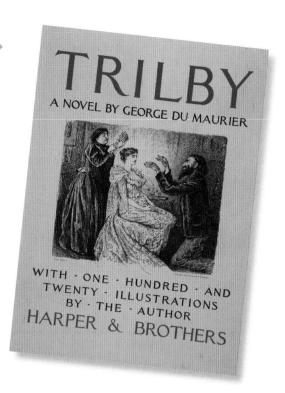

Poster advertisement for George Du Maurier's novel *Trilby*.

Guy-Blaché directed the first *Hunchback* film adaptation, the short *Esmerelda*, in France. By 1908, the first *Dr. Jekyll* adaptation, sixteen minutes in length, was released. Other shorts retailed mayhem. In *The Doll's Revenge* (1907), an angry toy grows large, then dismembers and eats its tormentor, while *In the Bogie Man's Cave* (1908) features cannibalism.

Émile Cohl, the father of the film cartoon, made the first animated horror film, a short titled *Le cauchemar de Fantoche* (*The Puppet's Nightmare*), in 1908. American fantasy and horror film of the day, when not cadging from European sources, adapted the spooky work of American writers such as Edgar Allan Poe (*The Pit and the Pendulum*, 1913), Washington Irving (*Rip van Winkle*, 1903), and Nathaniel Hawthorne (*The House of the Seven Gables*, 1910; *Feathertop*, 1912).

By 1910, the first film had been made in Hollywood (D. W. Griffith's *In Old California*), just as the first *Frankenstein* film, fourteen minutes long, came to life in the Edison Studios back in New York. "INSTEAD OF A PERFECT HUMAN BEING THE EVIL IN FRANKENSTEIN'S MIND CREATES A MONSTER," proclaims one of the movie's intertitles. The film is largely stage-

OPPOSITE: Poster for 1896's *The Haunted Castle*, aka *The House of the Devil*.

Cecil B. DeMille (hand on hip) directing one of his early motion pictures, ca. 1920. He directed the first film adaptation of *The Ghost Breaker* in 1914.

bound, but there are a few good tricks in it, including showing the creation of the monster through the simple but effective technique of making a wax dummy of the creature, burning it, and then running the film backward. The Monster is defeated by being sucked into a mirror—a foreshadowing of the mystic use of mirrors in future films by the directors of macabre moments such as Jean Cocteau and Wes Craven.

Around 1912, film technique became confident industrywide in the United States. Early Hollywood film studios organized themselves. The production process streamlined itself, and an efficient web composed of studio-sponsored and independent film-distribution companies grew and spanned the country. Moving picture houses opened up everywhere. Film lengths grew, and productions became more ambitious and complex. Twenty-five years of trial and error resulted in a film industry that produced a steady stream of viable full-length narratives. The studio era had begun.

Many of film's future Golden Age directors—Maurice Tourneur, Cecil B. DeMille, Michael Curtiz, F. W. Murnau, Kenji Mizoguchi, and Ernst Lubitsch—got their start grinding out horror films. In fact, among the eight films Tourneur made in 1913, his first year as a director, one was *Le systeme du docteur Goudron et du professeur Plume* (*Dr. Goudron's System*), a horror short based on Poe's story "The System of Doctor Tarr and Professor Fether," the original "lunatics take over the asylum" tale. (Tourneur's director son, Jacques, would have a major impact on the horror film thirty years later.) The popular German serial *Homunculus* (1916), directed by Otto Rippert and written by Robert Reinert, centered on the story of the world's first test-tube baby, who grows up to find he is immensely powerful but soulless, and swears revenge on humanity—a prototype of the supervillain if there ever was one.

The Golem: How He Came into the World (1920) poster.

The Germans triumphed at horror first. Paul Wegener, the first horror-film star, was a six-foot-six-inch tall, thick-bodied man with a rough-cut,

high-cheekboned, almost Mongolian face, and intense, expressive eyes. After playing the lead in his first film, the devilish doppelganger story *The Student of Prague*, filmed on location in 1913 (and credited as the first true independent film), he became entranced with the legend of the Golem.

In the Golem legend, the chief rabbi of Prague crafts a superman of clay which he brings to life using Kabbalistic magic. Wegener wrote, directed, and starred as the Golem on film three times over the course of six years, with the final version, released in 1920 and cowritten by Henrik Galeen

DER GOLEM
Das Lichtspiel
der gebildeten Welt
wird
infolge des enormen Erfolges
und der
nicht zu bewältigenden Nachfrage
in den

Kurfürsten-
damm 26   **U.T**   Friedrich-Ecke
Taubenstr.
LICHTSPIELEN
weitere 7 Tage
vorgeführt
Ausserdem findet die Vorführung in den
U.T
Weinbergsweg 16-17 und Moritzplatz statt.

and codirected by Carl Boese, being the one remembered today. A blend of fable, fantasy, and social commentary, *The Golem: How He Came into the World* gives us a Frankenstein prototype—a slow, shuffling hulk of a monster, arms askew, a morally neutral force that can be bent to the will of its master. The Golem saves a scoffing Holy Roman Emperor and his court, and wins the Jews of Prague reprieve from being driven out of the city. Then the rabbi's assistant uses the Golem to attack his romantic rival and kidnap his beloved. But the monster stands over the captive girl, lustfully running his hand down her body. He fights off the assistant with a torch and sets the city ablaze, running amok. Only a child, unafraid and curious, is capable of getting close enough to him to accidentally remove the magic amulet that animates him, turning him to clay again.

Wegener would go on to play evil characters in films such as Richard Oswald's *Figures of the Night* (1920), Rex Ingram's *The Magician* (1926), Gennaro Righelli's *Svengali* (1927), and his collaborator Galeen's *Alraune* (1928), and he would finally spoof his horror-icon status in his first sound film, Oswald's 1932 *Eerie Tales*. (Galeen, no horror slouch himself, wrote the

scripts for the first three screen versions of *The Student of Prague*, Murnau's *Nosferatu* in 1922, and Leni's *Waxworks* in 1924. He then directed the definitive version of *The Student of Prague* himself in 1926. It featured Conrad Veidt as the cursed student, in the role originated by Wegener.)

Golem, filmed in an epic style at the base of crowded, convoluted urban sets, bears all the hallmarks of the fright-inducing Expressionist style. That style had been cemented onscreen five months earlier than *Golem* when director Robert Wiene used the toolkit of Expressionism

Paul Wegener as the Golem in a scene from *The Golem: How He Came into the World* (1920).

Cesare (Conrad Veidt) kidnaps Jane (Lil Dagover) in *The Cabinet of Dr. Caligari* (1920).

to illuminate the disturbing content of *The Cabinet of Dr. Caligari* (1920). This no-budget masterpiece of a nightmare features a sinister, insane hypnotist and his murderous sleepwalking slave, Cesare (Conrad Veidt). The movie attacks authority and questions reality, but what makes it memorable is its stark, disorienting style and the grotesque, puppet-like acting of its principals.

Expressionism was an artistic symptom of the trauma World War I brought to Europe. A stylized, severe, and serious aesthetic, it emphasized abstractions and angles, an attempt to express off-kilter and intense emotional content rather than balanced, symmetric, mundane realism. *Caligari* production supervisor Rudolf Meinert enlisted artists Hermann Warm, Walter Reimann, and Walter Röhrig to create a completely artificial and exaggerated set design for *Caligari*. They painted all the settings in flat perspective on the canvas, including bolts of light and shadow. Everything, even outdoor scenes, was shot inside cramped studio confines. The result was a claustrophobic style that was to permeate not only the horror film, but would percolate into film noir as well. The style is nightmarish, a physical embodiment of the madness overtaking the characters externalized, an artistic effort that's a sustained attack on the senses and is just

(from left to right) Werner Krauss, Conrad Veidt, and Lil Dagover in a scene from *The Cabinet of Dr. Caligari* (1920).

as disturbing as the story it tells. The result? The first great horror film.

Many persistent traits of the horror film are already present here; science is a form of magic, and in *Caligari* we have a mad scientist of operatic proportions. His suspect specialty is mesmerism. He's a despised and resentful outcast from official society, part con man and part conjurer. He weaponizes his unnatural powers for evil purposes; his somnambulist subject is by turns a serial killer, a zombie, a robot, a child. The creator/monster dynamic is in full bloom here. The creature acts out the impulses that the mastermind dictates.

As in many horror movies to come, the female lead in *Caligari* is present only as a passive, feeling victim. Her innate femininity keeps Cesare from killing her; he takes pity on her, drops his phallic knife, and kidnaps her instead. Failing even in that, Cesare collapses, a puppet with severed strings. It remains only to expose Caligari's secret identity—he's the director of the local insane asylum!

The screenplay was written by pacifists Hans Janowitz and Carl Mayer, whose World War I experiences left them with a profound distrust of authority. *Caligari* can be read as a pointed attack on the dangers of unquestioning obedience. Fritz Lang (*Metropolis*) was originally slated to direct before backing out at the last moment. Prior to his departure, Lang modified a framing story already present in the script, implementing the now-familiar "it-was-all-a-dream" twist that neuters the film's anti-authoritarian thrust. (This trick is found as long ago as 1910 at the end of prolific Danish director August Blom's *Dr. Jekyll and Mr. Hyde*.)

Director Wiene created a horror trilogy of sorts with his *Raskolnikow* (based on Dostoyevsky's *Crime and Punishment*) in 1923 and *The Hands of Orlac* the following year, about a pianist who loses his hands and is given new ones that belonged to a killer. Wiene's production design grew more naturalistic with each film. It's instructive to see that he didn't need scenic affectation to make his films frightening. Horror

requires an almost musical sense of editing, a firm grip on the rhythm of tension, shock, and release. That rhythm is already present in Wiene's films.

Richard Oswald is an overlooked but important early horror director, prolific if pedestrian. He made the first vampire feature film, *A Night of Horror*, in 1917, as well as *The Picture of Dorian Gray*; *Eerie Tales*, one of the earliest horror anthology films, co-starring *Caligari*'s Conrad Veidt and the bizarre avant-garde dancer Anita Berber, in 1919; the perverse *Figures of the Night*, with *Golem* star Wegener, in 1920; and another *Eerie Tales* in 1932, again starring Wegener, another horror anthology film, but done with tongue firmly in cheek.

After *Golem* and *Caligari*, European movie horror took off. Not yet a despised genre, horror film wasn't just a means to an end—it was treated as a legitimate art form, or as an element to be integrated into a larger film work. For example, Swedish actor/director Victor Sjöström's *The Phantom Carriage* (1921) is not a horror film, but a redemptive drama that contains terrifying supernatural elements.

It's a variant of the *Christmas Carol* template. In it, a callous drunkard rides in Death's coach at midnight on New Year's Eve and faces up to the consequences of his wicked past. The gritty, deeply felt material is evoked by the outstanding camerawork. The film's extensive special effects were excruciatingly difficult to execute at the time. The gloomy and reflective tone of the film, containing a quiet horror of the soul, would be transmitted through future Scandinavian directors such as Carl Theodor Dreyer and Ingmar Bergman.

Danish director Benjamin Christensen's *Häxan: Witchcraft through the Ages* (1922) was intended to be a documentary about the mistaken persecution of witches in the Middle Ages. However, it rapidly morphs into a devil's march of terrifying, transgressive fantasy sequences that illustrate the period's conceptions of witchcraft. Lit with deep black shadows and highlights like the paintings of Caravaggio, Christensen's striking compositions illustrate dark rites, perversions, and gore to a degree unequaled until decades later. It was banned in the US for many years; finally, it was released in trippy 1968 with a new narration track recited by outlaw poet William S. Burroughs.

Other unique examples of silent horror include the remarkable *A Page of Madness*, an avant-garde, intertitle-less Japanese 1926 feature by Teinosuke Kinugasa, written by Nobelist Yasunari Kawabata and others, about a man who works as a janitor in an insane asylum to be close to his mentally ill wife. In France, Jean Epstein's *The Fall of the House of Usher* (1928) deviates in important ways from Poe's original story, but it's still unnerving, using slow-motion, multiple exposures, and model work to evoke an atmosphere of dread. It's more surrealist fantasy than horror tale, and bears the marks of Epstein's assistant and cowriter Luis Buñuel, about to make his shocking avant-garde masterpiece *Un Chien Andalou* a year later.

Three key German films made over the course of four years—*Destiny* (1921), *Nosferatu* (1922), and *Waxworks* (1924)—by three great German

A poster for Fritz Lang's *M* (1931).

directors (Fritz Lang, F.W. Murnau, and Paul Leni) also shaped the horror film for decades to come. Each one touches on death, sin, evil, monsters, madness, and the cruelties of fate. Each featured strong, painstakingly developed visual worlds. This is unsurprising when these directors' visual backgrounds are examined: Lang was a trained architect, Murnau an art historian, and Leni himself an artist.

Although Lang was not a horror director per se (his first sound film, *M*, 1931, tracks down a serial killer of children), his focus on the worlds of crime and fantasy led to complex, effects-rich adventure-film serials such as *The Spiders* (1919–20) and *Dr. Mabuse the Gambler* (1922), the latter concerning a supervillain. Lang was inspired by Louis Feuillade's serial-film adaptation of *Fantômas* (1913), another crime saga from the pulp adventure series of the same name by Marcel Allain and Pierre Souvestre. Lang's successes with these serials pointed to the virtue of tackling dark material, and helped spread the Expressionist aesthetic in film.

Lang captured the exotic on film with ease, his painterly background gave him an uncanny sense of composition and framing. Elaborate, unified stage productions, pioneered by Vienna theatrical impresario Max Reinhardt (1873–1943) and devoted to the Wagnerian ideal of *Gesamtkunstwerk* (stagings that were a complete synthesis of all available artistic resources), gave Lang and others a viable approach to make fantasy look convincing on film. Expressionism's triumph of subjectivity in art, combined with this dedication to creating coherent and detailed imaginary worlds, meant that films could become a kind of dream enactment. Lang put together complex, convincing narratives that proved film could carry mythic weight.

Lang's *Der müde Tod* ("Weary Death," or *Destiny*, as it was titled in the US) inspired both Hitchcock and Bunuel to become film directors. *Destiny* is the 1921 story of a woman who demands her lover back from Death, leading to three inset stories, each of which illustrates the futility of fighting fate. The subject is tragic romance, but the architecture of the film creates a template for horror anthologies to come. Its magical, cutting-edge special effects also inspired Douglas Fairbanks Sr. to copy them when he made *The Thief of Bagdad* (1924) with director Raoul Walsh. Fairbanks also bought the American distribution rights to *Destiny* and held it out of the American market for three years, until after *Thief* opened.[2]

Paul Leni was a stage designer for Reinhardt, and his command of settings and framing were also far ahead of his contemporaries. His *Waxworks*, also containing inset stories, was firmly in the Expressionist style but displayed a bit of whimsy as well. *Waxworks* starred Emil Jannings, Conrad Veidt, Werner Krauss (the original Caligari), and future Oscar-winning director William (then Wilhelm) Dieterle.

One thing a lot of the German horror efforts of the period have in common is actor Conrad Veidt. The willowy, anguished Romantic persona he embodied was put to great use in his many roles as a horror protagonist. Beginning as the murderous zombie Cesare in *Caligari*, he moved on to larger roles in *The Hands of Orlac* and *Waxworks*, as well as the 1926 doppelganger drama *The Student of Prague*. In the last, Henrik Galeen's Faustian story features a man who gets everything he wants but whose double climbs out of his mirror and commits crimes in his name. The film features *Golem* star Paul Wegener as the Devil's agent, and Veidt in the role Wegener originated in 1913.

In Leni's *The Man Who Laughs* (1928), adapted from the 1869 Victor Hugo novel, Veidt plays Gwynplaine, an orphan whose horribly mutilated face is shaped in a perpetual grin. (His makeup would become the template for the look of the iconic Joker in the *Batman* comics in their 1939 debut.) Veidt was forced out of Germany by his opposition to the Nazis, and is best

remembered as a Hollywood screen villain, the definitive evil wizard Jaffar in Alexander Korda's 1940 *Thief of Bagdad* and the despicable Major Strasser in *Casablanca*, released four months before his death in 1943 at the age of fifty.

Moving to America, for MGM Leni made *The Cat and the Canary* (1927), derived from a 1922 Broadway play. This film is one of the first in the "old dark house" genre, in which people gather at a mansion, usually in regard to the reading of a will, and are subsequently murdered, threatened,

Max Schreck as Count Orlok in a promotional image for *Nosferatu* (1922).

INSET: Promotional art for *Nosferatu* (1922), created for a German magazine by artist Albin Grau.

Most Valuable Monster

Dracula is by far the most popular horror character in film, with more than 170 appearances to date. (Of all literary characters, only Sherlock Holmes appears more often.) Of all the actors to portray the bloodthirsty Count, Christopher Lee holds the record for longest tenure with 10 appearances. In comparison, Robert Englund played Freddy Krueger in the *A Nightmare on Elm Street* series eight times, and storied Kane Hodder played Jason Voorhees in the *Friday the 13th* movies only four times.

Taste the Blood of Dracula (1970) poster.

or driven mad. Leni continued to score with macabre work such as *The Man Who Laughs* and *The Last Warning* (both in 1928). Leni died of blood poisoning on September 2, 1929, at the relatively young age of forty-four.

F. W. Murnau, perhaps the best silent-era director, also studied with Reinhardt and took his lessons completely to heart. He crammed every frame with beauty and signifiers that enrich the action, coupled with an instinct for keeping the story moving. This resulted in the memorable *Nosferatu: A Symphony of Horror* in 1922. This film was suppressed for years due to the fact that it blatantly plagiarized Stoker's *Dracula*, which resulted in legal action by Stoker's widow.

Nosferatu uses a panoply of special effects: pixilation, inverted negatives, superimposition, and a symbolic language of objects and settings that adds viewing layers to the experience. Most of the future vampire-film clichés are here, among them the frightened villagers in archaic costume, Gothic atmosphere, and death by sunlight.

The centerpiece of the film is the eerie yet commanding performance of actor Max Schreck as the grotesque, bald, scalloped-eared, rat-toothed gremlin of a vampire, Count Orlok. (*Schreck* means "fright" in German.) His wide-

Max Schreck as Count Orlok, being destroyed by sunlight, in *Nosferatu* (1922).

eyed imperturbability is a marked contrast to the panicked mortals he confounds. The restored print—replete with original intertitles, a decent translation of same, and proper color tinting of the scenes—is a fresh and powerful statement. Unlike *Caligari*, which never breaks the feeling of a dream, *Nosferatu* begins with the mundane and scales up to the realm of the fantastic.

Here, the female lead Ellen (Greta Schröder) is a classic Romantic heroine: wan, winsome, melancholy, empathic, and passive. She saves her husband, and humanity itself, by actively luring and succumbing to the vampire long enough for the cock to crow—and if that isn't symbolism, I don't know what is.

(Iconoclastic filmmaker Werner Herzog remade the *Nosferatu* as *Nosferatu the Vampyre* in 1979, using the intensely strange actor Klaus

Kinski as a vampire, now properly named Dracula, using much the same makeup approach as Schreck.)

Before relocating to America, Murnau made an adaptation of Goethe's *Faust* (1926), which remains definitive. From the compressed, tormented perspectives of the sets to the sweeping, subjective flying shots concocted from miniatures, smoke, and in-camera effects, it seems that everything Murnau could conceive of visually could be manifested on film. *Faust*'s epic story of temptation and redemption featured top-notch performances by Gösta Ekman as Faust and Emil Jannings as Mephisto, his tempter. (Later, Jannings and other film figures, including Werner Krauss, Lil Dagover, and *M* screenwriter Thea von Harbou, would star in their own real-life horror stories when they collaborated with the Nazis.)

Leni, Murnau, and other European horror directors were lured to hungry Hollywood in the 1920s, in talent sweeps the American studios made in Europe during the decade. (Lang would later flee the Nazis, joining a second wave of European film-industry emigrants to Hollywood in and after 1932.)

Meanwhile, the craft of animation, so important to the future of horror films, was in the process of evolving. In San Francisco, cartoonist, boxer, and sculptor Willis H. O'Brien began to

===== 🐾 =====

Top Ten Horror Films of the 1920s

The Cabinet of Dr. Caligari (1920)

The Golem: How He Came into the World (1920)

Destiny (1921)

Häxan: Witchcraft through the Ages (1922)

Nosferatu: A Symphony of Horror (1922)

The Hunchback of Notre Dame (1923)

Waxworks (1924)

The Phantom of the Opera (1925)

The Cat and the Canary (1927)

The Unknown (1927)

=====

develop stop-motion creature animation in such shorts as *The Dinosaur and The Missing Link: A Prehistoric Tragedy* (1915) and *The Ghost of Slumber Mountain* (1918). He gained renown after his work was seen in the feature-film adaptation of H. G. Wells's *The Lost World* (1925). That success would lead to O'Brien's chance to realize King Kong eight years later for its creators, Merian C. Cooper and Ernest Schoedsack.

For decades to come, until the development of computer-generated animation, the creation of monsters and the staging of fantasies in American film would rest on O'Brien's groundbreaking work.

As movies exploded in popularity, the theatrical stigma of working in "the flickers" waned. The 1920 adaptation of *Dr. Jekyll and Mr. Hyde*, directed by John S. Robertson, featured Broadway star John Barrymore, whose transformative performance enlivens an otherwise unremarkable film. (Barrymore was playing Richard III at night and filming *Hyde* during the day, which led him to a nervous breakdown that closed the Shakespeare production early.)

The screenplay derives from the 1887 stage adaptation made for Richard Mansfield—the same production that made Mansfield a suspect in the Jack the Ripper killings in England. That stage adaptation, the very first, added a "good girl/bad girl" dichotomy to the storyline, in the interest of adding a romantic subplot. Instead, to Robert Louis Stevenson's discomfort, it redefined Jekyll's problem as one of sexual frustration, which is how all succeeding movie adaptations would play it.

When up-and-comer Leonidas Frank "Lon" Chaney, a versatile character actor and master of makeup, assumed star status with his roles in Universal Studios' big-budget fare such as *The Hunchback of Notre Dame* (1923) and *The Phantom of the Opera* (1925), it became clear that horror was a genre with potential and permanence. Chaney, teamed with rogue director Tod Browning, would push the horror film into new, ever-darker places.

BROWNING AND CHANEY

THE FATHER OF *FREAKS* AND THE MAN OF A THOUSAND FACES

The careers of director Tod Browning and actor Lon Chaney Sr. cross each other at right angles, like intersecting, perpendicular lines on a graph. One died young and famous, the other lingered long in self-imposed obscurity. One epitomizes expressive grace, the other is still regarded half-hesitantly as an unhinged midwife of aberrations. Together, they created powerful films of horror and suspense.

Much has been made of silent-film great Chaney's childhood in Colorado Springs, Colorado, as the son of deaf parents as a factor in the sharpening of his pantomimic skills. However, a careful examination of his early stage career shows him, surprisingly, to have initially worked as a song-and-dance man and comedian. He was not a tall man, nor a hulking one, but he was strong and limber, with a broad and strong-featured, mobile face. The tragic onstage suicide attempt of his mentally disturbed then-wife, Cleva Creighton, at the Majestic Theater in Los Angeles on April 30, 1913, sped him from life on

Lon Chaney Sr., ca. 1925.

the boards to Hollywood, where his adept work with makeup kept him busy in exotic bit roles until his breakthrough in George Loane Tucker's *The Miracle Man* in 1919.

In *Miracle Man*, Chaney plays The Frog, a contortionist who is part of a gang of con men who seek to cash in on a genuine spiritual healer's successes. Nothing remains of that film but a pair of three-minute snippets, one of which showcases Chaney's remarkable transformation. From a prone and twisted shape in the dust, he snaps his limbs back into place in theatrical spasms, enthralling the onlooking crowd until he rises, seemingly whole and cured.

Seven films later, Chaney was given his second big break. He played the legless and vengeful arch-criminal Blizzard in Wallace Worsley's *The Penalty* (1920), a role that taxed him emotionally and physically. The performance put the seal on his popular appeal; it was after this appearance that he began to be dubbed "The Man of a Thousand Faces."

Hollywood's star system had only been inaugurated a decade before, but film actors were already typed, many playing the same kind of familiar audience-tested and -approved roles that guaranteed ticket sales, over and over again. Chaney's versatility was motivated by practicality—the more roles he could play, the more frequently he could work.

Chaney's popularity was not due solely to his disguise gimmicks. Although he approached

OPPOSITE:
Lon Chaney Sr. in *The Hunchback of Notre Dame* (1923).

Director Tod Browning, ca. 1932.

Lon Chaney Sr. in *London After Midnight* (1927).

INSET: *London After Midnight* (1927) poster.

his screen appearances technically, via makeup and prostheses, Chaney could also be termed a prototype of the "Method actor." Chaney studied real-life models for his subjects surreptitiously, picking up their mannerisms and attitudes. "It was not merely the applying of grease paint and putty noses to the face but mental makeup as well. Grotesqueries as such do not attract me; it is vivid characterizations for which I strive," he wrote in 1927.[1]

Chaney wielded a strong intelligence, intense commitment, and an eloquent athleticism. His strong, plain features communicated meaning clearly, and he used his entire body in front of the camera, just as an athlete would. A good exercise for the viewer is to focus exclusively on his hands in films such as *Oliver Twist* (1922) or *The Phantom of the Opera* (1925); in these movies, his hands are constantly at work, reinforcing his characterizations.

The bulk of Chaney's film work can be classified either as crime dramas or melodramas. Chaney's screen persona is often that of a criminal or other antiheroic "sinner" whose goodness is confirmed at film's end by an act of redemptive sacrifice (*The Penalty, He Who Gets Slapped*). Chaney biographer Michael Blake rightly terms that persona "a grotesque character who is eventually destroyed by love."[2] (These strident morality tales of the "avenging conscience" were as close as the movies of the time could get to psychological realism.)

Chaney plays double roles in *A Blind Bargain*

(in this lost 1922 film, he played both the screen's first mad scientist and his hunchbacked, half-ape assistant), *The Blackbird*, and *London After Midnight*. He even murders himself in split screen in *Outside the Law*. These patterns would define most of his screen vehicles, films crafted around his transformative abilities. Director Browning "claimed that when he was working on a story for Chaney, he conceived the character first and the plot would follow," wrote Blake.[3]

If horror was, at least in part, about transformation, then Chaney was the genre's great original chameleon. He fit the archetype of the Player—the man who is everyone and no one, a perception Chaney reinforced by remaining aloof from the press. His cinematic shapeshifting was powerful and disturbing, and naturally pushed him toward portrayals of the uncanny.

This led to his casting as the tormented, deformed bell-ringer Quasimodo in the period extravaganza *The Hunchback of Notre Dame* in 1923. This immensely expensive production was green-lit by the ambitious Universal movie executive and "boy wonder" Irving Thalberg, who approved the budget while studio head Carl Laemmle was out of town. Wallace Worsley directed the adaptation. It's in the early Hollywood Grand Style, featuring Chaney's pathos-laden performance as a deformed bell-ringer in the Middle Ages in love with a Roma girl, as well as an immense standing set that would appear in other Universal movies for decades. The shoot employed 750 crewmen, occupied nineteen acres of studio ground, took six months (including two months of night shoots), and employed somewhere between 2,000 and 3,500 extras. Instead of a megaphone, for the first time ever a Western Electric Public Address Apparatus System was used.

Hunchback is not really a horror film. Chaney's Quasimodo is deformed but not evil; he is a hero trapped in a monster's body. Chaney's brilliance lies in his ability to project his character's inner sensibilities through the layers of makeup, prostheses, and appliances—a capacity for sympathetic portrayal that grounds all his characters and makes them compellingly watchable, no matter how hideous or depraved they may seem to be on the outside.

The blazing financial success of the *Hunchback* gamble set the stage for Universal Studios' longtime association with the horror genre. For actors, finding pathos in the portrayal of monsters and villains onscreen would prove to be the key to success for much of the rest of horror-film history. Classic-era stars of

The Phantom of the Opera (1925) poster.

the genre, such as Boris Karloff and Vincent Price, would nearly always find a humanizing element beneath their characters' grotesque actions, making them far more affecting than the extroverted, happy-go-lucky heroes of the adventure and romance films of the period—say, the Fairbankses, Powers, and Flynns.

In *The Phantom of the Opera* (1925), Chaney dares himself to be even more alienating. It's another big-budget affair, incorporating a reconstruction of the interior of the Paris Opera House, another mammoth set that ended up standing for ninety years. Rupert Julian's film is an elaborate adaptation of Gaston Leroux's 1910 novel about a shadowy, masked figure living beneath the Paris Opera who becomes a mentor to, and tormentor of, a young soprano.

As the mad, sadistic, corpse-faced Erik, Chaney distills his torment through his eyes alone—an accomplishment rivaled only by Conrad Veidt in *The Man Who Laughs*, made three years later. Chaney blackened his eye sockets and nostrils, pulled his nose up with wire, and distended his mouth with false teeth. The result is a gruesomely skeletal

Lon Chaney Sr. in *The Phantom of The Opera* (1925).

Phantom's sumptuous "jewel" prestige production values included seventeen minutes of primitive color footage. Time and again, remakes attempted to duplicate the original's grandeur and appeal, with little success. However, Broadway beckoned. The original film might still only be a curio if not for Andrew Lloyd Webber's immensely successful 1986 stage musical version.

After *Phantom*, Chaney moved to MGM, where he would reunite with a director he had worked with twice before, pleasantly—Tod Browning.

look that frightened a whole generation of film-going children. His shocking unmasking scene, built up to carefully, is justifiably legendary.

Phantom bears all the hallmarks of the classic horror stories. The villain/monster is romantic and brooding, mysterious and powerful, malign yet tragic. "Feast your eyes—glut your soul on my accursed ugliness!" he exclaims via title card. He inhabits a lair—an uncanny, gloomy, and hauntingly beautiful world within and underneath our own. His schemes are elaborate. (In the film, it is explained that he is criminally insane, an escapee from Devil's Island and a "master of Black Art." And hey, he sleeps in a coffin. Big clue there.) And he is capable of love, obsessively but touchingly.

Personal Best

Lon Chaney, Sr.

The Penalty (1920)

The Hunchback of Notre Dame (1923)

The Phantom of the Opera (1925)

The Unknown (1927)

West of Zanzibar (1928)

Browning was developing his reputation. A boy who literally ran away with the circus, Browning found himself in the film business in 1913, appearing in approximately fifty movies before being sidelined for two years in 1915, due to a crippling car accident that killed one of his passengers and maimed another. (Periodic descents into alcohol would pepper Browning's career.) When he returned to work, he did so as a director.

Browning was obsessed with the freakish. He often portrayed the world of the con artist, the sideshow performer, and other marginal members of society. He worked with themes of mutilation, missing or non-functioning limbs, and sexual dysfunction.

Browning was also an early advocate of "rational" lighting, that is, using identifiable light sources in the scene instead of just a uniform wash of illumination. This made his footage dimmer and more mysterious, akin to the Expressionist style brought over from Germany. He could dream up and execute the kind of nightmares Chaney was born to embody.

Browning and Chaney wound up making ten films together.

Their key achievement was the outlandish but compelling *The Unknown,* in 1927. Costarring with twenty-two-year-old Joan Crawford, Chaney plays a criminal distinguished by a double thumb, a man on the lam who disguises himself as an armless freak, starring as a knife-thrower in a traveling Roma circus in Spain. His partner in his act is the circus owner's young and beautiful daughter (Crawford). He loves Crawford's character, but is unable to reveal himself. She, in turn, has been a victim of incessant sexual harassment and has a phobia of being touched by men. (Yes, you read that correctly.) As he seemingly has no arms, "you are the one man I can come to without fear," she tells him.

Unable to reveal his incriminating secret, Chaney finally has his arms amputated in order to be with her. When he recovers, he returns to find that she has overcome her phobia and is engaged to the circus strongman. In anguish, Chaney plans vengeance. Of course, it involves

a plan to rip the strongman's arms by the roots. Chaney/Browning films often sported such grotesque symmetries in their plots.

Somehow, Browning and Chaney pull off this absurd plot convincingly. Browning could film the most extravagant imaginings in a very straightforward, matter-of-fact way—almost as if John Ford were tasked with filming a script by David Lynch. Chaney's acting is at its most intense here, but he never loses his link with real feeling. His profound, palpable anguish explodes off the screen.

The streak continued. *London After Midnight* (1927) was the highest-grossing film Chaney and Browning made together. Chaney's shark-toothed Man in the Beaver Hat looks terrifying. The film, unfortunately lost, can only be examined via Rick Schmidlin's meticulous 2002 partial reconstruction that uses production stills from the shoot; the character's rapid, prowling stoop in the film reportedly gave Groucho Marx

Bela Lugosi as the titular character in *Dracula* (1931).

the inspiration for his own distinctive stride. (Browning remade it, ineffectively, in 1935 as *Mark of the Vampire*.)

In *West of Zanzibar* (1928), Chaney is Phroso, a crippled, cuckolded magician who takes the only child of his unfaithful, dead wife and his enemy and raises her in a brothel for revenge—only to find out she's his own child. It's the most disturbing of the Chaney/Browning collaborations after *The Unknown*. Their last collaboration, *Where East Is East* (1929), features Chaney killing his ex-wife with a trained gorilla. (And who wouldn't?)

Among all the silent-film stars, only Chaplin waited longer than Chaney to go into sound. When Chaney made a talkie in 1930, he chose to remake his and Browning's successful 1925 feature *The Unholy Three* (though Jack Conway, not Browning, directed). As ventriloquist and conman Professor Echo, Chaney got to use five different voices in the film, a bravura performance that seemed to assure that he would profitably make the transition to sound. Ironically, during filming he was so ill he could sometimes barely speak. Chaney and Browning had begun preliminary work together on a sound version of *Dracula* when Chaney succumbed

to throat cancer on August 26, 1930. Browning proceeded with the project, filming *Dracula* with Bela Lugosi in 1931.

The first of the mainstream American horror booms commenced with *Dracula*, as did the status of the tragic figure of Lugosi. (Some horror critics claim that the Spanish version, filmed at the same time, at night on the same sets, is superior.) The Count is the opposite of one of Chaney's pathetic monsters; to the contrary, he is a commanding, pitiless figure. As it turned out, unrepentant villains could be interesting as well.

Reports indicate that, despondent at not being able to work with Chaney as he had planned, Browning left most of the day-to-day duties on the *Dracula* set to his cinematographer, Karl Freund. Freund was a recent émigré who was steeped in Germany's gloomy, angular Expressionism, and had served as director of photography on Wegener's *The Golem*, Lang's *Metropolis*, and Murnau's *The Last Laugh*, and would go on to direct the horror landmarks *The Mummy* (1932) and *Mad Love* (1935). (In a final, grand departure from his norm, Freund served as the cinematographer for the classic TV comedy *I Love Lucy*.)

The results are stylistically disjointed. The camera is agile in scenes without dialogue, but stodgy and stage-bound when a microphone is present. Despite this drawback, Lugosi's creepy intensity carries the film. *Dracula* was a hit, and it gave Browning the chance to make his dream project.

Browning had been working on the *Freaks* film project for five years before he finally got the green light in 1932. In it, a gold-digging trapeze artist exploits a circus midget, cynically marrying him for his money while carrying on with the circus strongman. The plot is discovered, incurring the wrath of the little man's

Director Tod Browning (top) with some of the cast of *Freaks* (1932).

sideshow "family." It's not long before the freaks come squirming after her and the strongman in a driving rainstorm, a sequence that forms the harrowing climax of the picture.

Browning's circus past permeated his cinematic sensibilities. The filmmaker posits that society's outcasts and mutations are not the real freaks, and that it's the "normal" world that harbors the deadliest monsters. It's still a subversive idea, and one accentuated here with disturbing details. Browning hired a clutch of actual circus freaks to play themselves, and the camera lingers voyeuristically on the faces of the deformed and disabled performers, even as it insists on their humanity. Browning seemed obsessed with indicting the audience, pointing fingers at its complicity in iconizing, isolating, and ostracizing outward variance from the norm.

It was far beyond anything that was on film to date. At a deeper level, Browning was far ahead of his time in thinking about "body horror"— the instinctive, abdominal repulsion that the sight of physical abnormality triggers, the shock and shame that physical difference brings out in both the beholder and the beheld. In this, he and Chaney were on the same wavelength. Browning's insistence that the mutated represent a kind of pure-hearted, ideal society of the scorned is still haunting.

Browning's repellent masterpiece destroyed his career. One woman at a preview screening of the original ninety-minute cut of the film

threatened to sue MGM, claiming it caused her to suffer a miscarriage. The film, even in its radically truncated sixty-four-minute version, the only one that survives today, is still a direct assault on the senses and the sensibilities. Vilified, Browning made only four more films, two of them in the horror genre—*Mark of the Vampire* (1935) and *The Devil-Doll* (1936)—though neither of them is absorbing. By 1939, Hollywood was done with him. He had twenty-three more years left to live.

Freaks lived on in special, forbidden showings. Exploitation director, producer, and distributor Dwain Esper dragged prints of the film around the back roads of America, presenting it as *Forbidden Love* or *Nature's Mistakes*, sometimes pairing it with a "stag film" (early nudist or pornographic footage), or with Esper's own painfully bad horror film, and the first "exploitation" film, 1934's *Maniac*, aka *Sex Maniac*. The reconsideration of *Freaks* came via midnight screenings in the 1960s. By 1994, it had been added to the National Film Registry.

Freaks is still hard to take. Oddly, though, its attempt to take the moral high ground distinguishes it from its exploitation-film descendants.

With the beginning of the effective enforcement of Hollywood's Production Code in 1934, the window onto transgressive images and ideas in mainstream American film slammed shut. It would take the box-office bounce of *Psycho* twenty-six years later to unleash such defiant transgressions again.

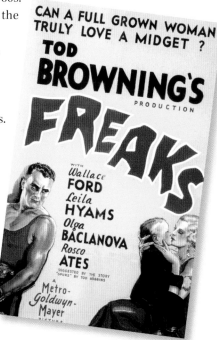

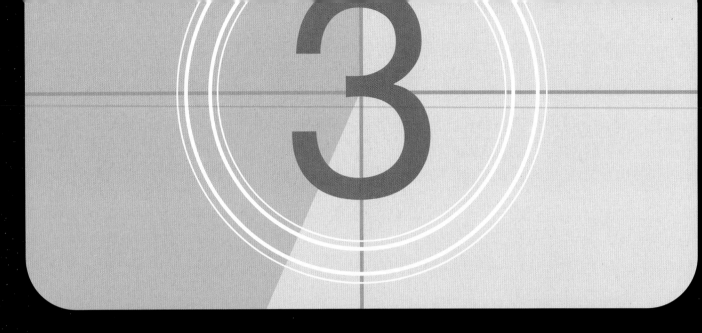

MONSTER CENTRAL

THE GREAT HORROR CYCLES BEGIN

Carl Laemmle, president of Universal, and his son, Carl Laemmle Jr., general manager, in 1931.

Once upon a time (1884, to be exact), a nice little man named Carl Laemmle (pronounced LEM-lee) came over from the Old Country (Germany, in this case) to America. In 1906, he opened a movie theater in Chicago. He branched out. He founded a cozy little Hollywood film studio, Universal, in 1914. Carl loved nothing more than making movies, creating imaginary worlds that audiences could sit in the dark and climb into—for a price.

Universal rapidly became one big happy German-American family. At one time, Uncle Carl had more than seventy relatives on the studio payroll.

And Carl loved his son Junior very much, so much so that he made him the studio's head of production. He had a problem: he kept letting Junior spend more on big-budget films than they made back. For a while, every once in a while, though, the studio hit paydirt—especially with horror films.

Beginning with *The Hunchback of Notre Dame* in 1923, Universal became known as the home of horror, just as the Warner brothers seemed to produce most of the gangster films, and MGM handled the bulk of family-friendly fare. Universal's horror lineup was so popular that it spawned a genre full of sequels and spinoffs. Even after Carl and Junior were forced out of the studio in 1936 by creditors, the film factory kept cranking out stories about monsters, ghosts, and ghouls (after an unprofitable three-year moratorium by the new Universal execs).

This was the Golden Age of horror: characters including Dracula, Frankenstein, the Invisible Man, the Mummy, and the Wolf Man were all born at Universal, in glorious silver and gray tones. Certain dependable genre directors helmed a healthy part of the output— James Whale, Karl Freund, and the Ernest B. Schoedsack and/or Merian C. Cooper efforts were the best known. There were others, such as the versatile future Oscar-winner Michael Curtiz (*Doctor X*, 1932), and pros like Victor Halperin, who churned out horror (*White Zombie*, 1932;

Supernatural, 1933; *Revolt of the Zombies*, 1936; *Torture Ship*, 1939) even though he despised the genre. It wasn't a genre ruled by auteurs but by archetypes, and these resonated so strongly that they persist to this day.

With the exceptions of the Wolf Man and the Creature from the Black Lagoon, all of the "Universal monsters" were crafted in the short span of four years, between 1931 and 1935. These were the worst years of the Great Depression, when people needed cheap, distracting thrills— in other words, imaginary frights to take their minds off very real, everyday ones. It helped, too, that for most of this period, up until July 1, 1934, when Hollywood started self-enforcing the censorships of the Motion Picture Code, the subject matter and the imagery in American film were largely unrestrained—bolder than they would be again for twenty-six years.

Every beast had a backstory. Frankenstein's Monster was an abandoned child; the Mummy suffered for forbidden love; mad doctors such as Jekyll were led astray in a quest to improve man's lot; Larry Talbot became the Wolf Man simply by being in the wrong place at the wrong time, the ultimate unlucky bystander. (Only Dracula seemed unperturbed by his lot; significantly, he spawned the fewest sequels.)

Five actors—Bela Lugosi, Boris Karloff, Peter Lorre, Lionel Atwill, and Dwight Frye—would create an indelible sextet of characterizations— the Vampire, the Monster, the Mummy, the Killer,

OPPOSITE: The marquee of the Old Rialto Theater on Broadway, New York City, ca. 1940. The Rialto is showing a horror double bill of Tod Browning's *Dracula* and James Whale's *Frankenstein* (both 1931).

the Mad Doctor, and the Lunatic, respectively —on film.

Bela Lugosi became, fatally and forever, enslaved to his most memorable role, Count Dracula. Lugosi, a classically trained stage actor from Hungary, made his name in America with his portrayal of the bloodthirsty noble on Broadway in 1927. (His nemesis, Doctor Van Helsing, was played by Edward Van Sloan, who essayed similar roles in films such as *Frankenstein*, *The Mummy*, and *Dracula's Daughter*.)

Dracula, the film, was adapted from the 1927 Broadway adaptation of Bram Stoker's novel. (Interestingly, the playwright, actor, and director Hamilton Deane, a friend of Stoker's, wrote the stage version as a vehicle for himself; its profitability led Deane to commission Peggy Webling to adapt *Frankenstein* for the stage almost immediately; it was this stage version that was the source for James Whale's 1931 *Frankenstein* film.)

Dracula concerns the undead Transylvanian count who seeks fresh blood in England, chiefly by feeding on vulnerable young maidens. Lugosi's undeniable charisma made him a natural in

the part; his Dracula is a suave, slick European noble, cutting in on the girlfriends of his enemies, casually preying on his social inferiors, taking his bloody, symbolic droit de seigneur (the right of first intercourse with a bride) from the peasant class—an act of exploitation simultaneously sexual and classist.

Lugosi is often faulted by critics for refusing to shed his thick Hungarian accent. However, he does quite well with complex dialogue in films such as the early Charlie Chan vehicle *The Black Camel* (1931), and as the rare hero in the serial

RIGHT: Bela Lugosi as Count Dracula in *Dracula* (1931).

INSET: *Dracula* (1931) poster.

The Return of Chandu (1934). But Hollywood had one idea about what Lugosi was good for and refused to let it go, oft sticking him in a sequence of increasingly embarrassing horror vehicles.

Meanwhile, Lugosi turned out a number of strong performances in a short span of time. For example, he's the sinister Dr. Mirakle in Robert Florey's *Murders in the Rue Morgue* (1932). The doctor is a scientist interested in genetics . . . well, he wants a woman and a murderous ape to make a baby together. Based on Poe's stories, this feature was so bloodthirsty that, even though it was made in the pre-Code era, a quarter of it was removed before release.

Lugosi is also Haitian voodoo master "Murder" Legendre in Victor Halperin's *White Zombie* (1932), who enslaves souls to work for him on a sugar cane plantation. Lugosi then essayed the small but key role of the bestial Sayer of the Law in Erle C. Kenton's *Island of Lost Souls* (also 1932) and stood out as the tormented hero of Edgar Ulmer's *The Black Cat* (1934).

Boris Karloff's turn in the spotlight was next. An appealing and sensitive player from England who reached Hollywood by way of a traveling repertory theatre in Canada, he knew, as did Chaney, that the key to making a monstrous character connect with the viewer was to use pathos. Shelley's original Frankenstein's Monster is quite a different critter—eloquent, philosophical, melancholy, and prone to brooding on barren mountaintops. Karloff's Monster is mute and must express himself through pantomime.

Personal Best

Bela Lugosi

Dracula (1931)

Murders in the Rue Morgue (1932)

White Zombie (1932)

The Black Cat (1934)

Son of Frankenstein (1939)

White Zombie
(1932) lobby card.

Karloff made the most of the opportunity. "The Monster was inarticulate, helpless, and tragic . . . how could one not feel sympathy for such a creature?" Karloff stated.[1] He cannily played up the Monster's vulnerability. From the moment in the film when the Monster holds his hands up to the light that filters down into his imprisonment, when he supplicates fumblingly, he becomes someone we can all identify with: the uncertain, awkward, unwittingly destructive, uncomprehendingly despised child.

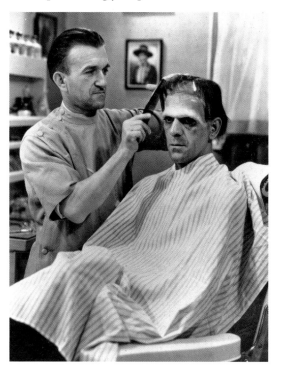

Makeup artist Jack P. Pierce (left) applies makeup and combs the hair of Boris Karloff for Karloff's role as the monster in *Frankenstein* (1931).

Director James Whale, ca. 1934.

It didn't hurt that master makeup artist Jack Pierce was on the job at Universal. His brilliant efforts took time and were grueling to the actors being altered, but he created several iconic monster "looks," beginning with Frankenstein and including the Mummy and the Wolf Man.

Frankenstein turned out to be so resonant, so indelible, that it's difficult to look at with fresh eyes. But it celebrates a very different, darker kind of life, one that fuses dead bodies and live wires. Whale celebrates the bizarre, bathes us in it. All the normative characters in the film, who serve as sounding boards and plot advancers, are terribly, horribly boring. Would you rather hang out with lip-chewing, furrow-browed fiancée Elizabeth, or Fritz the hunchback (Dwight Frye)? One has a much bigger stock of interesting stories, undoubtedly.

Colin Clive's Dr. Frankenstein is a nervous wreck, intoxicated with the possibility of creating life but fearing damnation as well. Later film Frankensteins would be more commanding (Peter Cushing, for one), but Clive is both literally

Elsa Lanchester (left) and Boris Karloff in *Bride of Frankenstein* (1935).

and figuratively overshadowed in Frankenstein by Karloff.

This *Frankenstein* exists in a hybrid world—modern amenities exist side by side with Old World trappings, establishing a kind of proto-steampunk vibe that hangs over the entire series. Kenneth Strickfaden's flashing, sputtering electrical laboratory props for the creation scene became iconic in themselves (they were dusted off and fired up for Mel Brooks's 1974 parody *Young Frankenstein*). More essential but less often cited is Charles D. Hall's forbidding Gothic art

Claude Rains in
The Invisible Man
(1933).

direction. This harum-scarum juxtaposition of old and new would become a hallmark of the monster movie.

Director Whale was on a roll. He next tackled the comedy-horror film, making an "old dark house" film titled, appropriately, *The Old Dark House* (1932), very much in the mold of silent hits such as *The Ghost Breaker* (1914) and *The Cat and the Canary*.

The Invisible Man (1933) is Whale's most amusing and pointed horror film. In it, scientist Jack Griffin experiments on himself, and his see-through formula unexpectedly drives him to antisocial madness. His mad, arrogant genius stands in sharp contrast to the ignorant, horrified attitudes of the lumpenproletariat villagers amongst whom he finds himself stranded. The suggestion is that Griffin's contempt for humanity is entirely justified.

The film made a star out of actor Claude Rains, even though he isn't visible until the film's last minute. (The role of the Invisible Man was never really owned by a particular actor, and the character wound up cheapening into a special-effects gimmick faster than any of the others.) Horror-film regulars such as Rains, Basil Rathbone, and Cedric Hardwicke, all of whom were stage-trained with extensive classical experience, could easily take on the high-flown dialogue and Gothic rigors of the horror genre, but were in essence brilliant generalists.

At the time, *The Invisible Man* was the special-effects equivalent of a moon shot, pulled off thanks to the efforts of visual specialists John P.

Fulton, John J. Mescall, and Frank A. Williams. In the pre-digital era, this meant wrapping the lead actor in black velvet and shooting him against a black background, among other uncomfortable and painstaking procedures. As technologies advanced, so did the ability to create more effective-looking horror on film.

Bride of Frankenstein (1935) is Whale's masterpiece and his last horror film—his ultimate commentary on love, loyalty, and familial relations, all twisted grotesquely out of proportion. Its grimly comic tone and exuberant performances elevate it above its predecessor.

Dr. Frankenstein is forced to tinker with the dead again, blackmailed by his mentor, Dr. Praetorius (the wonderfully bitchy Ernest Thesiger). Praetorius finds the Monster, who survived his immolation in a windmill in the first film, and plans to build him a mate. "To a new world of gods and monsters!" Praetorius exclaims as he toasts his fatal, deity-supplanting plan. Whale was as subversive as Browning, but much more subtle. The twisted Christian imagery that dots the film is slyly placed, and religion, science, and authority are all mocked on a near-subliminal level.

The plan of Praetorius is thwarted when the Bride rejects the Monster, obviously attracted to Dr. Frankenstein instead. Inconsolable, the Monster releases Frankenstein and his human fiancée—"Go! You live! Go!"—before seemingly destroying himself, the Bride, and Praetorius in an explosion ("We belong dead!"). In his final moments, the Monster proves his humanity by making moral judgements and acting compassionately towards his creator. It was the

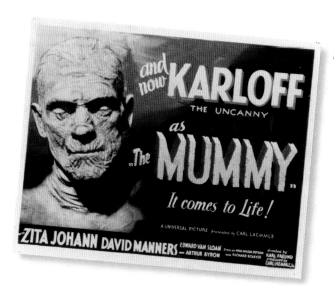

A publicity poster for *The Mummy* (1932).

Monster's high-water mark. After this film, the Monster would be little more than a towering, mute, killing machine, manipulated by others.

Though Karloff wound up as thoroughly typecast as Lugosi, he accepted it and worked the distinction to his advantage. So powerful was his original portrayal in *Frankenstein* that he quickly followed it up with a slew of choice villainous roles, creating other iconic characters such as the Mummy.

In the original film *The Mummy*, Karloff plays the ageless Imhotep, an ancient Egyptian high priest who comes back to life in convenient bandage-wrapped form when a forbidden scroll is read, intent on finding his lost love. (This story was inspired by the world-famous discovery of Egyptian king Tutankhamun's tomb in 1922). The Mummy makes an astute and subversive political point—colonize us, pilfer our holy sites, make museum specimens of us, and vengeance will fall.

The idea of the ageless, unfulfilled romance came right out of H. Rider Haggard's 1887 novel *She*. Here it provides a poignant backstory for Karloff as the cursed, cadaverous immortal, Ardath Bey (aka Imhotep, the Mummy). His gaunt face and blazing stare are compelling, as is his passion for the beauty of Zita Johann as his unwilling intended. Like Dracula and Frankenstein, he seeks a forbidden female. In another notable role, Karloff essayed the stereotype of the "fiendish Oriental mastermind" in *The Mask of Fu Manchu* (1932).

Karloff and Lugosi are at their best together

in Edgar Ulmer's *The Black Cat* (1934). Ulmer was a prolific and inventive B-movie master. *Black Cat* is bizarre, brutally disturbing. Lugosi is the hero, Vitus Werdegast, a psychiatrist who returns to face architect Hjalmar Poelzig (Karloff), who betrayed his fellow soldiers in World War I, and stole Werdegast's wife from him.

Poelzig's sleek Art Deco palace squats atop an ancient dungeon that holds the preserved, glass-encased remains of Poelzig's ex-lovers ... including Werdegast's wife! It turns out that Poelzig has taken Werdegast's daughter to bed as well, and that he leads a Satanic cult, for the trifecta.

The antagonists play out their games of death through the fate assigned to a young couple who conveniently get trapped in the middle of things. The hijacking and endangerment of innocent bystanders was already a familiar horror plot point. The couple is straight out of an "old dark house" film. He's a mystery writer, there's a storm, the road is impassable, she's cute, and a sacrifice to the Devil is mandated. The resulting climax involves torture so graphic that Universal insisted Ulmer reshoot some of it. He did—but he made it even more extreme. Somehow it escaped into general distribution anyway.

An overlooked tour de force for Karloff was his *The Black Room*, directed by Roy William Neill in 1935. Neill, best known for his Sherlock Holmes films with Basil Rathbone, had a penchant for gloom-filled frames and doom-filled plots that presaged film noir. Karloff plays twin barons—one good, one evil—in a tale that creeps along like a demented bedtime story.

Karloff's rich, stage-trained baritone voice was perfect for his work as filmdom's go-to Mad Doctor (*The Invisible Ray* and *The Man Who Changed His Mind*, 1936; *The Man They Could Not Hang*, 1939; *The Man with Nine Lives* and *Before I Hang*, 1940; and on and on . . .). Increasingly, his appearances spoofed his forbidding image. His biggest stage success was in the absurdly menacing role of Jonathan Brewster in Joseph Kesselring's hit 1941 Broadway comedy-horror play *Arsenic and Old Lace*, which was written with him in mind. A victim of bad plastic surgery, his character becomes violent when others remark that he looks like—Boris Karloff.

The sound era's pioneer in playing deranged STEM professionals was the prolific and honored English stage actor Lionel Atwill, who made, in rapid succession, *Doctor X* (1932), and *The Vampire Bat*, *Murders in the Zoo*, and *Mystery of the Wax Museum* (all 1933), as insane doctor, scientist, and sculptor, respectively. In *Wax Museum*, one of the last and best of the early two-strip Technicolor films, a mad sculptor finds that his statues look much more lifelike when they contain a core of dead body.

Fellow Englishman Colin Clive's more famous characterization of Dr. Frankenstein was a hyped-up ball of anguish, but Atwill's greatest asset in horror was his blithe matter-of-factness, which could normalize even his characters' strangest behaviors and assertions. Even if an Atwill character is in the middle of dissecting his own mother, he is convinced that everything is perfectly fine, and frankly and testily wonders why everyone around him is acting so nervously. Atwill would confidently steal scenes in movies (he is the unforgettable, monocled, one-armed Inspector Krogh in *Son of Frankenstein*) until scandal and illness broke his health. He died at age sixty-one in 1946.

A vital component of the mad-doctor scenario is of course the assistant, with or without hunchback. The actor with the greatest impact on the horror film in proportion to his screen time is Dwight Frye, the original Renfield in *Dracula*, the original hunchbacked assistant (then named Fritz, not Ygor) in the original *Frankenstein*. He appeared in supporting roles in sixty-two other films, including *The Vampire Bat* and *Bride of Frankenstein*, which called for lunatics, thugs, creeps, and maniacs—and all in over the course of just seventeen years. He bore nicknames such as "The Man with the Thousand-Watt Stare" and "The Man of a Thousand Deaths." Frye died at the age of thirty-four in 1943.

Peter Lorre joined the mix the last of all, in America at least. A short, bug-eyed, primarily comic stage actor who worked in Berlin during the unstable Weimar period, he made his mark in 1931 with his portrayal of serial killer Hans Beckert in Lang's *M*. While *The Cabinet of Dr. Caligari* and Hitchcock's *The Lodger* dealt with maniacal murderers, *M* was focused entirely on the (offscreen) killing of children. Lorre had the guts to play the unplayable—a compulsive murderer and sexual pervert. Furthermore, he played him without attempting to excuse him, so penetratingly that he inspires the tragic sympathy once inspired by the blood-spattered examples of tragic Greek heroes such as Oedipus and Orestes.

M is classified as a thriller, but it becomes a horror film as it widens out to reveal the structure of society around Beckert. Life is organized in a pitiless class system (the victims all come from the slums). The cops and the criminals are simply rival firms at work here, a cynical Brechtian assessment in tune with a culture on the verge of Hitler's rule. Beckert's kangaroo-court trial at the end of the film is at once an obscene parody of the justice system and an effective analysis of that system's hypocrisies and limitations. In the final analysis, the crowd is just as bloodthirsty as the accused.

This once-in-a-lifetime performance was Lorre's ticket first to film work in London, then in Hollywood. In 1935's *Mad Love*, his first American film, he patented his archetype: the intelligent and perverse social misfit, trammeled by sexual problems, and barely in control of his nihilistic impulses. In this second and best film adaptation of Maurice Renard's 1920 novel *The Hands of Orlac*, *Mad Love* (Karl Freund's last feature film as director, and his only other horror film besides *The Mummy*) explores the

Peter Lorre in *M* (1931).

The giant ape is displayed on stage in New York by his captors in a scene from *King Kong* (1933).

Fredric March with and without makeup in a publicity photo for 1931's *Dr. Jekyll and Mr. Hyde.*

sadistic, voyeuristic pleasures of Grand Guignol. Lorre's Dr. Gogol is a devotee of Guignol, a brilliant surgeon but also a spurned would-be lover. Colin Clive is all nerves as the concert pianist who loses his hands and gets new ones—ones that belonged to a murderer—thanks to the good doctor.

Lorre's star would wane and wax: first, he would get lost at Columbia with a string of "Mr. Moto" detective movies, then catch fire at Warner Brothers with *The Maltese Falcon* (1941) as a supporting player, peter out, and finally come back one last time in Roger Corman's Poe films, as comic relief and for nostalgia value. Still, his distinctive features would become synonymous with horror, and through him the figure of the killer would eventually come to the front and center in American horror film.

Three key horror films made outside Universal's stable demonstrate the power and popularity of the genre at the time: *Dr. Jekyll and Mr. Hyde* (1931) and *Island of Lost Souls* (1932) at Paramount, and *King Kong* (1933) at RKO. *Jekyll/Hyde*, directed by Rouben Mamoulian, was a prestige production that won Fredric March an Oscar and made his career. (He evaded horror typecasting, remaining within the leading-man category for the duration of his film career.) Mamoulian was not intimidated by the new strictures of sound; his freewheeling camera starts the story with a long, handheld, traveling point-of-view shot; dissolves and split-screens push the cinematic language in the service of the story.

March's *Jekyll* is saintly and idealistic to begin with. He seeks to eliminate the "lower" impulses of the psyche through chemistry. His ingestion of his concoction doesn't strip him of his evil impulses, but distills them into an essence of malice. March shrinks and twists in front of the camera as he transforms, degenerating into an ape-like savage who lives for sensual pleasure and selfish aggressions. The contrast is mirrored in his bifurcated pursuit of two very different women: his demure fiancée and a slatternly tavern girl. Faust-like, he destroys one of the women and damns himself in the process.

Strong stuff for the time. This adaptation of *Jekyll/Hyde* emphasized sex and violence, to the point that eight minutes of it was trimmed when it was rereleased in 1936 after the Production Code was instated.

The giant ape known as King Kong was dreamed up by adventurer-turned-moviemaker Merian C. Cooper one day as he gazed at the Empire State Building. With his filmmaking partner Ernest B. Schoedsack,

Cooper conceived of the story of an enormous throwback anthropoid worshipped as a god on a Pacific island, captured, then dragged back to civilization for profit, where he wreaks havoc. Kong is an enormous dark savage who falls in love with a demure white woman. Whether or not you read anything symbolic into this, the film itself is still a staggering achievement.

This is in large part due to the determination of Willis O'Brien. Using an articulated model constructed by sculptor Marcel Delgado, O'Brien spent hundreds of hours manipulating it and other small-scale creatures frame by frame, creating creature battles and an urban rampage—all in miniature.

King Kong is better understood as a "monster" movie, but it shares all the elements of the horror story: the search for forbidden knowledge, the dabbling in things best left unknown, and the unleashing of transgressive, destructive powers. Fortunately, co-creator Cooper was wise enough to endow the stop-motion title character with humanizing traits, giving the audience a figure to root for amid the extensive, primitive, but finally convincing animation and special-effects work.

Kong is the ruler of Skull Island, but in the big city, he's just another awkward rube. His tenderness toward the leading lady redeems him and dooms him at the same time. As the movie progresses, the humans increasingly come off as petty and Kong grows nobler. Who wouldn't identify with the heroic ape's struggle against the pygmies who crucify him? "It was Beauty killed the Beast" is the final line spoken in Kong, and that fairy-tale substratum underlines the transformation of a forty-foot-tall gorilla into a sympathetic hero.

Yet another H. G. Wells novel, 1896's *The Island of Doctor Moreau*, formed the basis for another perverse masterpiece, *Island of Lost Souls* (1932). It's an ominous inquiry into what constitutes human identity. Set on the seemingly obligatory jungle island, a castaway discovers that an exiled scientist there is experimenting ruthlessly on animals, attempting to turn them into men, but begetting only grotesque hybrids.

Charles Laughton (standing) as Dr. Moreau, Leila Hyams (left) as Ruth Thomas, and Richard Arlen as Edward Parker in the 1932 film *Island of Lost Souls*.

Acting great Charles Laughton is seen in one of his finest roles here, as the cheerfully sadistic mad doctor.

This horror film is all about sex and the body. The hero is sexually tempted by Lota, a woman created from a panther. His rage when he discovers the truth about her contains the shock and revulsion that the contemplation of bestiality prompts. Dr. Moreau is far past that state of unacceptance; his human/animal hybrids are to him merely problems to be solved, clinical subjects to be controlled. His rule is a parody of monotheism. "What is the law?" he shouts as he cracks his whip. "Not to walk on all fours," respond his creatures in fear. "Not to spill blood. Are we not men?"

The mad scientist dooms himself in the midst of his hellish Eden by forcing his subjects to kill for him. It is Moreau's hypocrisy that destroys everything, sparking a revolt that ends with him being vivisected without anesthetic by his own creations in his very own "House of Pain."

"Don't look back," one survivor says to another as the film ends. It's a line that could be applicable to the whole disturbing pre-Code era. After a short hiatus, the monster factory would start up again, but when it did it had to be much more covert and coded about what it tried to convey.

4

CRANKING OUT THE CREEPIES

HORROR IN THE 1930s AND 1940s

Two factors caused the great American horror movie drought of 1936–1939. The first was censorship. Although the restrictive Motion Picture Production Code was adopted by the major studios on March 31, 1930, it wasn't strictly enforced until July 1, 1934, from whence all films needed a certificate of approval from the Production Code Administration prior to US release. Films such as *Island of Lost Souls*, *Frankenstein*, and *The Black Cat* (the last of which was one of the three Universal's top moneymakers of the year) all suffered cuts. Soon, no one was proposing subjects, approaches, or elements that were likely to keep a film from earning its needed release certificate.

This was too little and too late for the British Board of Film Censors, which slapped a discouraging "H" certificate on all American horror films, banning viewers age fifteen and younger. As Britain represented 40 percent of a US film's potential foreign revenues, the result was an effective embargo on the horror product overseas.

Second, money. Universal's founder lost his studio to the bank. Carl Laemmle took out a $750,000 production loan in 1936, exposing his company to purchase by an East Coast firm, Standard Capital. On March 14, 1936, they exercised their option and bought him out, kicking Carl Sr. upstairs and Carl Jr. to the curb.

What Universal's new owners knew about finance, they did not know about making successful movies. They slashed budgets across the board and nixed all horror films for the time being.

It took one thoughtful exhibitor to change horror-film history. On August 5, 1938, Emil Ulmann, manager of the 659-seat Regina Theater on Wilshire Boulevard in Beverly Hills, decided on a four-day run of old prints of Universal's *Dracula* and *Frankenstein* combined with RKO's 1933 *Son of Kong*— history's first horror triple feature.

Eager audiences clamored to get in, and the theater stayed open twenty-one hours a day for a time to meet the demand. Four nights stretched into five weeks. Three weeks into the run, the cagey Ulmann even booked an unemployed and destitute Bela Lugosi to make personal appearances between shows, keeping the crowds coming and incidentally reviving the Hungarian actor's career. Universal printed off 500 copies of *Dracula* and *Frankenstein* and distributed them nationally, raking in profits.

All the studios took note; demand created fresh supply. Karloff, Atwill, Rathbone, and Lugosi were all summoned off the bench. On January 13, 1939, *Son of Frankenstein* opened, spawning a string of formulaic, increasingly corny horror sequels by Universal that didn't play itself out until the end of World War II.

OPPOSITE: *Son of Frankenstein* (1939) poster.

(from left to right) Bela Lugosi, Boris Karloff, and Basil Rathbone in a scene from 1939's *Son of Frankenstein*.

Son of Frankenstein, directed by the dependable mainstream producer/director Rowland V. Lee, is stylistically brash but narratively confused. This was perhaps due to the fact that the dialogue was written on the fly during production. The original screenplay was written by Willis (aka Wyllis) Cooper, much better known as a masterful writer and producer of radio horror series such as *Lights Out* (1934-47) and *Quiet Please* (1947–49). Director Lee tossed out Cooper's script and made it up as he went along, causing production delays and inflating costs to twice their original estimate.

In the finished film, Frankenstein's son (Rathbone) returns to wrestle with his dubious heritage at his father's castle and laboratory somewhere in a blighted, backward Mitteleuropa. He is surrounded by colorful, vaguely Germanic peasants in one of the most aggressively stylized horror settings in film history. Jack Otterson's outsized sets, a remarkable mix of modernism and Gothic

Tom Tyler in costume for *The Mummy's Hand* (1940).

sensibilities, dominate. George Robinson's cinematography comes as close to *Caligari* as a mainstream horror film ever would, with its slanted shadows and aggressive use of negative space. All the characters seem isolated, struggling among and through patches of darkness.

In this tale of redemption and revenge, the Monster, after gaining speech in the preceding *Bride of Frankenstein*, has been reduced to mute status. Karloff, in his last outing as the Monster, still imbues the character with an inner life, but he serves merely as an instrument of revenge for the crippled blacksmith, Ygor (Lugosi), who uses him to kill all the jurors who sentenced Ygor to death by hanging. (He got better!) "They hanged me once, Frankenstein," he chortles, "because I stole bodies, they said . . . They broke my neck. They said I was dead."

Lugosi, reaping a substantial role for once, steals the film in one of his most nuanced performances. "He . . . does things for me," explains Ygor to Frankenstein as they stand over the unrevived Monster. (Legend has it that the homoerotic implication of the line on the first take caused Karloff to break character—in British stage slang, "corpse"—and crack up, triggering a round of unprofessional giggles among three of the cinema's biggest bogeymen, and many retakes.)

Avoiding double jeopardy, Ygor is dead but alive, the embodiment of the cold hand of the past that throttles Frankenstein's dreams of redemption—until the very end, at least. The weaponizing of a Universal monster for a villain's personal ends would become a common plot point of future fright-flick installments from the studio.

The keynote of all Universal horror films made after *Son of Frankenstein* was thrift, thanks to the fiscal excesses of directors such as Whale and Lee. From now on, horror was demoted to B-movie status. Instead of being made as stunning A-list features, they were treated as predictable moneymakers, genre fare, suitable for auditoriums girdling the dependable audiences of kids, idle lovers, and pioneer horror aficionados. Monetizing horror film's popularity on a budget meant that the quality and look of the films declined from the grand, prestigious productions of the silent-era *Phantom* and *Hunchback* to low-budget, cheesy-looking fodder that played the bottom half of a double bill in backwater burgs across the continent.

Another studio stalwart, director Christy Cabanne, was at the helm of *The Mummy's Hand* (1940). The character was ripped out of the context established in the Karloff *Mummy* and given a new storyline. Gone was the grand romantic concept of obsessive love thwarted across the millennia. This reboot featured the bandaged bogeyman as an obedient, silent monster who serves as the murderous pawn of whoever can get him the tanna leaves he needs in order to keep on shuffling.

Here the mummy is controlled by evil high priest Andoheb (George "Pinky" Zucco, the beetle-browed villain of many a low-budget feature), who uses him to attempt to gain an eternal girlfriend in the form of actress Peggy Moran. Former cowboy star Tom Tyler plays the mummy, renamed Kharis, here, opposed by rather ineffective leading man Dick Foran. The impressive sets are redressed from James Whale's

career-ending jungle-adventure flop *Green Hell*. Lon Chaney Jr. would take over the lead role for the next three installments, each worse than the one before.

Chaney the younger was the only actor who joined the horror pantheon during this period, and he backed into fame reluctantly, not on his own terms. His tragic story deserves a more detailed retelling. Much of the anguish Chaney Jr. channeled into his monster characters welled up from his personal life.

Overshadowed by his brilliant father and unintentional namesake, and haunted by the mental instability of his mother, Chaney Jr. wanted to work in movies and be judged as an actor on his own merits. However, the studios would only let him pursue success at the cost of dropping his original Christian name, Creighton, and tacking on his more marketable father's moniker instead.

He did not inherit his father's intense screen presence and transformative abilities, but he was an actor of depth and complexity when given the right role. Anyone who has seen his astonishing work as the giant simpleton Lenny in Lewis Milestone's 1939 *Of Mice and Men*, or his marvelously resigned stolidity in a supporting role in the iconic Western *High Noon* (1952), can only imagine what else he might have achieved without so many demons eating away at him.

The younger Chaney was also crippled by a lifelong dependence on alcohol. Towards the end of his career, he advised his directors to get all the work they could out of him by midafternoon, as he was usually too incapacitated to continue productively after that.

In *Man-Made Monster*, directed by George Waggner in 1941, Chaney Jr.'s horror film debut

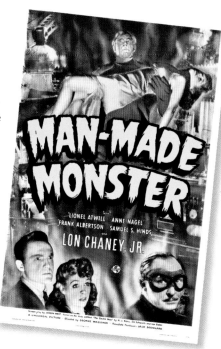

Poster for *Man-Made Monster* (1941), Lon Chaney Jr.'s horror film debut.

sets the tone for all his future roles in the genre: a regular guy turned into a monster by compassionless science, driven to destruction by the whims of fate. He is Dynamo Dan, the Electric Man, resistant to the deadly force, which prompts Lionel Atwill's mad scientist character to pump Dan full of juice as he dreams of creating a race of electrified, obedient, zombie supermen. ("What is one life compared to this discovery?" he exclaims at one point.) All and sundry receive their comeuppances in less than an hour's runtime. With Universal, you got the goods quick and hard.

Chaney Jr. made his mark as Larry Talbot, the doomed hero of *The Wolf Man* (also 1941, with Waggner at the helm again), an innocent man condemned to become a monstrous, immortal, bestial killer. The movie's oft-quoted couplets proclaim: "Even a man who is pure in heart / And says his prayers by night / May become a wolf when the wolfbane blooms / And the autumn moon is bright . . ."

Neither the Wolf Man nor the Mummy are characters derived from literary sources, but each was powerful enough to forge its

The Wolf Man (1941) poster.

own modern mythology. In Wolf Man's case, something struck a nerve. (Universal's original attempt at a Wolf Man movie, Stuart Walker's 1935 *Werewolf of London*, was a damp squib.)

The Wolf Man was released in the week following Pearl Harbor, and the studio thought the movie might tank. Instead, people flocked to indulge in a portrayal of humanity's suddenly very palpable dark side.

The Wolf Man's true creator was screenwriter Curt Siodmak, an escapee from Hitler's Germany. He saw the fatal sign of the Pentagram, a forbidding five-pointed star that appeared on the persons of werewolves and in the palms of their victims, as a metaphor for the stigma of Jewish identity. For Siodmak, Germany had become monstrous as well—a nation of normal people transformed into wolfish beings by the full moon of Nazism.

"I am the Wolf Man," Siodmak later said. "I was forced into a fate I didn't want: to be a Jew in Germany. I would not have chosen that as my fate. The swastika represents the moon. When the moon comes up, the man doesn't want to murder, but he knows he cannot escape it, the Wolf Man destiny. Something happens that you know is going to happen, but you cannot escape it, like going to a concentration camp."[1]

To explain Chaney Jr.'s inability to master an English accent, Wolf Man makes his Larry Talbot the happy-go-lucky second son of the definitively English Sir John (Claude Rains). Larry's been estranged from the family, living away in America for eighteen years. He returns

home after the death of his older brother. In the process of protecting a village girl from a (were)wolf's attack, he himself is bitten. Now he's condemned to undergo long and painful stop-motion makeup sessions during the full moon, transforming into a matted-haired beast with claws, paws, and snout.

Monster makeup master Jack Pierce was still king of his department at Universal. The innovative yet curmudgeonly little man would put Chaney Jr. through hell for *The Wolf Man*. In those days, a transformation sequence could still be most effectively done mechanically, via

stop-motion, in the camera itself. Here's how it worked: a few frames of an image is shot; the image is altered slightly; another few frames are shot; and so on until the sequence is complete. In the case of Chaney Jr., it took four hours a day to put on the Wolf Man makeup, and an hour to get it off. Chaney Jr. went along reluctantly with Universal directives, but he suffered mightily through Pierce's hours-long makeup ministrations.

Bela Lugosi has a blink-and-you'll-miss-it role in *The Wolf Man*, as the Roma who transmits the curse of lycanthropy to Larry. The real acting revelation in the film is Maria Ouspenskaya, who plays the tiny Roma fortune-teller Maleva, who becomes a kind of mother substitute for Larry. Ouspenskaya was a soulful early Method actress who studied under Stanislavski at the famed Moscow Art Theatre and who became a noted acting teacher in the States.

Her stone-faced seriousness in the role helps the audience to suspend disbelief, and she projects her personality strongly even when encumbered with earrings the size of demitasse saucers. Whenever a werewolf dies in the film, like a pagan priestess she stands over the body and intones, "The way you walked was thorny, through no fault of your own, but as the rain enters the soil, the river enters the sea, so tears run to a predestined end. Your suffering is over. Now you will find peace."

Once the studio saw Chaney Jr. as a marketable simulacrum of his father, he was shoved into almost every iconic monster role in films such as *The Ghost of Frankenstein*, *The Mummy's Tomb* (both 1942), and *Son of Dracula* (1943). He also got a chance to star in six low-budget thrillers based on the popular radio horror series *Inner Sanctum*: *Calling Dr. Death* (1943), *Weird Woman* (1944), *Dead Man's Eyes* (1944), *The Frozen Ghost* (1945), *Strange Confession* (1945), and *Pillow of Death* (1945).

Chaney Jr. reserved his affection for his portrayal of the Wolf Man, whom he called "my baby." Indeed, his mournful and desperate take on Larry Talbot, the unwilling and tormented shapeshifter, elevated the character to tragic status. Eventually, though, even that dignity would be taken from him.

Throughout the World War II era, Frankenstein, Dracula,

the Mummy, and the Invisible Man returned from utter destruction time and time again, producing cycles, spinoffs, and variants, and even finding themselves costarring in the same films, so-called "monster rally" vehicles. Films about ghouls, ghosts, zombies, and mad doctors swarmed close behind.

Between 1939 and 1946, there were four more entries each in the Frankenstein's Monster, the

Jack Pierce (left) applies paint to Lon Chaney Jr.'s costume on the set of *The Mummy's Ghost* (1944).

Mummy, and the Invisible Man series, and three of Dracula. A new crop of supporting horror actors developed, including John Carradine and J. Carrol Naish. Other regulars included early "scream queens" such as *King Kong*'s Fay Wray, *Wolf Man*'s leading lady Evelyn Ankers, Anne Gwynne (*Black Friday,* 1940; *House of Frankenstein,* 1944), and the exotic Acquanetta (born Margaret Davenport in Norristown, Pennsylvania), who starred as the titular Ape Woman in the first two (*Captive Wild Woman*, 1943; *Jungle Woman*, 1944) of a trilogy on the subject.

Of course, as with most film series, the sequels got worse as they progressed. Part of this was due to the studios' financial need to get the monsters back up there on the screen on any pretext, no matter how slim; the popular returning character in film was a money-maker as old as the silent era's Broncho Billy.

There were prolific studio writers who whipped out genre scripts with lightning speed. One such writer, Griffin Jay, disgorged seven horror scripts, and sixteen in total, over a span of only four years (1940–44), which might have contributed to his demise at age forty-nine in 1954. (Returning, unkillable characters litter other serial narratives, such as superhero comics and soap operas. Stan Lee's Marvel Comics maxim that characters should seem to change but don't is an ever-profitable one.)

A straight-faced timeline of the personal ups and downs of the Universal monsters would be full of convoluted leaps across chasms of internal logic. In many cases, these original and compelling characters are reduced to mere plot points—forces set in motion by the vengeful, set up to be knocked down and burnt/drowned/ staked/shot/clubbed/frozen, with the sure and certain hope of their resurrection for the next sequel.

Likewise, Universal's standing sets were dressed and redressed, but became recognizable to habitual horror fans as a kind of scary Brigadoon to which they returned repeatedly. Each remake was populated with the same

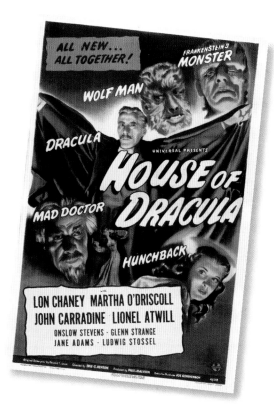

House of Dracula
(1945) poster.

burgomasters, maidens, elders, pitchfork- and torch-wielding peasants, wives sobbing into their aprons, and children God-knows-where, probably in the clutches of the monster.

The last entry in the original Universal monster series is representative of the whole. *House of Dracula* (1945), directed by the dependable Erle C. Kenton, features John Carradine as Dracula, Chaney Jr. as the Wolf Man, Glenn Strange as the Monster, and Onslow

Top Ten Horror Films of the 1930s

Dracula (1931)

Frankenstein (1931)

Dr. Jekyll and Mr. Hyde (1931)

M (1931)

The Mummy (1932)

Freaks (1932)

The Invisible Man (1933)

King Kong (1933)

Bride of Frankenstein (1935)

Mad Love (1935)

Stevens as the obligatory, soon-to-be-mad doctor. (For a welcome change, an actress, Jane Adams, played the doctor's hunchbacked assistant.) The entertaining but confusing mish-mash of storylines and turnabout conflict ends with the death of everyone involved—except Larry Talbot! Not only does he live, but he's cured of his lycanthropy, finally finding the peace he sought in movie after movie.

In 1948, *Abbott and Costello Meet Frankenstein* would use Chaney's Wolf Man and other Universal monsters as straight men for the antics of the popular comedy duo, a smash hit that again revived Universal's fortunes. The *Abbott and Costello Meet . . .* formula proved so profitable for the studio that it repeated it ad nauseam, with the duo meeting "the Killer, Boris Karloff," the Invisible Man, Dr. Jekyll and Mr. Hyde, and the Mummy. Now the creatures of nightmare were reduced to profitable punch lines.

Beyond Universal, few studios took a chance on making horror films. Most notably, RKO

Frankenstein's monster lifts comedy team Bud Abbott (left) and Lou Costello (right) off the ground in a promotional still for *Abbott and Costello Meet Frankenstein* (1948).

Top Ten Horror Films of the 1940s

The Wolf Man (1941)

Cat People (1942)

I Walked with a Zombie (1943)

The Seventh Victim (1943)

The Body Snatcher (1945)

Dead of Night (1945)

Hangover Square (1945)

Isle of the Dead (1945)

The Picture of Dorian Gray (1945)

Bedlam (1946)

rolled out a new version of *The Hunchback of Notre Dame* in 1939, featuring Charles Laughton in the role of Quasimodo. MGM's 1941 *Dr. Jekyll and Mr. Hyde*, directed by Victor Fleming, was an overblown prestige production featuring Spencer Tracy, whose performance wasn't a patch on Fredric March's.

There was, however, a small burst of "gaslight" thrillers in American film during World War II that was successful.

The Picture of Dorian Gray (1945), adapted from Oscar Wilde's novel, directed by Albert Lewin, and starring the undistinguished Hurd Hatfield, gathered a bouquet of awards and nominations. The foggy comforts of Victorian-era horror settings would become a trend solidly leaned into a few years later at Britain's Hammer Studios.

England held a place in the American imagination as a domain of intelligible but remote, mysterious, and weird social superiors, perhaps the residue of a resentment borne since colonial times. The Victorian era, the height of British imperial culture, produced a teeming, sometimes disturbing onslaught of vivid

The Picture of
Dorian Gray
(1945) lobby card.

social system in which goodness still resides and is in need of protection. Sin could be expiated, or at least avenged. And in Laird Cregar . . .

In Laird Cregar, this particular type of evil character found its perfect expression. It's interesting to speculate about where his career might have taken him—a victim of compulsion himself, he died before *Hangover Square* opened, at the age of thirty-one.

The most illuminating and comprehensive examination of Cregar's life is found in Gregory William Mank's *Hollywood Cauldron*.[2] A born actor, Cregar rose quickly through the ranks, making sixteen films in only six years. Large (six-feet-three-inches tall, he weighed as much as 300 pounds at times), flamboyant, and sonorous, he excelled in supporting roles ranging from the comic (*Charley's Aunt*, 1941) to the Satanic (*Heaven Can Wait*, 1943). Cregar was a throwback: a hearty, Victorian-era kind of actor with impeccable diction, florid gestures, and grand poses to spare. Naturally suave and well-spoken, he could transmit complexity and menace with the best of them.

His performance as a psychotic, murderous police detective in *I Wake Up Screaming* (1941) made his studio, 20th Century Fox, think of ways to explore his facility for mayhem. A team of director John Brahm, producer Robert Bassler, and screenwriter Barré Lyndon got to work.

The Lodger was a tried-and-true property, based on the 1911 story by Marie Adelaide Belloc Lowndes. The story centers on the character of Jack the Ripper. Hitchcock made the first and most noted film adaptation of the story in 1927; this, the third, remains the most effective.

The film's success rests squarely on Cregar's shoulders. As the mysterious and disturbed lodger Slade, he veers from clipped, frosty politeness to fits of near hysteria. Cregar plays him as a creature of deep feeling. He is obsessed with avenging his brother's death—implied as being due to venereal disease picked up from a prostitute—in a way that suggests undernotes of an incestuous homosexual desire. Awareness of this kind of subtext sailed gaily by the oblivious

imaginative writing from the likes of Stevenson, Stoker, Doyle, Wilkie Collins, H. Rider Haggard, Sax Rohmer, and H. G. Wells. The number of archetypal horror, mystery, and fantasy characters created during the period—among them Sherlock Holmes and his nemeses, the Invisible Man, Dr. Jekyll and Mr. Hyde, Fu Manchu, Dracula, and She Who Must Be Obeyed—guaranteed that fog-shrouded London cobblestone streets would remain the hunting ground of monsters and villains in popular culture.

German émigré John Brahm had directed an unmemorable werewolf film, *The Undying Monster* (1942), for 20th Century Fox. He was yoked to screen heavy Laird Cregar with amazing results in *The Lodger* (1944) and *Hangover Square* (1945), two creepy masterpieces that take full advantage of Cregar's uncanny ability to project darkness, aided immeasurably by the cinematography of two greats: Lucien Ballard in the first case and Joseph LaShelle in the second.

Both *The Lodger* and *Hangover Square* fall technically into the category of thrillers. As in film noir, both movies feature a protagonist drawn to doom by a beautiful and seductive woman. However, unlike the cynical and disillusioned leading men of noir, these two films feature tragic antiheroes, victims of compulsions they can neither understand nor fight, and unwilling monsters, full of old-school pathos. The two films' cityscapes are gritty, as in film noir, but there is still a status quo of normalcy in them, a solid censor, who was much more concerned with the scantiness of leading lady Merle Oberon's gowns. Cregar is pitiful without being pitiable, modulating his performance until by film's end he is both worked up and reduced to the status of a snarling, cornered beast.

Psychopaths and serial killers were not fodder for leading men at the time. With the exception of Lang's *M*, few such explorations existed on film, barring rarities such as *Night Must Fall* (1937), *Gaslight* (1944), *The Scarlet Claw* (1944), *Leave Her to Heaven* (1945), and *The Spiral Staircase* (1946). After this, no significant "psycho-killers" would be featured until *Psycho* and *Peeping Tom* in 1960. It would take a decade or so more of cultural decay after that until the serial killer became a staple onscreen.

In Cregar's case, the parallel between the keeper of guilty secrets onscreen and offscreen could not be more pronounced. Cregar was flamboyantly gay at a time when variant sexual identities were kept under wraps,

Laird Cregar as the tortured soul at the center of John Brahm's *The Lodger* (1944).

especially in Hollywood, and feelings of conflictedness and alienation radiate from him throughout his final two screen performances. In both, he is a hopeless outsider who can't conform to social norms and who must be destroyed in order to preserve the status quo. In fact, Cregar would, in the pursuit of a more "normal" life, destroy himself.

Cregar, terrified of being trapped professionally and personally as quite literally a "heavy," yearned to be accepted as a leading man, and also hoped that he could "cure" himself of his homosexuality. Part of his plan involved a crash diet, abetted by amphetamines. Though the same producer, director, screenwriter, and star worked together again on *Hangover Square*, due to Cregar's ups and downs, filming was much more troubled than it was on *The Lodger*.

Hangover, based on the 1941 novel by Patrick Hamilton, tells of London composer George Harvey Bone (Cregar, now a relatively skeletal 225 pounds). The premise of the film seems flimsy—a composer blacks out and becomes homicidal when he hears dissonance—but this perfectly crafted story is made plausible and deeply disturbing.

Bone as his normal self is passive and meek, a catspaw for the seductive Netta (Linda Darnell), a vulgar music-hall girl who distracts Bone from his serious music, repurposing his elegant melodies for her own tawdry hit songs. The more conflicted Bone grows, the more frequent and long-lasting his murderous blackouts become. Netta turns him from the film's "good girl," leads him on, uses him, and jilts him.

The bravura visual centerpiece of the film is its Guy Fawkes sequence. (The day, which celebrates King James I's deliverance from an assassination attempt in 1605, features a dummy dubbed "the Guy" which is heaped on a bonfire and set alight.) Bone, in his murderous trance, wraps Netta's body in a cloak and mask and hoists it to the top of the pile as a joyous, torch-bearing crowd urges him on. The intersection of bloodthirsty public ritual (the crowd chants, "Guy! Guy! Stick him in the eye! Put him on the

fire and watch him die!") and private crime is tantalizing.

Brahm's camera eloquently moves through a broad vocabulary of swoops, pans, zooms, in-camera smears, and point-of-view shots to communicate the tension and disconnection in Bone's mind. And it doesn't hurt that Bernard Herrmann's score is one of the best ever for any film, much less a horror film. (Herrmann had already composed the score for *Citizen Kane*, and would create many more classic scores for Hitchcock and other directors.) Using the score of Bone's "Concerto Macabre" as the soundtrack for the film as well, Herrmann effortlessly wields and interweaves themes, splashes of emphasis, and subtle audio underlines that ratchet up the film's tension tenfold.

By film's end, Bone completes the first performance of his concerto as audience and orchestra flee him and the burning building he occupies. Bone achieves his creative peak at the moment of his death, the fire he used to destroy the evidence of his crime now devouring him. "It's better this way," intones the nominal hero, a police surgeon played by George Sanders. As sentiments go, it's rather weak, but the closing visual of the composer lost in the flames, stabbing out his final, minor chords, is as elegant an image as one is likely to find in a horror film.

And it was Cregar's last film. Already weak from his crash diet, Cregar followed principal shooting on *Hangover Square* with gastric bypass surgery. The strain on his heart was too much, and he died in the hospital on December 9, 1944.

It's impossible to know whether Cregar would have achieved the leading-man status he craved or found himself trapped in the villainous roles he was so good at and which he disdained. His eulogy was delivered by a friend whose performances would share elements with Cregar's grand, gloomy style, and who would soon make a name for himself in similar roles— another up-and-coming actor of the time named Vincent Price.

An important but overlooked thread in the development of the horror genre is the film serial. Though serials were mainly Westerns and crime thrillers, which were cheaper to make, fantastic and frightening elements crowded into the hyperactive and repetitive pleasures of serials such as 1935's *The Phantom Empire* (singing radio cowboy Gene Autry battles a futuristic underground kingdom in his first, most cognitively dissonant film project), *The Phantom Creeps* (1939), and *Drums of Fu Manchu* (1940). Olympic swimmer-turned-actor Buster Crabbe's embodiment of Art Deco-steeped sci-fi heroes Flash Gordon and Buck Rogers did much to ignite young imaginations of the time as well— and few horror-movie villains were as terrifying as bald-pated, goateed Charles Middleton in grim and deadly Ming the Merciless mode.

Horror was in the zeitgeist. A horror boom launched network radio shows such as *The Witch's Tale* (1931–38), *The Hermit's Cave* (1930–44), *Inner Sanctum* (1941–52), *Lights Out* (1934–47), and *The Mysterious Traveler* (1943–52). Pulp horror magazines such as *Weird Tales* (1922–54) proliferated; the magazine *Horror Stories* (1931–38) was part of a gruesome trend of "shudder pulps," trading in stories of sex and violence, that died out at the beginning of World War II.

While all this hullabaloo was going on, the least likely Hollywood studio, cheapo Columbia, produced the best horror films of the decade, and a few that rank with the best ever. Enter Val Lewton.

VAL LEWTON AND THE TERRORS OF THE UNSEEN

CAT PEOPLE

SHE WAS MARKED WITH THE CURSE OF THOSE WHO SLINK AND COURT AND KILL BY NIGHT!

A shadow unfurls along a wall. A light from below throws startled features into high relief. Bars of darkness cross a face; in the tree is a hanged creature. A knife, a clock, an open grave. Figures writhe; blood creeps under a doorframe.

These are some of the sinister charms of suggestion at work in the horror films produced by Val Lewton between 1942 and 1946. Of these nine films, only five are regularly included in the horror canon, *Cat People*, *I Walked with a Zombie*, *The Seventh Victim*, *The Body Snatcher*, and *Bedlam*; the others are referred to as "atmospheric," meaning not scary at all.

However, these gems contain the distilled essence of truly effective horror. By placing the monsters just beyond the edge of the frame, Lewton recaptured the power of the image, in a way not seen since the silent days. Like big-shot producers such as Darryl F. Zanuck and Irving Thalberg, Lewton placed his unique stylistic stamp on every film he made—but unlike them, he did it all on a B-movie budget, typically one-quarter of the allotment usually set aside for making a respectable feature film.

Lewton, born Vladimir Ivan Leventon, emigrated from the Ukraine to America in 1909 with his parents, at the age of five. Lewton was a voluminous reader and compulsive performer. (His aunt Adelaide became one of

Best Horror Movies for Scaredy Cats

The newer a horror film is, the more likely it is to contain disturbing content. Short of hiring a friend to warn you when the scary parts are coming, these selections won't freak you out . . . too badly.

The Phantom of the Opera (1925)

Dr. Jekyll and Mr. Hyde (1931)

Cat People (1942)

The Innocents (1961)

The Mephisto Waltz (1971)

the early twentieth century's most celebrated actresses and flamboyant personalities, under the stage name of Alla Nazimova.) Lewton cranked out a number of novels, some a bit unsavory (his *No Bed of Her Own*, published in 1932, was burned in Germany on Hitler's orders), before finagling his way into a job as what is variously described as editorial assistant to, or story editor for, producer David O. Selznick.

In 1942, he took on the responsibility and challenge of helming a low-budget production unit at RKO Studio. Lewton's task: to create a series of inexpensive and successful horror features. He was given three key constraints: his films could not cost more than $150,000 each to make, had to be less than seventy-five minutes long, and would have to be based solely on titles given to him by the studio heads. He achieved his goal in spades.

Cat People is populated with Lewton's personal fears and idiosyncrasies. An outwardly affable man, Lewton suffered from bouts of anxiety, hostility toward authority figures, and a number of phobias—including, most significantly, an aversion to being touched and a terror of cats. These obsessions coalesced into the thematic center of *Cat People*.

When the completed *Cat People* was first screened for RKO president Charles Koerner in the autumn of 1942, Koerner wouldn't speak to producer Lewton or director Jacques Tourneur, "then left in a hurry."[1] Critics were not bowled over by it, either. It resonated with audiences, though, grossing an estimated $4,000,000, and saving a studio left seriously in the red by the indulgence of Orson Welles's expensive but unprofitable masterpieces *Citizen Kane* (1941) and *The Magnificent Ambersons* (1942).

Cat People's incredible popularity at the time can be ascribed to its raising the topic of

Producer Val Lewton, ca. 1945.

OPPOSITE:
Cat People (1942) poster.

sexual feeling, however covertly. It's the story of a young Serbian woman, Irena, who fears that she turns into a murderous panther when sexually aroused. The idea that a woman's sexual desire could turn her into a murderous beast was radical for the time, an acknowledgment of female power that wouldn't be seen in film again for decades. The brief shot of water glistening on the heroine's naked back as she crouches in the tub, sobbing, after a kill, is one of the more disturbing moments in a 1940s-era film.

Dana B. Polan asserts that "*Cat People* is a tragedy about a world's inability to accept, or even attempt to understand, whatever falls outside its defining frames."[2] Studio heads certainly couldn't understand how an absence of onscreen monsters might actually be more frightening to viewers, who would complete the equation with their imaginations. They definitely couldn't understand Lewton, who based another of his film's premises solely on a nineteenth-century symbolist painting, Arnold Bocklin's "Isle of the Dead," and another on "Bedlam," a 1734 engraving by William Hogarth taken from his famous "Rake's Progress" series.

Cat People's doomed antiheroine's struggle is similar to that of *The Wolf Man* from the previous year: both are cursed protagonists who change into beasts, and struggle to warn those around them who scoff at their supernatural assertions. In Irena's case, the burden of proof increases exponentially due to her gender. The completely unacceptable source of her transformative power, and the ease with which she is dismissed,

insulted and preyed upon, mark important points, culturally, for pre-feminist America.

Another, more disturbing, idea is that Lewton is playing out his mental obsessions through his antiheroine. Irena is, as Lewton was, passive-aggressive; the only way she can convince anyone she is dangerous is by allowing her animal self to be aroused. Her aversion to touch is, in this sense, a protective move.

Her dark, impassioned warmth is no match for the wooden, obvious, two-dimensional characters by whom she is surrounded. Her strange tales are easily pooh-poohed. Even when she returns to her estranged husband, Oliver, ready to engage with him sexually, he blandly informs her that it is too late, and leaves her to ominously and reflexively shred the fabric of the couch on which she is sitting.

Cat People (1942) star Simone Simon plays a doomed anti-heroine.

Irena's otherness only reaches those she kills or nearly kills. The film's most unbelievable moment is also its most visually impressive. We see a drafting room, lit at night only by beams shining up from the now-antiquated "light tables" used by design firms. Behind these cower Oliver and the "regular gal" he is friends with at work (and to whom he turns to when his marriage is stymied). The two of them are stalked by Irena in the form of a black panther.

Oliver lifts a T-square as one would a crucifix and sings out, "In the name of God, Irena, leave us in peace!" (This line is delivered none-too-convincingly, thanks to actor Kent Smith.) *Cat People* reaches a kind of nutty transcendence. A pragmatic tool is pressed into supernatural service, and a beast relents.

Lewton made his own luck and turned his limitations into virtues. He found and nurtured undeveloped talents (directors Jacques Tourneur, Mark Robson, and Robert Wise; Robson and Wise jumped from editing to directing duties under Lewton's command), and he gave leeway and encouragement to movie veterans who rarely received either.

In a one-of-a-kind contrast, Tourneur's father Maurice, who had long ago made a name for himself in France and the US as a silent and then a sound director, was making a horror film the same time as his son was making *Cat People. Le Main du diable,* aka *Carnival of Sinners,* (1943) was filmed in France during the Nazi occupation. It's a variation on Robert Louis Stevenson's 1891 short story "The Bottle Imp," in which a lucky talisman must be sold for less than it is bought for to avoid catastrophe—a "tag-you're-it" strategy used by novelist Koji Suzuki in his 1991 *Ringu* novel as well, later to spawn its own film series. In *It Follows* (2014), the curse is transmitted by sex.

The Wolf Man screenwriter Curt Siodmak turned in perhaps his best horror script for *I Walked with a Zombie* (1943). Jacques Tourneur helmed again. "*Jane Eyre* in the jungle" was Lewton's original conception, but so much riveting ritual makes it into the film that it

resonates beyond those parameters. Honest talk about slavery, and the illustration of segregated cultures and where they touch, is transgressive material that could never have made it into the mainstream films of that day.

In the film, a nurse is summoned to a Caribbean isle to take care of a planter's catatonic wife. Despite her best efforts to cure her, she fails, and it's gradually revealed that the wife was considering leaving her husband and was bewitched in revenge. Of course, the nurse is drawn to the planter, who tries to enlist her help in destroying his helpless spouse. Once again, the prospect of a woman exercising sexual freedom puts her in the patriarchy's crosshairs.

Cinematographer Nicholas Musuraca routinely made something grand out of scant resources over the course of the Lewton horror cycle. Boris Karloff, recently cast free from his Universal contract and sick and tired of playing the same old clichéd bogeymen, credited Lewton with giving his career new life with a range of complex, layered roles that made maximum use of his considerable dramatic talents.

With incredible rapidity, Lewton's unit turned out film after extraordinary film. *The Leopard Man* (Tourneur directs again, 1943) is a very early serial-killer saga set in the unfamiliar landscape of New Mexico. In *The Seventh Victim* (directed by Robson, also 1943), a very young Kim Hunter goes searching for her lost sister in New York

I Walked with a Zombie (1943) poster.

The Seventh Victim (1943) lobby card.

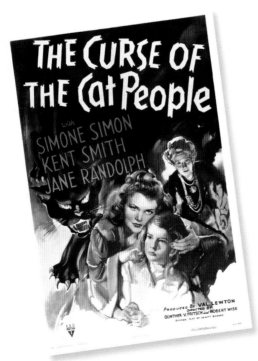

Personal Best

Val Lewton

Cat People (1942)

I Walked with a Zombie (1943)

The Seventh Victim (1943)

The Body Snatcher (1945)

Bedlam (1946)

City. It turns out the sister is on the run from a Satanic cult she's joined, which demands that she kill herself for revealing its secrets. (That the cult is a bunch of squeamish nerds makes their murderous intent all the more bizarre and ludicrous.) Studio interference made the narrative fragmented and incoherent, but its atmospheric impact was not lessened.

The Ghost Ship (Robson again, 1943) is a psychological thriller, featuring Oscar nominee Richard Dix as a domineering ship's captain. Is he nuts, or isn't he? Another great Lewton theme is the idea of the dangers of submission to unjust authority, and here, again and again, as in a

nightmare, an innocent man's questioning of the order of things is denied, devalued, and ignored, dooming him. Look for the great character actor Skelton Knaggs, who plays a mute who speaks only in haunting voiceover.

The Curse of the Cat People (1944) is a ghost story with murder at its heart, a sinister fairy tale about the ghost of Irena of *Cat People* haunting the daughter of the couple that triggered her death.

The Body Snatcher (1945), based on the 1884 Robert Louis Stevenson short story, marks the apogee of the Lewton cycle. It's a fictional paraphrase of the gory careers of the real-life Burke and Hare, who infamously supplied corpses for surgeons to dissect in 1828 Edinburgh—sometimes augmenting the supply, and their incomes, through murder.

At the time of the story, the dissection of the human body was condemned by church and state alike, stunting science's ability to gain understanding about its workings. Karloff is at his best here as the murderous "body snatcher" and cabman Gray, who resents his lowly status and lack of power. He sells his grisly wares to Dr. MacFarlane, who is desperate for bodies to work with so that he can forward his research in order to cure spinal disorders.

Henry Daniell, a talented beagle-faced character actor of the period, is superb as the guilt-stricken, irascible medico. A bad man almost redeemed by his best intentions, MacFarlane doesn't ask too many questions about how he gets his subjects until a younger,

The Curse of the Cat People (1944) poster.

Boris Karloff in character as the sinister grave robber John Grey in the 1945 thriller *The Body Snatcher*.

an iron hand. Who is sane? Who is mad? It depends on who wields power. It takes a revolt of the insane, and a trial that mocks the rituals of justice, to deliver the villain his comeuppance.

These elements, combined and guided under the supervision (and incessant late-night rewrites) of Lewton, present a paradigm present in all the films—a bland daylight world that is seduced and turned upside down by the narcotic enticement of darkness outside the scope of vision.

No matter what kind of happy resolution is imposed at the end of these films, there is a terrible feeling of incompleteness to them. Under Lewton, the horror film opens out and speaks about far more than it was initially designed to do. Lewton leverages the mind of the viewer to fill in the blanks, knowing of course that what is imagined might be behind that door or lurking above is far more terrifying than anything shown. At the end of a Lewton film, the toll of the unseen adds up disquietingly.

Director Jacques Tourneur went on to many successes in all manner of genres, and specifically in horror with *Night of the Demon* (1957) and *The Comedy of Terrors* (1963); Wise, of course, went on to make *The Day the Earth Stood Still* (1951) and *The Haunting* (1963) (and *West Side Story*, 1961 and *The Sound of Music*, 1964).

Karloff's three appearances in Lewton's films show him at the height of his powers. The Karloffian trio of bitter sadists—the cabman/murderer John Gray in *The Body Snatcher*, the paranoid General Pherides in *Isle of the Dead*, and the asylum keeper Master Sims in *Bedlam*—all resonate on a remarkable number of levels, turning these seemingly simple horror tales into disquisitions on morality, power, hypocrisy, and the flimsy social mechanisms that so easily crumple when evil pushes at them.

idealistic student assistant discovers the truth.

Snatcher is also about class and society. "I am a small man, a humble man," Gray intones with a mixture of threat, pain, resentment, and envy. "Being poor I have had to do much that I did not want to do. But as long as the great MacFarlane comes to my whistle, that long I am a man. If I have not that, then I have nothing. Then I am only a cabman and a grave robber. You'll never get rid of me, Toddy."

As the principals' schemes unravel and collide, fantastic bravura sequences underline the horror. Gray stalks a blind street singer whose song is cut off mid-verse; later, Gray strangles potential blackmailer Joseph (Bela Lugosi) in ominous shadowplay. The final sequence, in driving rain and flashing lightning, is one of horror's most indelible moments.

In 1945, the Robson-directed *Isle of the Dead* traps a disparate group, one of them perhaps a vampiric demon, on a remote Greek island. Catalepsy and madness ensue. The final entry in the canon, *Bedlam* (Robson, 1946), uses a madhouse as a metaphor for the corrupted body politic. In it, a social reformer is imprisoned by the sadistic Karloff, who rules his subjects with

ATOMIC-AGE MONSTERS

THE SCI-FI/HORROR BOOM

After the soul-shocking obscenities of Auschwitz and Hiroshima, where could horror film go? The genocidal terrors that mankind unleashed upon itself during World War II dwarfed anything the most darkly inspired horror storyteller could conceive.

In response, horror got edgy again during the first postwar decade, as though the collective unconscious needed to spit up a fresh load of bile. A deep mistrust of both technological progress and mankind's inhumane tendencies was manifest. For some time to come, horror would be heavily tinged with science fiction.

Up to this time, science fiction had focused on flights of fantasy rather than on bug-eyed monsters and death. The opening of the space age filled people with curiosity and an appetite for speculative fiction (a previously marginal genre) on the subject. Horror film took note. In outer space, there was a whole new realm in which fears could breed.

The film industry itself changed at the same time. A landmark antitrust decision of 1948 meant that studios could no longer command exhibitors to show what the studios wanted, when and where they wanted. This removal of leverage meant that there was no longer a guaranteed market for studio films.

The American film industry was also fighting for the eyes that had turned to television directly after World War II. The inroads television was rapidly making on film audiences meant that movies had to provide the viewer with something they couldn't see at home.

The vastness of the movie theater's screen surface, in comparison to TV's dinky, grainy, black-and-white box, was emphasized. That meant epics and intermissioned, overtured "road shows"—in other words, films as grand, destination events. Various gimmicks were floated. There were widescreen innovations such as Cinerama, CinemaScope, VistaVision, and Panavision. There were super-widescreen and 3D projection systems.

There was more sex, more violence, and an exploration of controversial topics, as the Motion Picture Production Code began to crumble. "Art houses"—small boutique theaters that featured foreign, experimental, and vintage films—and a new filmgoing culture were springing up as well, encouraging the incursion of more broad-ranging fare.

The expertise, time, and money spent on these horror films from the nifty 1950s (horror-comedy king Joe Dante's 1993 *Matinee* is a tribute to the period) were scant. The results looked cheap and cheesy, but that didn't seem to bother moviegoers one bit. Fright flicks, and other genre films, were now a staple of the drive-in movie theaters that multiplied across the country. These movies were rites of passage for teenagers, who were already cynical and developing postmodern sensibilities—and incubating the concept of camp.

The sci-fi/horror film broke down roughly into three categories: 1) an alien invasion, seeking to subdue/enslave/consume/erase mankind; 2) scientific experiments (usually atomic) that create or awaken a nonhuman, giant monster; or 3) The creation of an altered self—a shrinking/colossal/transparent/all-seeing man, warped out of shape and usually out of his mind as well.

OPPOSITE:
The Day the Earth Stood Still (1951) poster.

Attack of the Crab Monsters (1957) poster.

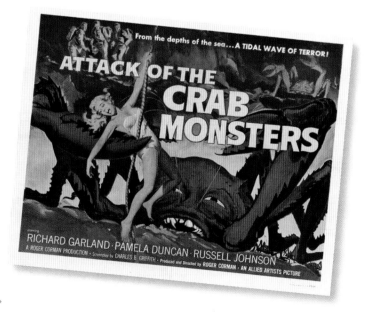

James Arness as *The Thing from Another World* (1951).

The idea of alien conquest was as old as *The War of the Worlds*, but the 1950s turned planet Earth into a locus of high-volume alien interest, a delicious destination that inspired an imaginary onslaught of bug-eyed invaders. The positive and negative poles of that speculative subgenre were embodied in two films released in the same year, 1951—Robert Wise's *The Day the Earth Stood Still*, about a Christlike ambassador from outer space, and Howard Hawks and Christian Nyby's paranoid *The Thing from Another World*.

The Thing was based on John W. Campbell's terrifying 1938 story "Who Goes There?" (done justice years later by director John Carpenter). Despite Nyby's directorial credit, *The Thing* is a Hawks film, containing many Hawksian touches: the culture of manliness, the fast, overlapping, wisecracking dialogue, the idealization of teamwork, and the achievement of a definite mission. But *The Thing* also contains all the hallmarks of '50s horror, among them aliens with unknown powers, pervasive paranoia, and a slam-bang violent conclusion.

A military crew and scientists examine a crashed alien starship in the Arctic, unleashing a blood-drinking being, the possible harbinger

The Thing from Another World (1951) poster.

of an invasion bent on destroying them all. All the archetypes are present. Robert Cornthwaite plays to perfection the egotistical, dour intellectual, the Nobel Prize-winning "egghead" scientist with well-formed vowels who insists on making friends with the creature, in the process endangering all humanity in the name of knowledge (a more well-behaved but no less mad scientist type). Kenneth Tobey plays the hypermasculine leader, fond of following orders and sticking to practical solutions. There is a chauvinist cast to the whole enterprise; the Arctic research station's greenhouse door is locked because "the Eskimos are too fond of our strawberries." Someone says at one point, "You look like a lynch mob."

Margaret Sheridan is simultaneously the scientist's secretary and the leader's love interest—the typical Hawksian tough girl, who can drink and smoke and banter with the best of them—and a prehistoric predecessor of the fabled "Final Girl" in horror film. (As the decade progressed, this new female archetype quickly waned, mirroring the culture's swing toward sexism, and devolved rapidly back into the archetype of the Helpless Female Victim. To kill monsters during the 1950s, you needed a penis, and were preferably white, American, and Christian—in that order.)

Hawks legitimized the science-fiction genre simply by making a good, solid film within its strictures, filming the unreal in an everyday, deadpan style. Hawks showed that new ideas

and gimmicks could be slotted into a standard Hollywood action-film template.

The heart of *The Thing* is not science fiction but horror—the threat of destruction, the fear of what's on the other side of the door. In fact, the Cold War subtext comes right to the surface in the final line: "Keep watching the skies!" The price of freedom in the America of the 1950s was eternal paranoia.

Again and again, humanity repulsed alien attacks in films such as *Invaders from Mars* (1953), *Phantom from Space* (1953), *Target Earth* (1954), *Earth vs. the Flying Saucers* (1956), *It Conquered the World* (1956), *Invisible Invaders* (1959), *Plan 9 from Outer Space* (1957), and even *Teenagers from Outer Space* (1959). Only three of this subgenre distinguished themselves—Jack Arnold's *It Came from Outer Space* (1953), William Cameron Menzies's *Invaders from Mars*, and Don Siegel's splendid *Invasion of the Body Snatchers* (1956).

It Came from Outer Space was based on an unpublished story treatment by author Ray Bradbury, "The Meteor." It was Universal's first 3D production, and

its premise is clever and counterintuitive. When the aliens turned out to be benign travelers stuck unintentionally on Earth with the cosmic equivalent of a flat tire, it's our own paranoia and hostility that serves as the engine of threat.

Menzies invented the job of film production designer, and the gorgeous color values of *Invaders from Mars* read like a gaily illustrated folk tale or a dream (the story, like that of *Frankenstein*, originated in a nightmare). It's told from the perspective of a boy who sees a flying saucer land and then finds everyone around him . . . changing. The idea that all the grown-ups are actually stern, brutal monsters under the control of something strange, compatriots in a weird conspiracy, is an accurate metaphor for the confusions and anxieties of childhood. The subtle paranoia, coupled with an original, open-ended conclusion, makes it an anxiety-stoking delight. (The equivocal "was it all a nightmare?" ending was changed for British audiences.)

Whether *Invasion of the Body Snatchers* is taken as a metaphor for the encroachments of communism, fascism, the Church, political correctness, or conformity, the idea of a secret invasion of alien "pod people" that grow like

giant, grotesque embryos to resemble the very humans they kill and replace remains resonant. Director Don Siegel's gritty film-noir instincts pull the film into a lean, hard-hitting style normally allotted to crime film. (The original and highly negative ending was nixed by the studio, which shot a new closing scene assuring the audience of the inevitable destruction of the invaders.)

The scariest part of *Snatchers* is how easy a takeover seems to be. Significantly, the "change" happens when humans fall asleep; staying awake is the only way to keep from being destroyed. The protagonist, Dr. Bennell (Kevin McCarthy), muses, "In my practice, I've seen how people have allowed their humanity to drain away. Only,

it happens slowly instead of all at once. They didn't seem to mind." The invaders see feeling and individuality as barriers to efficiency, traits that are better off eliminated. And as their ranks grow, it seems more and more mad to oppose their calm and logical domination. By film's end, Bennell is a raving prophet of doom.

The new wave of giant-monster pictures was launched by two men. First, there was Ray Bradbury, whose 1951 short story "The Fog Horn" tells the tale of a lonely dinosaur that mistakes the blare of a fog horn for the voice of a fellow

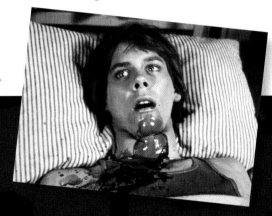

Before They Were BIG

Many stars got their start humbly, in horror films. Here are some familiar names with some of their no-so-well-remembered early film appearances.

Leonard Nimoy: *Zombies of the Stratosphere* (1952)
Clint Eastwood: *Revenge of the Creature and Tarantula* (1955)
Steve McQueen: *The Blob* (1958)
Kevin Bacon: *Friday the 13th* (1980)
Tom Hanks: *He Knows You're Alone* (1980)
George Clooney: *Grizzly II: Revenge* (1983)

Johnny Depp: *A Nightmare on Elm Street* (1984)
Patrick Dempsey: *The Stuff* (1985)
Patricia Arquette: *A Nightmare on Elm Street 3: Dream Warriors* (1987)
Leonardo Di Caprio: *Critters 3* (1991)
Hilary Swank: *Buffy the Vampire Slayer* (1992)
Jennifer Aniston: *Leprechaun* (1993)
Michelle Williams: *Species* (1995)
Renee Zellweger: *Texas Chainsaw Massacre: The Next Generation* (1995)
Paul Rudd: *Halloween: The Curse of Michael Myers* (1995)
Charlize Theron: *Children of the Corn III: Urban Harvest* (1995)
Matthew McConaughey: *Texas Chainsaw Massacre: The Next Generation* (1995)
Adam Scott: *Hellraiser: Bloodline* (1996)

ABOVE LEFT: *The Blob* (1958) poster; ABOVE RIGHT: Kevin Bacon is an unfortunate victim in *Friday the 13th* (1980).

creature. Next, budding special-effects artist Ray Harryhausen drew up a project inspired by that story, and by the successful 1952 re-release of *King Kong*.

Harryhausen had studied with Willis O'Brien, the creator of the original 1933 *King Kong* model work, and he developed a "monster from the sea" concept drawn from Bradbury's premise. The battle this time was against a stop-motion dinosaur brought to life by atomic testing. Against it, the film pits Kenneth Tobey, again a decisive alpha male, accompanied by most of the US military. (Tobey was one of a squad of square-jawed, manly sci-fi/horror heroes of the period, a list that included John Agar, Richard Carlson, Hugh Marlowe, Grant Williams, and the ever-popular Whit Bissell.)

The result, *The Beast from 20,000 Fathoms* (1953), cost $210,000 to make, and grossed $5,000,000. Harryhausen was launched on a multi-decade career as a special-effects legend. Everybody started making stop-motion monsters. Not long after, Japan's Toho Studios whipped up a live-action, miniature-scaled, monster-suited one in *Godzilla* (1954), creating Japan's *kaiju* (strange beast) subgenre.

This new generation of monsters enlisted none of the sympathy the previous one did. These monsters were nonhuman: giant and/or mutated reptiles (*Reptilicus*, 1961), insects (*Them!*, 1954; *Beginning of the End*, 1957), crustaceans (*Attack of the Crab Monsters*, 1957), arachnids (*Tarantula*, 1955), cephalopods (*It Came from Beneath the Sea*, 1955), mollusks (*The Monster That Challenged the*

Personal Best

Roger Corman

House of Usher (1960)

Little Shop of Horrors (1960)

Tales of Terror (1962)

X: The Man with the X-Ray Eyes (1963)

Masque of the Red Death (1964)

PREHISTORIC SEA-GIANT RAGES AGAINST CITY! A THRILL STORY BEYOND ALL IMAGINING!

WARNER BROS. PRESENT The Beast from 20,000 Fathoms

The Beast from 20,000 Fathoms (1953) lobby card.

World, 1957) minerals (*The Monolith Monsters*, 1957), and even undifferentiated masses of protoplasm (*The Blob*, 1958).

These creatures had no backstory, no pathos. They were unintelligible, but undeniably aggressive. As in the 1940s, the monsters of this era were used as gimmicks, soulless plot devices that propelled the special effects . . . such as they were. Films such as *Them!* were breeding grounds not only for monsters, but for up-and-coming actors such as Clint Eastwood, James Arness, James Whitmore, Fess Parker, and Leonard Nimoy.

The only distinguished movie monster to join the canon besides Godzilla in the 1950s was the Creature from the Black Lagoon. The director of *Creature* was Jack Arnold, who helmed a number of '50s sci-fi and horror hits, most in tandem with producer William Alland.

The Amazonian Gill-Man is hunted by eager biologists who want to rip him away from his quiet backwater hangout. Somehow, despite his preposterous, inexpressive appearance, the amphibious humanoid inspired fear and affection in three films (*Creature from the Black Lagoon*, 1954; *Revenge of the Creature*, 1955; *The Creature Walks Among Us*, 1956) as he pursued love unsuccessfully in plots clearly taken from the Beauty and the Beast/King Kong playbook.

The Gill-Man's fate is repeatedly tragic. In a way, he's the ultimate nerd monster—a put-upon soul, a literal fish out of water, the kind who trips over his own claws, gets tangled in fishing nets, and never, ever gets the girl.

The epitome of the no-budget sci-fi/horror flick of the 1950s is Roger Corman's *It Conquered the World*. An alien-invasion story featuring one of the shortest monsters on record, this ludicrous production is anchored by the stalwart performances of cheapie veterans such as Peter Graves, Beverly Garland, and Lee Van Cleef, the last of whom is forced to spit out lines like: "I welcomed you to this Earth. You made a charnel house!" (Fortunately, the alien leader is easily dispatched with a common hardware-store blowtorch.)

The "mutation" subgenre of horror films of the period resembles the Jekyll/Hyde template, the exception being that most of those affected in these films are passive victims: they are not scientists taking a conscious risk but rather "regular" people exposed to radiation or experimental medicine by chance. This series of films really began with Britain's *The Quatermass Xperiment*, aka *The Creeping Unknown*, in 1955. In this film, a hapless returning astronaut is the

carrier of a hungry alien life force which turns him into one of their own.

These films are usually distinguished by the adjectives in their titles: *The Amazing Colossal Man* (1957), *The Incredible Shrinking Man* (1957), *The Hideous Sun Demon* (1958), *Attack of the 50 Foot Woman* (1958), *The Amazing Transparent Man* (1960) . . .

By 1962, in *The Brain That Wouldn't Die*, a scientist keeps his girlfriend's accidentally decapitated head alive in a pan full of nutrients in an effort to hook her up to a "suitable" body. She is not happy, and neither is anyone else by the end of the film, especially the viewer.

The best of this subgenre is *The Incredible Shrinking Man*. It's the story of a man exposed to a combination of radiation and insecticide who begins to decrease in size. The metaphor of shrinking is a powerful sexual one—stature equals status, and protagonist Scott Carey finds himself progressively ridiculed, ignored, made impotent, and finally forgotten as he shrinks away to nothingness. (The outsized props and clever technical work make the story surprisingly plausible.) The riveting story is a great adventure, as well as a profound meditation on masculinity,

Gill-Man from *Creature from the Black Lagoon* (1954).

power, and identity. Grant Williams, who worked less often than he should have, masters the title role.

As he grows smaller, Carey finds that he possesses an existential worth that transcends his stature. He struggles for survival, first versus the family cat, then against a terrifying spider that, relative to him, is the size of a Buick. The studio wanted an ending in which the hero returns to normal size, but director Jack Arnold stuck to a more mystical conclusion, in which Carey asserts, "Smaller than the smallest, I meant something, too. To God, there is no zero. I still exist!"

In the cases of films such as *The Fly* (1958) and *X: The Man with the X-Ray Eyes* (1963), we are firmly on the familiar path of the mad doctor who destroys himself. *The Fly* is Ground Zero for the body-horror subgenre. In it, a scientist (David Hedison) working on teleportation mixes his atoms with those of an errant housefly. The first film was given a much stronger, more complex and justly celebrated remake years later by David Cronenberg, but the original has its moments. (That small, shrill voice screaming, "Help me! Help me! . . .")

X: The Man with the X-Ray Eyes is a Jekyll/Hyde story for a new generation. An arrogant scientist (Ray Milland) creates eye drops that give him powerful vision, but it turns out to be both a boon and a curse. His optical powers keep increasing, and he can't stop them. Cleverly filmed, the story has a nihilistic ending—one that anticipated the increasingly black tone of horror films to come.

To a man (and including the 50 Foot Woman), science's mutated victims become hostile, resentful, alienated, and aggressive. There is no way to reintegrate them into society. Like the alien invaders and the giant inhuman monsters (and like other real-world international threats), they become amoral forces that seek to destroy our treasured way of life. They deserved no mercy. Sometimes they were even teenagers (AIP's awful, but profitable, bang-bang *I Was a Teenage Werewolf* and *I Was a Teenage Frankenstein*, both 1957.)

The horror films of the 1950s were focused on the human protagonists instead of the monsters, emphasizing both their responsibility for creating the movie's problem in the first place and highlighting their ingenuity in eliminating the resulting threat. There's wish fulfillment in that scenario. The nuclear age was at once exhilarating and terrifying. Could we put the genie back in its bottle? On film, mankind usually triumphs. In *Invasion of the Body Snatchers*, an "everything is under control" ending was tacked awkwardly onto the end; in other films, a familiar "The End?" title would be seen, leaving room for doubt, if not for a sequel.

A few eager movies tried to pile all these elements together. In *Not of This Earth* (1957*),* *It! The Terror from Beyond Space*, and *Night of the Blood Beast* (both 1958), alien creatures are murderous rampagers, foreshadowing the threatening monsters of *Planet of the Vampires* (1965) and *Alien* (1979). In *Forbidden Planet* (1956), ostensibly a straight science-fiction film, a horror/monster element blends nicely with the iconic space-age style, and enjoys parallels with Shakespeare's *The Tempest* as well.

Significantly, *Forbidden Planet*'s murderous monster is created by a scientist's unconscious thoughts. Soon, American horror movies would make a sharp turn downwards into the depths of the human psyche, into the realms of insanity and bloodshed.

Robby the Robot meets actor Earl Holiman as the ship's cook in *Forbidden Planet* (1956).

BLOOD AND BOSOMS
THE SUCCESS OF HAMMER HORROR

IT'S COMING FOR <u>YOU</u>
from Space to wipe
all living things from
the face of the Earth!
CAN IT BE STOPPED?

Hammer film stars (from left) Christopher Lee, Hazel Court, and Anton Diffring at the Hammer Films Christmas party in 1958.

OPPOSITE: Poster for *The Quatermass Xperiment*, aka *The Creeping Unknown* (1955).

"The best horror films are adult fairy tales, no more, no less," said veteran Hammer horror director Terence Fisher.[1] For all the futurism in the films of the 1950s, the most significant trend of the decade in film horror was a return to the past. A decision to revive classic monsters, tied together with sumptuous Technicolor gore and the fortuitous intersection of a remarkable number of talents, propelled Britain's Hammer Studios to the top of the horror heap. Over the course of two decades, in more than four dozen horror, sci-fi, and thriller movies, Hammer formed a bridge between horror's Gothic past and horror cycles of the future—including Roger Corman's Poe films, the Italian *gialli* crime/horror sagas, exploitation films, and the inevitable slide to more graphic horror as censorship standards eroded.

Ironically, Hammer's first horror hit was a typical '50s sci-fi/horror hybrid. Hammer Film Productions was one of Britain's many low-budget domestic movie companies when it struck gold in 1955 with its adaptation of a highly successful BBC television alien-invasion series with a scientist hero, Dr. Bernard Quatermass. (American character-actor great Brian Donlevy was cast in the lead role for insurance; in non-US films, a Designated American Star in the credits was seen as prime box-office bait.)

The Quatermass Xperiment—the missing "E" emphasizes the "X" rating of the film, a new designation that restricted British viewers to those sixteen and older—is an effective hybrid, featuring a brilliant, nearly wordless performance by Richard Wordsworth as an astronaut who returns to Earth infected with a murderous, energy-absorbing extraterrestrial life form. The British censors found the shooting script "outrageous," but audiences didn't seem to mind the graphic presentation of a mutated human being.

Hammer studio head James Carreras decided to capitalize on the opportunity. Emboldened further by the success of Warner Brothers' Victorian-period, color, 3D horror film *House of Wax* in 1953, the Hammer team decided to resuscitate the Frankenstein franchise. Cleverly, they stayed away from the Universal Studios aesthetic so that copyright lawsuits would not be filed. Furthermore, they shot the bloody details in color, using vivid hues that intensified the scares. (Unfortunately, they used Eastmancolor stock, which is highly unstable and prone to fading, making it very difficult to find well-preserved copies of these early Hammer efforts.)

Four key figures set the tone for Hammer horror: director Fisher, screenwriter Jimmy Sangster, cinematographer Jack Asher, and production designer Bernard Robinson. Fisher was chosen for the Frankenstein project due to his experience with London's Gainsborough Pictures, which cranked out a number of notable costume melodramas between 1942 and 1946. Sangster was a production manager turned screenwriter, and, as such, he knew how to write a screenplay that used scant resources to maximum effect. Asher and Robinson are the particular unsung heroes: faced with skeletal budgets and the limited confines of what became the Bray Studio, a sixteenth-century country house on the Thames, west of London, the two men created a lavish look for most of the films in the series, dressing and redressing the same rooms ingeniously. Meanwhile, Hammer house composer James Bernard's contributions, his distinctive percussive emphases, horn runs, and clashing strings did much to carry home the sweeping, magisterial threats peddled in Fisher's sequences. (Hammer musical director Harry Robinson turned out some decent scores as well.)

Horror of Dracula (1958) lobby card.

At the same time, Hammer producers put together two actors whose names would become as synonymous with horror film as Karloff's and Lugosi's. For *The Curse of Frankenstein* (1957), the hulking, six-foot-five Christopher Lee was cast as Frankenstein's Monster, and the charming and polite Peter Cushing took on the role of the mad doctor himself.

Fortunately, director Fisher had never read Mary Shelley's original book or seen any of Universal's original Frankenstein entries—and had no desire to. Sangster's script focuses on the unscrupulous doctor, who will do anything in the pursuit of science, and who uses his creature to satisfy his murderous ends. (The doctor is the continuing character from film to film; Lee did not play the Monster again.) And Herr Doktor's ruthless toying with the affections of two women in the film is definitely a new twist. Some of the legacy of the monster movies of the 1940s is here, though—the Monster is still silent and violent, a

Peter Cushing in The Curse of Frankenstein (1957).

soulless tool that furthers the plot. *The Curse of Frankenstein* was widely despised as graphic and obscene, and slapped with an X rating. It was, of course, wildly popular.

The Hammer aesthetic was cemented with the next horror entry, *Dracula*, aka *The Horror of Dracula* (1958). Christopher Lee was cast as the Count, and Cushing as his Van Helsing. Lee's is a very different Dracula from Lugosi's. Lee's interpretation makes him a proud, commanding figure, irresistible to women, able instantly to flash into a state of demonic bloodlust. (Lee was not just the definitive Dracula for many; he could play a range of genre characters, from sober heroes to raging maniacs, to a last great turn as the wizard Saruman in the *Lord of the Rings* film trilogy.)

In contrast, Peter Cushing's heroes are much like his villains—calm, cool, logical— and his Van Helsing is a workmanlike scientist, rigged out with a complete set of

Personal Best
Peter Cushing

The Curse of Frankenstein (1957)

(Horror of) Dracula (1958)

The Flesh and the Fiends (1960)

The Brides of Dracula (1960)

Twins of Evil (1971)

vampire-fighting paraphernalia in a handy carrying case. Whether playing a Frankenstein or a Van Helsing, Cushing had an absolute, no-nonsense conviction about his character that carried him through the most implausible scenarios, combined with a restraint that made his performances subtle and modulated.

The Hammer production crew did an outstanding job of projecting a rich, Gothic feeling onto celluloid in *Dracula*, and the camerawork is free and fluid. The color work, the most talked-about aspect of the early Hammers, is garish and meant to provoke. The Hammer characters, unlike most of those in the Universal entries, are three-dimensional. There are few subplots, and almost no comic relief. Underneath it all, there's a dedication to quality that commands respect and still hangs together. Simultaneously streamlined and overwrought, this new Dracula would spawn eight Hammer sequels.

The Hammer films mark a return to a less-enlightened historical period. Like the 1950s, the Victorian era was another superficially super-rational period, consciously focused on reason and progress, but also one plagued by an irrational undertow. In sci-fi/horror, rational forces overcome the aberrations of nature and the hellspawn of science. In Hammer films, the protagonists have to reject dry reason. They first have to acknowledge that there are monsters among them. They have to believe the unbelievable in order to defeat it. Even Hammer's "scientific" horror films hinge on a rejection of science and a reversion to faith in the primitive, the mystic, and the macabre, a reattunement to more ancient concepts of tragic blindness and cosmic revenge. In this way, Hammer prepared the ground for England's forthcoming "folk horror" boomlet.

The twin successes of *The Curse of Frankenstein* and *Dracula* resulted in Hammer forging an alliance with Universal in America, and brought investors to their business office. Soon most of the Universal and other classic horror icons—such as the Mummy, the Phantom of the Opera, and werewolves—joined the Hammer stable. In livid, gory, and graphically violent form, they ruled the horror box office for nearly fifteen years.

The Mummy (1959) wisely returned to the

original concept of a doomed lover seeking his mate across the centuries. Christopher Lee is an impressive Kharis, the monster of the title. He finally gets some dialogue in flashback, handles it well, and then becomes mute but perfectly expressive as the central character, tapping into pathos more effectively than any horror performer since Karloff. Amazing production design on a small budget reinforced this solid, fast-paced reboot of the Mummy franchise (and sparked three sequels).

Perhaps the most unrestrained Hammer entry is *The Brides of Dracula* (1960).

George Pastell (left) as Mememet Bey and Christopher Lee as the title character in *The Mummy* (1959).

The most evil DRACULA of all!

The BRIDES of DRACULA

Starring PETER CUSHING · FREDA JACKSON · MARTITA HUNT · YVONNE MONLAUR

Screenplay by JIMMY SANGSTER, PETER BRYAN and EDWARD PERCY · Directed by TERENCE FISHER
Executive Producer MICHAEL CARRERAS · A Hammer Film Production Released by Universal International through Rank Distributors Ltd

The Brides of Dracula (1960) poster.

It's not exceptionally coherent, but it's filled with striking imagery and ideas, including weird themes of polygamy and incest. Instead of Lee's Dracula, we have David Peel as a suave, perverse Baron Meinster, and veteran actress Martita Hunt as his doting mum. There is much to unpack, including the idea that status and wealth insulate and sustain perverse and anti-human tendencies. Cushing is back as Van Helsing at his most swashbuckling. Featuring self-branding and burning windmills, it's a fever dream of a film.

Other significant contributors to Hammer were directors Freddie Francis (*Paranoiac*, 1965), Roy Ward Baker (*Quatermass and the Pit*, 1967), John Gilling (*The Plague of the Zombies*, 1966), and Pete Sasdy (*Taste the Blood of Dracula*, 1970). There were key writers and producers as well, such as Tudor Gates, who penned Hammer's strange and erotic "Karnstein trilogy" (*The Vampire Lovers*, 1970; *Lust for a Vampire*, 1971; *Twins of Evil*, 1971), and Anthony Hinds, who produced under his own name but cranked out horror screenplays as John Elder.

The Hammer repertory company of actors was superb. One standout was Anton Diffring (1959's *The Man Who Could Cheat Death* and 1960's *Circus of Horrors*), whose cool Aryan manner made him perfect for roles as mad doctors and Nazis, both of which he regularly played. (Ironically, Diffring escaped Hitler's Germany due to the threat to his life he faced for being gay and Jewish.) Actresses such as Ingrid

Pitt, Hazel Court, Barbara Shelley, Veronica Carlson, and Kate O'Mara are unmistakable as screaming victims and/or as vampiric acolytes. Actors such as Michael Gough, Michael Ripper, Ralph Bates, André Morell, and Andrew Keir were regulars as well. (Oliver Reed's first starring role was in Hammer's 1961 *The Curse of the Werewolf*.)

Quatermass and the Pit, aka *Five Million Years to Earth*, is the most successful of Hammer's three Quatermass films, and the most outrageous. This time, the gruff Andrew Keir portrays the professor, who must investigate an alien spacecraft uncovered by underground construction in London. It seems that Martians colonized Earth, created mankind, and are the Satanic source of all evil. Which means, in a sense, that mankind is essentially evil as well. As their malevolent influence tears up the urban infrastructure and makes humanity go berserk, the question becomes—can they be destroyed? The beautiful Barbara Shelley and perpetual good-guy sidekick James Donald are wonderful, and the innovative special effects are a highlight.

Another compelling entry is *The Devil Rides Out* (1968), an adaptation of the popular 1934 novel by Dennis Wheatley. Christopher Lee gets to play the hero for once, as he leads the fight against a cult of Satanists led by the saturnine Mocata (Charles Gray). There are plenty of arresting special-effects sequences, but the

Hammer Horror's Best

The Curse of Frankenstein (1957)
(Horror of) Dracula (1958)
The Mummy (1959)
The Brides of Dracula (1960)
Quatermass and the Pit (1967)
The Devil Rides Out (1968)
The Vampire Lovers (1970)
Vampire Circus (1972)
Countess Dracula (1971)
Captain Kronos – Vampire Hunter (1974)

highlight of the film is a simply staged scene in which Mocata, sitting quietly in an armchair, attempts to hypnotize and control the troupe of protagonists.

Now . . . about the sex. Another important aspect of Hammer was its emphasis on revealing the female body, and exploring the sexual subtext (later on, there was nothing "sub" about it) that was implicit in horror narratives. Hammer heroines were often blonde and always bosomy, showing off their anatomies in diaphanous, low-cut gowns and peignoirs.

It was very clear that something forbidden and erotic was taking place when the Hammer version of Count Dracula had his way with his prey. He was a hypnotic seducer who unleashed his female victims' carnality while he sucked their blood. It was this vampiric release of repressed sexuality that was the most threatening aspect of all.

Eventually, sex in Hammer films moved into the foreground. *The Vampire Lovers* featured Ingrid Pitt as the vampire Carmilla, who preferred to dominate innocent young women, mentally and sexually. The so-called "Karnstein trilogy" continued with *Lust for a Vampire* and *Twins of Evil*, and Pitt went on to star as Countess Dracula (also 1971), bathing in the blood of her victims to maintain eternal youth. Though Pitt only had these two substantial horror roles for Hammer, her performances were so indelible that they vaulted her into the horror canon.

As the sequels multiplied, ideas began to run out, and cheap, unmotivated gore, violence, and sex began to dominate. Hammer was now competing with bolder imitators, both in Britain and abroad, and losing the battle. It began to parody itself in increasingly outrageous and campy takes such as *Vampire Circus* (1972), *Dracula A.D. 1972* (1972), and *Frankenstein and the Monster from Hell* (1974).

The most enjoyable late-period Hammer feature is *Vampire Circus*. A vanquished vampire vows revenge, and it comes fifteen years later in the form of a . . . you guessed it: a circus. Owned, operated, and underwritten by vampires.

Complete with a maniacal dwarf, shapeshifters, a bare-naked lady/leopard, and hallucinations, it's a potpourri of self-indulgent spectacle, a tasty treat chock-full of empty calories.

A wonderful late entry written and directed by Brian Clemens, *Captain Kronos—Vampire Hunter* (1974), showed a possible new direction for Hammer, adding adventure and humor to the usual formula, in a movie designed to be the first in a series. It sets up a daring duo: Kronos, the man of action (Horst Janson), and his brainy, hunchbacked assistant Professor Grost (John Cater). But it was too late. The original run of Hammer horror films petered out in 1976 with *To the Devil a Daughter*, featuring a nude fifteen-year-old Nastassja Kinski.

Hammer's "blood and bosoms" formula still works. Despite its occasional absurdities and lapses into bad taste, the studio's generally literate and high-toned approach gave it class and distinction, a shuddery thrill associated with mist, velvet, lace, and splashes of vivid red. At their best, Hammer films are glorious, diverting mashups of high- and low-art elements. It's trash, but it's highfalutin' trash, and it's apparent that everyone involved created the films with the deep seriousness and shared enthusiasm of children at play. The Hammer horror films are grown-up dress-up and make-believe parties; games played so seriously that they convince.

Christopher Lee in *Dracula A.D. 1972* (1972).

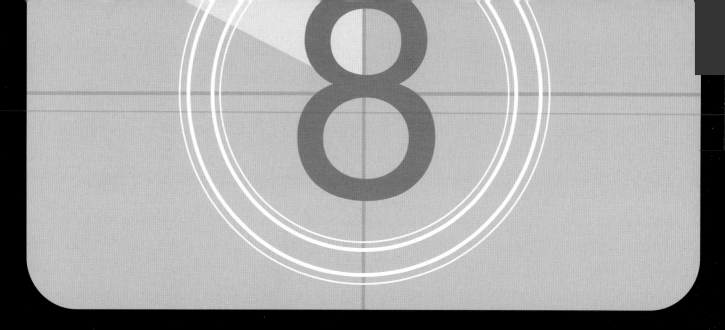

THE MOMENT OF SHOCK

OF SHOCK

PSYCHO AND *PEEPING TOM*

The year 1960 was pivotal for film horror. No fewer than four groundbreaking movies—Britain's *Peeping Tom*, America's *Psycho*, Japan's *Jigoku*, and Italy's *Black Sunday*—were released, each of them seismically disturbing to censors and audiences alike, and all deeply frightening in a completely new way. (The last two films mentioned inaugurated their own national horror cycles, to be discussed later on.)

European and Asian film industries gained massive amounts of global ground in the 1950s. As nations rebuilt themselves after World War II, they found America ready and willing to absorb their cultural products. Soon lumped in with more serious foreign "arthouse films," genre pictures from around the world played in America—and made money. Then, when Britain's Hammer Studios succeeded by reviving the classic movie monsters, it emboldened other European, Asian, and American film studios to leap hard into the horror genre.

Horror film was dormant for decades on the continent, due partly to government censorship and partly to a learned lack of demand. But

Black Sunday (1960) poster.

a new feeling was slowly developing across national cinemas, edgy and disturbing. Actor Charles Laughton's single directorial effort, 1955's *The Night of the Hunter*, though classified as a thriller, is a scary, subversive, and influential horror film. It's a dark, Expressionistic children's nightmare, a cautionary tale with mythic overtones. Legendary film critic James Agee's script, one of only four he would ever write, tells the story of a serial-killer preacher who stalks two children in a quest for stolen money. In the process, the adult world is revealed to be oblivious both to truth and to understanding. Robert Mitchum plays one of his signature roles as the villain, "LOVE" tattooed on one set of knuckles and "HATE" on the other. Hunter combines a strange, silent-era dreaminess with a scathing portrayal of hypocritical evil.

Henri-Georges Clouzot's *Les Diaboliques*, also made in 1955, was a game-changer. The story of a wife and mistress who combine forces to kill the abusive man who rules over them was adapted from a popular 1951 murder mystery by the team of Pierre Boileau and Thomas Narcejac. (Their work would be adapted into other memorable films such as *Vertigo*, 1958, and *Eyes Without a Face*, 1960.) In its claustrophobia, *Diaboliques* was a throwback to the "old dark house" mystery/horror films of the 1920s. However, it differs from everything that came before it in three key ways.

First, the plot. *Diaboliques* was among the earliest films to implore its audience (with a final title card) not to reveal its twist ending. The film

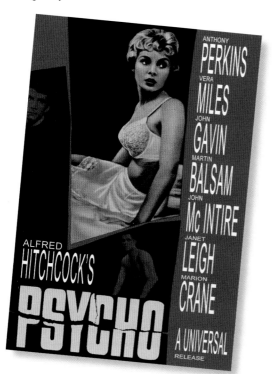

OPPOSITE: British poster for *Peeping Tom* (1960).

Psycho (1960) poster.

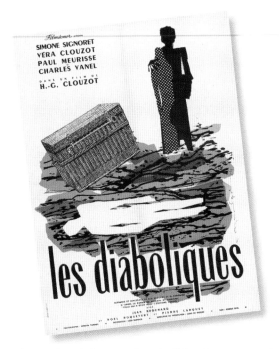

Les Diaboliques (1955) poster.

is constructed as one long buildup to a traumatic payoff, which calls into question everything the viewer has seen and believed. It pulls the rug out from under its audience, assaulting its sense of logic and continuity. Clouzot's twisty mystery founded the cinema of shock—an entire movie constructed to provide a disturbing climax.

Second is Clouzot's emphasis on the subjective experience of the film's central figure, its guilty protagonist, the wife Christina. Played by the brilliant Vera Clouzot, the director's wife, the film is shot from her perspective. The gloomy, banal setting of an oppressive boys' school, the film's dank, sodden, and moldy atmosphere, and the fragmented and shadowed interiors evoke the unexpressed feelings that ferment underneath as the principals attempt not to panic. Clouzot again and again concentrates on small details and atmospheric touches, as well as pauses that linger just a shade too long. In so doing, the director creates a sense of impending and inescapable doom.

Third and most important is the unrepentantly dim view of humanity that *Diaboliques* embodies. There is a despair in the film about the inherent selfishness of human motivation akin to that found in the film noirs of the day, but Clouzot goes deeper. His past provides clues for his attitude. Clouzot started

out translating German films into French, but was fired by his German studio for his friendship with Jewish producers. Later, he worked for a German film company in France during World War II and was then condemned afterwards, and for a time blacklisted, as a German collaborator.

In *Diaboliques*, all actions seem destined to frustration. Emotions are irrelevant in the struggle for domination. No one is safe or worthy of trust, and paranoia rules the day. Instead of an attack from without, Clouzot gives us the horror from within, made manifest in the scope of the daily lives and petty ambitions of "normal" people.

Crowds flocked to the film, and it encouraged many repeat viewers, who were eager to see just how the film had tricked them the first time. In Clouzot's hands, film was a blatant tool of manipulation and assault. From now on, triggering a visceral response, not simply an emotional one, was an essential component of film horror.

The stage was set for the psychological-thriller boom. Alfred Hitchcock made stylish, witty mysteries and thrillers for decades—and in

Alfred Hitchcock holding up a clapperboard on the set of *Psycho* (1960).

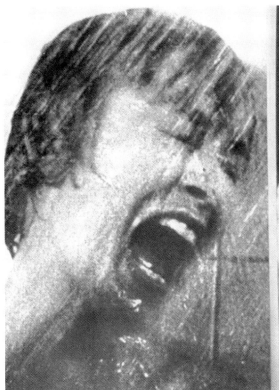

It runs in the family! Janet Leigh (left) in *Pyscho* (1960) and her daughter Jamie Lee Curtis (right) in *Halloween* (1978).

1960 he made the most influential horror film up to that point.

Psycho is the quintessential transgressive film. It was a low-budget affair, disdained by Hitchcock's studio Paramount as too perverse a script to film. As a result, Hitchcock produced it himself and made millions. Based on Robert Bloch's 1959 novel, which was in turn based on the real-life career of American serial killer Ed Gein, *Psycho* put sex, sexuality, mental illness, and (seemingly) graphic violence front and center. It was a bold step for Hitchcock.

A young woman steals from her employer and goes on the lam. She ends up staying the night at the Bates Motel, whose boyish proprietor, Norman, is terribly shy and mother-dominated. Without warning, the woman is brutally murdered while she showers.

This infamous and iconic "shower scene" contains a blizzard of edits that disorient the viewer and make the brutal crime a shock impossible to turn away from. The feeling of

helplessness and randomness that the scene instills keeps the audience off-balance until the end of the film. The ladling-on of ever-more-perverse details is almost sadistic; the director was intent on manipulating, almost punishing, the viewers for their curiosity. *Psycho* is film as blunt instrument.

To add to the confusion, the film gave viewers protagonists that vanished abruptly, and encouraged identification with the villain, himself a victim. Hitchcock took the "don't reveal the ending" gimmick and pushed it hard, forcing exhibitors to refuse to seat viewers after the film started. Promotional, life-sized cardboard cutouts of the director pointing at his watch stood in every theater lobby that showed the film. It became Hitchcock's most successful movie. In response, the shock-laden exploitation film market exploded into life.

Hitchcock doubled down on Clouzot's cynicism. The victims in the film are random, and the crimes depicted are discovered and stopped

Anthony Perkins as Norman Bates (in silhouette) in *Psycho* (1960).

almost by chance. The audience's desire to see the innocent saved and the guilty punished is repeatedly frustrated; in fact, there is no culpable "guilty party" left by the end of the film, and no sense of a happy ending. The only resolution is found in the final image of a car and the body it contains being pulled out of a swamp.

Hitchcock's effortless technique, developed by decades of experience, helped make *Psycho* a hit, cementing his status as a master filmmaker. Conversely, the similarly experienced, brilliant, and honored British director Michael Powell's *Peeping Tom*, made the same year, destroyed his career. Both films featured mentally ill serial killers motivated by voyeurism and sexual excitement. Why was the reaction to *Peeping Tom* so different?

Peeping Tom is the embodiment of Terence Fisher's definition of a horror movie as an adult fairy tale. It's a visual poem about sex and death, created by Powell, best known for his work with writer/producer Emeric Pressburger

(*Black Narcissus*, 1947; *The Red Shoes,* 1948). Powell took a daring script by polymath and cryptographer Leo Marks and turned it into a transgressive masterpiece.

The main character in *Peeping Tom* is, like *Psycho*'s Norman Bates, an adult child scarred psychically by a parent. A young cameraman, Mark Lewis turns out to have been observed and tormented by his psychologist father his entire life, examined and documented relentlessly in a study of fear. Mark works as a focus puller by day at a low-budget movie studio making silly comedies, but he supplements his income by taking and selling pornographic pictures. He lives in one room of his father's mansion, renting out the other rooms and keeping to his creepy, soft-spoken self. In his spare time, Mark films women as he stalks and kills them (the viewfinder of his camera has crosshairs, just like the sight of a rifle), capturing their fear-soaked reactions to their own death as they see it in a mirror attached to the camera.

He earns the affection of a lodger, Helen, who gradually discovers his secret. Mark is a pitiable figure, a tragic antihero who is aware of his compulsions but is unable to break away from them. His camera is always with him; he even films the investigation of his crimes. As played by Carl Boehm, he is Peter Lorre-like, quiet and thick-lidded, almost whispering his lines, as invisible as he can make himself. (We never see Mark in the act, as it were—he is perpetually placid.)

Helen, played by Anna Massey, is a "plain Jane." Excluded as an object of desire and therefore as a potential murder target, only she has the power to divert Mark from his obsessions even temporarily. She becomes his confessor, and he shields her from his violence as best he can. "Don't let me see you are frightened," he implores her. For Mark, fear is the only palpable emotion, the only thing that can excite him sexually, and what provokes him to guiltily kill the object of his sexual impulse.

Top Ten Horror Films of the 1960s

House of Usher (1960)

Jigoku (1960)

Peeping Tom (1960)

Psycho (1960)

The Innocents (1961)

What Ever Happened to Baby Jane? (1962)

Planet of the Vampires (1965)

Kill, Baby . . . Kill! (1966)

Night of the Living Dead (1968)

Rosemary's Baby (1968)

When *Psycho* ends, evil is captured (if not yet brought to justice), and the return of normality is implied. *Peeping Tom* goes much deeper, equating image-making with death. Taking a woman's picture turns her into an object to be used, for sexual gratification, or Mark's substitute for sexual gratification, which is playing the films of his kills over again.

"Whatever I photograph I always lose," he mourns. In the end, Mark kills himself in an elaborate set-up, recording his own fear as he runs himself through on the phallic blade attached to his camera, ironically completing the study his father began. "I'm afraid, and I'm glad I'm afraid," he cries.

And what does it mean that we're peering over Mark's shoulder throughout the film? The audience came to see violence, too. What is the extent and nature of the audience's complicity with the horror-makers, and, finally, the monsters themselves? Norman Bates's brand of madness is easier to digest than Mark Lewis's. It lets you off the hook.

Peeping Tom uses the device of the bold heroine who sees through a monster's disguise, straight out of *Beauty and the Beast*. Helen is at least physically intact at movie's end, the original "Final Girl" in horror film who survives not due to a man's rescue but due to her own intelligence and guts. Hers is a character that would get lost for decades. Horror's misogyny was about to increase exponentially.

Anna Massey (left) and Karlheinz Böhm in *Peeping Tom* (1960).

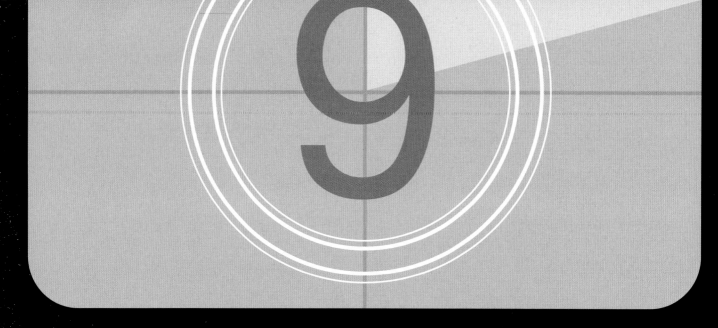

THE CORMAN POES AND THE PEERLESS VINCENT PRICE

Vincent Price said, "I don't play monsters. I play men besieged by fate and out for revenge."[1] This quote is the key to understanding his status as a horror-film actor. His ability to take a disreputable genre, at that time geared cynically to teenage audiences, and elevate it to the highest level of art, is a remarkable achievement.

This perfect marriage of his skills with sinister material was achieved during his work with director Roger Corman on Corman's so-called eight-film "Poe cycle," all but one of which featured Price and all but one of which were based, more or less, on works by Edgar Allan Poe.

A burst of 3D movies hit the market between 1952 and 1954. The technology enlivened *House of Wax*. This remake of *Mystery of the Wax Museum* gives us Price as the disfigured sculptor Henry Jarrod, whose statues look lifelike because, well, they're wax-coated corpses, OK? It was a huge success that typed Price forever, for better or worse, as a consummate film villain. *House of Wax*'s sumptuous, garishly colored period setting also influenced later efforts such as those of Hammer Studio.

The scrappy, beloved American International Pictures, founded by James H. Nicholson and Samuel Z. Arkoff in 1954, was an independent film production company with few artistic pretensions. They were the first in the movie business to identify the profit potential of making films specifically for teenagers. In the highly affluent postwar American economy, most teenagers now had spending money, transportation, some autonomy, and absolutely no desire to be stuck at home.

In a process similar to that which Columbia imposed on horror producer Val Lewton in the 1940s, AIP started with a title, worked up an arresting poster, raised money from investors, and only then wrote a script and made a movie. AIP actually asked teenagers what they wanted to see, narrowing the concept of their ideal customer down to that of a hypothetical nineteen-year-old male. It turned out that teenagers wanted to see characters like

themselves, and AIP cranked out thrill-laden cheapies in a variety of genres, featuring juvenile delinquents, drag racing, rock 'n' roll—and of course, sci-fi and horror.

Soon AIP was lighting up the drive-in screens of America with more than a dozen films a year, including fare such as *The Astounding She-Monster* (1957) and *Attack of the Giant Leeches* (1959). The wunderkind of the studio was director, writer, and producer Roger Corman, the so-called "pope of pop cinema" who could make decent films faster and less expensively than anyone before or since.

However, by the end of the decade, even the black-and-white B-movies that were AIP's bread and butter were losing their audiences.

Given the success of Hammer Studios' Technicolor horror epics, Corman decided to take a chance and make an "A" feature. Corman took advantage of the royalty-free, public-domain status of Poe's work, found inspired (and very liberal) screen adapters such as Richard Matheson, Charles Beaumont, and Robert Towne, and convinced the studio to let him shoot in widescreen and color, starting with *House of Usher* in 1960.

OPPOSITE:
Vincent Price in *House of Wax* (1953).

House of Usher (1960) poster.

The Tingler (1959) lobby card.

Screenwriter Matheson's contributions to the literature of the imagination cannot be overstated. A masterful genre writer, he specialized in science fiction and horror. His first published short story, 1950's "Born of Man and Woman," was a landmark horror tale, extensively honored and anthologized. Besides his five Corman/Poe screen adaptations, he wrote many novels that bred films (including *I Am Legend*, 1954; *The Shrinking Man*, 1956; *A Stir of Echoes*, 1958; *Hell House*, 1971; *Bid Time Return*, 1975; and *What Dreams May Come*, 1978).

He also produced dozens of short stories, and he defined the macabre in American television, creating timeless episodes for such anthology shows of the early 1960s as *The Twilight Zone*, *Thriller*, and *Alfred Hitchcock Presents*. He wrote classic made-for-television films such as *Duel* (1971), *The Night Stalker* (1972), and *Trilogy of Terror* (1975). For young horror aficionados, his name in the credits was a guarantee of mind-stretching thrills and enjoyment.

Vincent Price was also a natural choice for Corman. Price had trained as a stage actor, and in fact had made a big splash on Broadway in 1941 in the role of the manipulative villain Manningham in *Angel Street*, the popular thriller that would later be adapted twice into film as *Gaslight*. His first horror-film appearance was, ironically, as a victim—the hapless Clarence, who is dispatched by Basil Rathbone and Boris Karloff in 1939's *Tower of London*, a loose adaptation of Shakespeare's *Richard III*.

Price was hulking, handsome, and well-spoken—an adequate

House on Haunted Hill (1959) poster.

"straight" leading man, but especially effective as a tormented, mordantly mirthful antihero. In films such as *Dragonwyck* (1946), *The Baron of Arizona* (1950), *House of Wax*, *The Mad Magician* (1954), and William Castle exploitation films such as *House on Haunted Hill* and *The Tingler* (both 1959), he gained a reputation as an actor who presented as controlled, sophisticated, and intelligent—but who could also become a dynamic conduit of rage, fright, and open-mouthed madness. (He worked extensively in radio during the 1940s and 1950s, most notably as the detective hero "The Saint," and in memorable performances in such landmark radio horror plays such as "Three Skeleton Key," "Present Tense," "Bloodbath," and "Leona's Room.")

The Corman/Poe sequence starts strong with *House of Usher*. Its ambition is grand: Les Baxter's score features a pre-show overture, just like prestigious releases of the same year such as *The Alamo* and *Spartacus*. Corman makes a hundred bucks look like a thousand onscreen, and Matheson's adaptation supplies a romantic triangle with an incestuous hypotenuse.

Philip Winthrop (a wooden Mark Damon) visits the Ushers' ancestral manse to see his fiancée, Madeline Usher (Myrna Fahey). Her brother, Roderick (Price), seeks to prevent his sister's marriage, as he believes their bloodline is cursed.

Price fits Poe's description of his character to to an uncanny degree: "A cadaverousness of complexion; an eye large, liquid, and luminous beyond comparison; lips somewhat thin and very pallid, but of a surpassingly beautiful curve; a nose of a delicate Hebrew model, but with a breadth of nostril unusual in similar formations; a finely molded chin, speaking, in its want of prominence, of a want of moral energy . . ." Price's basso profundo voice gives gravitas to his gloomy pronouncements, and his sense of conviction carries the film.

(from left to right) Mark Damon, Vincent Price, and Myrna Fahey in *House of Usher* (1960).

The house itself is a malevolent character, and Winthrop nearly perishes several times due to its seeming lashings-out at him. Matheson makes Roderick's entombment of his sister far more sinister than the original story does, which gives the viewer the less ambiguous message that the wages of sin are death. The extremely inexpensive special effects make the climax more affecting; the ruins of Usher ratchet straight down into the tarn with the hallucinatory literalness of a child's nightmare.

On the surface, the Corman Poes are just another example of opportunistic filmmaking, working to the market. The Hammer "blood and bosoms" formula was strictly copied, with garishly colorful shocks and plenty of attractive, young, helpless heroines.

But Corman, despite his reputation as a purveyor of schlock, was actually quite a good director, and with a bigger budget and longer shooting time, he could really go to town. *Usher*'s rich, gloomy art direction by Daniel Haller and top-notch cinematography by Floyd Crosby,

augmented by robustly over-the-top dialogue and scoring, is startlingly effective.

Corman refreshed the popular memory concerning the American Gothic sense of horror created in the nineteenth century by Edgar Allan Poe, Nathaniel Hawthorne ("Young Goodman Brown;" "Rappaccini's Daughter"), and Washington Irving ("Rip Van Winkle;" "The Legend of Sleepy Hollow"). Through them comes the dark sense that even the virgin American landscape is fundamentally tainted, cursed with original sin. The single non-Poe adaptation in the Corman Poes is *The Haunted Palace* (1963), the first film based on work by the twentieth-century progenitor of the American Gothic revival, H. P. Lovecraft.

The disturbed and reclusive Howard Phillips Lovecraft (1890–1937) was a virtual unknown during his brief lifetime. His fetid, fertile mind created an entire mythos, an alternate, alien universe full of sleeping monsters whose lapsed attentions have allowed mankind, body and soul, to persist in a senseless, indifferent cosmos. The central deity is Cthulhu, a giant, vaguely man-like terror wielding a mixture of tentacles, wings, and claws. It sleeps at the bottom of the world, waiting for its time of dark dominance to recur on Earth. Cheery, eh?

Lovecraft has even staked imaginative claim to parts of New England now known as "Lovecraft country," cheek by jowl with Hawthorne and Irving. It would take several decades for cinema to become transgressive enough to tackle his work on a regular basis. A few scattered film versions turned into a torrent after the success of Stuart Gordon's *Re-Animator* (1985) and *From Beyond* (1986). We are in the midst of a Lovecraft boom: there have been at least a half-dozen Lovecraftian film and television productions per year since 2007.

House of Usher and its successors (*The Pit and the Pendulum*, *The Premature Burial*, *Tales of Terror*, *The Raven*, *The Haunted Palace*, *The Masque of the Red Death*, *The Tomb of Ligeia*—all shot between 1960 and 1964) are assured assertions that mankind is perfectly capable of creating and maintaining environments of evil, inescapable and tragic. (It helped that Price, whether sinister and restrained or wild-eyed and ranting, could always out-act any young male lead appointed to save the day, including very young Jack Nicholson.) Insanity, torment, trauma, sadism—to embody them, Corman collected a repertory company of horror stalwarts such as Basil Rathbone, Peter Lorre, Boris Karloff, Lon Chaney Jr., Hazel Court, and Barbara Steele.

Parodists have feasted on, and many critics take issue with, Price's plummy, acerbic delivery, and the petulant aggression he channels in his horror roles. However, his 200-plus film and television credits demonstrate that, with Karloff, Lorre, Carradine, and Chaney, he preferred steady employment as a designated "Merchant of

Menace" rather than virtuous penury. Like them, he enlivened almost every project with his professionalism.

He used his elegant bearing, his rich and expressive voice, and his haunted, hooded look to push his acting to the extremes demanded. If you buy into his style, it is riveting—and there is just enough stagey, ironic distance in his characterizations that we can sense a coziness, a hint of winking put-on, that allows him and us to relish the grand, melodramatic style even more intensely by throwing it into subtle comic relief. He is playing, in the purest sense. "I sometimes feel that I'm impersonating the dark unconscious of the whole human race," he once said. "I know this sounds sick, but I love it."[2]

Later Price films are a mixed bag, but there are a few gems. He is a weary and cynical vampire hunter in *The Last Man on Earth* (1964), the first adaptation of Matheson's 1954 novel *I Am Legend*. This adaptation was disowned by Matheson. Indeed, the movie is low-budget, gritty, and uneven, but its grainy matter-of-factness strongly influenced the look of George A. Romero's *Night of the Living Dead* four years later.

Other significant roles for Price include the brutal *Witchfinder General*, aka *The Conqueror Worm* (1968), and the gruesomely vengeful Dr. Phibes in two films (1971 and 1972). *The Abominable Dr. Phibes* gives us campy, over-the-top gore. It's a Roaring Twenties-era horror farce

Vincent Price (left) and Virginia North in *The Abominable Dr. Phibes* (1971).

Personal Best

Vincent Price

The Tingler (1959)
House of Usher (1960)
The Pit and the Pendulum (1961)
Masque of the Red Death (1964)
Theatre of Blood (1973)

about a disfigured surgeon (Price) who swears vengeance on the doctors he blames for his wife's death. Being a mad genius who speaks through a gramophone horn jacked into a hole in his neck, he of course patterns his murders after the Ten Plagues of Egypt . . . when he's not busy playing the organ, as every disfigured villain should. (The sequel, *Dr. Phibes Rises Again*, stumbles a bit but holds pleasures for the avid fan, i.e., myself.)

In the made-for-television *An Evening of Edgar Allan Poe* (1970), Price's staged readings of four Poe stories, totaling less than an hour in length, give the viewer the best look at what he was like in live performance.

His best work is in what he stated was his favorite film: 1973's *Theatre of Blood*, in which he plays the scorned actor Edward Lionheart—who comes back from the grave to murder his critics, each in a manner inspired by a Shakespeare play. One is knifed by a mob à la Caesar. Another is fed his own "children," in the form of beloved puppies, as in *Titus Andronicus*. The film features Diana Rigg as his daughter and conspirator, and many of England's best character actors play the doomed journalists.

It's by far the most literate horror movie ever made, and assuredly one of the most playful. The juxtaposition of deathless poesy and poetical deaths makes it a must-see for Bardolators and horror fans alike. And who doesn't love watching critics die? It also gave Price the chance to play a bit of Shakespeare onscreen. Though his delivery is deliberately broad and hammy, it leaves the viewer to wonder what he might have made

of roles such as Coriolanus, Titus Andronicus, Macbeth, or Lear.

Sweetly, and appropriately, he made his last significant appearance as the Inventor in Tim Burton's dark monster/comedy/romance flick *Edward Scissorhands* (1990).

By the time the bulk of his career was complete, a new kind of horror film, vastly more graphic and much less dependent on sonorous line readings and sweeping gestures, was coming. It was the age of *Night of the Living Dead* and *The Exorcist* (1973)—and horror was becoming much gorier and less sweepingly tragic.

Price had passions for art and good cuisine that rivaled his acting prowess, and he was an enthusiastic evangelist for culture. Near the end of his life, he returned to the stage and barnstormed across the country in a one-man show as Oscar Wilde, *Diversions & Delights*. I had the pleasure of seeing him command our attention and suspend our disbelief, and to shake his hand after the show. He was towering, charming, and polite. His enormous mitt swallowed up mine. My mental picture of him as the Master of Horror was pleasantly shattered, as he resembled nothing more than a nice guy from St. Louis, which in fact he was.

American culture is notoriously allergic to both tragedy and poetry, but in the hands of Corman and Price, horror movies brought popular culture as close as it ever would to those lofty pursuits.

Vincent Price (left) and Diana Rigg in *Theatre of Blood* (1973).

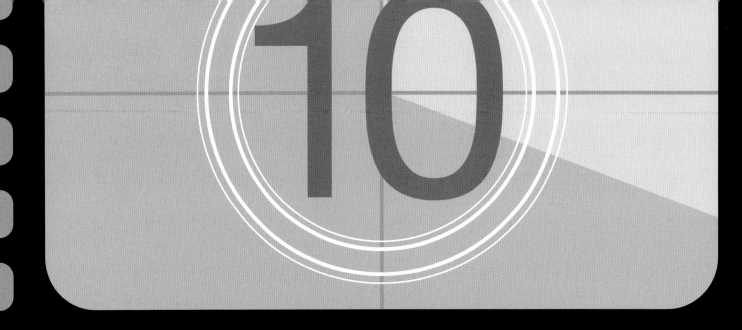

HORROR,
ITALIAN STYLE

Authoritarians don't like horror movies. After all, horror calls everything, including the status quo, into question. The strongest periods of horror-film production come during times of turmoil and change in a culture, not in ones paralyzed in a state of stable repression. In Italy, strict film censorship measures were in place as early as 1920, and continued through the fascist era, until the downfall of Mussolini in 1943. Only one horror film was made in Italy until 1957: the now-lost *Monster of Frankenstein* (1920).

When the Italian film industry finally started turning out horror films, it caught on with flair, more than making up for lost time. It not only created effective and influential horror films in the Gothic and sci-fi/horror styles; it also brewed a new subgenre, the *giallo*, which would affect the style, subject, and substance of all horror films to follow.

The Italian penchant for horror is deep-rooted, found as far back as ancient Rome, in Dante's *Inferno* and in the conventions of Romantic-era opera. Opera, in particular, is chock-full of horror, madness, murder, and vengeful ghosts. Gloomy castles and torment rampant were standard fare in musical tragedies such as *Lucia di Lammermoor* (Donizetti, 1835) and *Il Trovatore* (Verdi, 1853), and at least three grand operas end with a general slaughter (*Les Huguenots*, Meyerbeer, 1836; *I Vespri Siciliani*, Verdi, 1855; *Khovanshchina*, Mussorgsky, 1881, for those playing at home).

Personal Best

Mario Bava

Black Sunday (1960)

Black Sabbath (1963)

Planet of the Vampires (1965)

Kill, Baby . . . Kill! (1966)

A Bay of Blood (1971)

A scene from
I Vampiri, aka
*Lust of the
Vampire* (1957).

The success of Britain's Hammer horror films triggered a fast response from Cinecittà, the vast movie-making complex southeast of Rome. The first sound-era Italian horror film to roll off the line was *I Vampiri*, aka *Lust of the Vampire* (1957), a clunky effort shot in two weeks by director Riccardo Freda. By his side, though, was an already-experienced cinematographer, Mario Bava. Soon Bava would sit in the director's chair, ultimately fathering the Italian horror film. He and others such as Dario Argento would produce a number of significant Italian horror titles.

Italian horror has its own unique themes, informed by the Catholic concept of mankind's inherent sinfulness, and laced heavily with misogyny. Anglo-American horror was about the havoc unleashed by invading monsters, disturbing the placid certainties of the culture. Italian horror came from sin, generated from within, in the context of everyday life, rather than imposed from without. In these films, people, primarily men, are obsessed with life-altering, psyche-perverting memories. The Madonna/whore pigeonholing of female characters was strong in Italian horror for at least two decades, and the defining characteristic of these films is the graphic, numerous, and artfully staged assaults on, and murders of, attractive women.

OPPOSITE:
*The Horrible
Dr. Hichcock*
(1962) poster.

Eros and Thanatos merge here. In Italian horror films, sex equals death.

In these films, the villain's motivation often springs from sexual perversion. In 1960's *Mill of the Stone Women*, women are murdered to provide life (specifically, a sex life) for a sculptor's daughter. In 1962's *The Horrible Dr. Hichcock* (deliberately misspelled to suggest the involvement of *Psycho* director Hitchcock without incurring litigation), the theme is, unbelievably for that time and this, necrophilia. In Bava's 1963 *The Whip and the Body*, the theme, as you might expect, is sadomasochism.

Italian Gothic film pushed style to and past the max. Clotted, claustrophobic production design consistently overloaded every frame with a barrage of objects and surfaces. Lighting, notoriously spotty at first, evolved into an intriguing, intensely spare and atmospheric style, working first with noir-like shadows in black-and-white, and later with isolated spots of primary color, and still later in huge swathes and layers of vibrant and symbolic pigments, establishing tones and signifying underlying themes.

The archetypical actress of Italian horror during this period was England's Barbara Steele, who would star in nearly a dozen fright features in Italy and elsewhere. Her screen persona was perfect—her pale features, thin limbs, huge eyes, and long, straight, raven hair made her the embodiment of a Gothic femme fatale. She could play an innocent victim, a figure of evil, a ghost, or a monster with a convincingly brooding glare. In Bava's intense, impactful *Black Sunday*, aka *The Mask of Satan* (1960), Steele plays both villainess and heroine.

In *Black Sunday*, an ancient sorceress comes back from the grave to wreak vengeance on the descendants of those who executed her. Its convoluted plot is matched by its dark cluttered settings, which represent Italian Gothic style par excellence. Bava loved the Russian writer Gogol's 1835 horror story "Viy" and tried to infuse its grotesque, graphic spirit into his film. Certainly the shocking opening scene, in which spiked masks are hammered with a juicy squish into the faces of the guilty, put it in far gorier territory than had been explored previously (remember, 1960 brought us comparable frights in film form in *Psycho*, *Peeping Tom*, and *Jigoku*.)

These spurts of transgression punctuate a gloomy Romantic tale, a stylish mix of sex and sadism in the far-off confines of mythic Moldavia, rendered in stark shafts of light. The uncut version of the film was banned in Britain until 1992.

Dozens of directors swarmed to churn out variations on the genre conventions, including Freda, Camillo Mastrocinque (*An Angel for Satan*, 1966), Sergio Martino (*Torso*, 1973), and Pupi Avati (*The House of the Laughing Windows*, 1976). The prolific Antonio Margheriti could make distinctive

Barbara Steele in *Black Sunday* (1960).

Blood and Black Lace (1964) lobby card.

work in both the Gothic style (*The Long Hair of Death*, 1964) and the sci-fi/horror genre (his surreal *Wild, Wild Planet* of 1966 anticipates the body-horror films of David Cronenberg). Elio Scardamaglia's *The Murder Clinic* (1966) is a key transitional film from Gothic to *giallo* style. It steals the face-transplant gimmick from Georges Franju's *Eyes Without a Face*, and throws in a hooded serial killer.

The two key Italian horror-film directors of the period were Bava and Argento, and the subgenre they created and perfected was the *giallo*. The term, literally meaning "yellow," stems from the distinctive yellow covers of the popular pulp-fiction crime thriller books published in Italy from 1929 on.

The first true *giallo* film is considered to be Bava's 1963 *The Girl Who Knew Too Much*, but he didn't hit his stride until next year's *Blood and Black Lace*, in full color and with the emphasis switched to sex and violence instead of sleuthing and mystery.

In between those two films, Bava made a trilogy of terror of his own, *Black Sabbath* (yes, seeing that title on a theater's marquee is how the rock band got its name). The central story "The Wurdulak" is the best, and shows Bava cementing his voluptuous style: Bava's bold use of color and the dreamlike atmosphere he creates fully come to flower here. The segment gives us Karloff in one of his last effective performances,

as a rough peasant turned into a vampire who preys on his nearest and dearest. "Give Grandpa a kiss" is a line that seems obscene in context.

Blood and Black Lace is set in the present day, and the focus is on set pieces of violence tinged with eroticism, a hallmark of the *giallo* from then on. The murders of fashion models litter a plot about the possession of a deadly diary. Underneath its brutal murder scenes, it lays out an intricate and challenging plot of blackmail and betrayal. What Lawrence McCallum terms Bava's "terrible beauty"[1] makes the unpalatable riveting. Cameron Mitchell does a great job in the thankless role of the Featured American Star.

Bava's abilities grew prodigiously with each film. *Planet of the Vampires* is an exuberantly overdone, stylized sci-fi/horror film, created on practically no budget and with effects done entirely "in camera." It wound up directly influencing such films as *Alien*.

Black Sabbath (1963) poster.

Two spaceships crash-land on a seemingly lifeless planet. Parasitical alien life forms seek to kill, then command, the crews. *Planet* is ecstatically bizarre, right down to the latex-fetish design of the spacesuits. The title says it all (actually, they are more like zombies). The smoky, claustrophobic atmosphere turns a lonely planet into the equivalent of a haunted mansion. The international cast couldn't speak each other's languages. Everything was dubbed in post-production, but some confused looks during a few scenes are understandable. Barry Sullivan is the Featured American Star.

Kill, Baby . . . Kill! (1966) gave Bava a chance to make the definitive Italian Gothic horror movie. Despite the lack of a finished script, not to mention a shortage of funds, the result is a creepy and atmospheric masterpiece. A young doctor investigating a series of mysterious deaths uncovers a struggle for the souls of an entire village. Witches, ghosts, and maniacs abound, as our protagonists unravel a number of dark secrets. Bava's most disturbing effect is the use of a hollow-eyed, laughing girl ghost with a ball (played by a boy, no less) whose appearance presages another murder. (Federico Fellini stole this idea for his "Toby Dammit" segment of the horror anthology *Spirits of the Dead,* 1968.)

Bava's *Hatchet for the Honeymoon* (1970) is a clear forerunner of Mary Harron's *American Psycho* (1990), with a seemingly happy and successful central figure who narrates as he kills. The murderer owns a bridal shop, which is convenient, since he needs his victims to step into one of his gowns before he can bring himself to slaughter them. (Fortunately, he has cute little meat cleavers stashed around the place just for that purpose. Oh, and he needs to play a certain bulky, old-fashioned music box as he kills, too. Conditions have to be juuuuuust right . . .)

We will deal with Jess Franco more thoroughly later, but the filmmaker, on his way down into exploitation film, crafted the disturbing supernatural/erotic thriller *Venus in Furs* in Italy in 1969. James Darren plays a down-and-out trumpeter who finds a beautiful woman murdered on the beach, who later returns to life to seek vengeance. It's a carnival of perverse carnality. The film also features Klaus Kinski and Dennis Price, the latter of whom proves here that he can be tasked with almost any acting challenge and make it compelling.

Kill, Baby . . . Kill! (1966) poster.

Giallo plots became more and more incoherent as the genre progressed. By the time we get to Bava's *A Bay of Blood*, aka *Twitch of the Death Nerve*, in 1971, most of the slasher-film hallmarks are there: the point-of-view shots from the killer's perspective, the murder of sexually active teens, and the like. These were all elements soon to be adopted by American horror. However, strong plots have devolved into nihilistic murderfests, in which even small children can participate, as they do in *A Bay of Blood*.

Many *gialli* of the period veer into dream territory, becoming free-floating meditations on violence and evil. In Aldo Lado's debut feature *Short Night of the Glass Dolls* (1971), a paralyzed and mute journalist solves his own murder in his mind even as he's being prepped for an autopsy, a solution that involves Satanism and human sacrifice. Luigi Bazzoni's final film, *Footprints on the Moon* (1975), while containing *giallo* elements, is much more of an avant-garde film about identity à la the work of Michelangelo Antonioni.

Dario Argento returned focus to the form. Starting out as a screenwriter (he and famed director/producer/screenwriter Bernando Bertolucci wrote the script for Sergio Leone's magnificent 1968 spaghetti Western *Once Upon a Time in the West*), Argento brought a keen sense of structure to his *gialli*. Argento's plots are efficient machines—clear-eyed and cleanly edited; there is a constant sense of forward momentum in his films, plots racing like loosed arrows to their bloody conclusions.

Personal Best

Dario Argento

The Bird with the Crystal Plumage (1970)
Four Flies on Grey Velvet (1971)
Deep Red (1975)
Suspiria (1977)
Tenebrae (1982)

The Bird with the Crystal Plumage (1970) poster.

Argento takes the time to develop all his characters, to let them interact casually in order to establish relationships between them, as a director would in a "straight" drama. He uses humor and simple human detail to create a moviegoing experience that seems more wide-ranging, more relaxed than a by-the-numbers fright flick—until the viewer realizes it's all been part of one long delicious and nerve-wracking setup.

He started out brilliantly with his debut directorial effort *The Bird with the Crystal Plumage* (1970). This first "big" *giallo* is confident and visually stunning. The hunt for a murderer is complicated by the presence of several red herrings, and it's all wrapped up at the end with a convoluted psychiatric explanation that seems a parody of *Psycho*'s conclusion. What counts here are the distinctive action sequences.

The crimes in Argento's films usually take place in the art world—in *Plumage*, inside a gallery (Tony Musante is the primary witness, an author suffering from writer's block). As in film noir, the protagonist in the *giallo* is on a quest to discover the truth. As in a standard

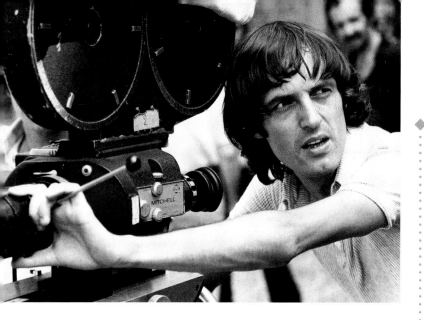

Dario Argento behind the camera on the set of *The Five Days* (1973).

murder mystery, we are presented here with a roster of suspects; however, faith in internal logic in a *giallo* is misplaced. In *Plumage*, the act of seeing—the witnessing of an attempted murder—is inherently flawed and dooms understanding until it's too late for the hero to act effectively. The solution is perfunctory; what's important are the bravura, graphic set pieces that made Argento's reputation. Whenever possible, Argento pulls us into long, hypnotic sequences that create apprehension for its own sake. Argento's cinematography is breathtaking. His soundtracks are compelling, juiced with delicious sound effects when not rife with clanging, clinking scores from prog-rock band Goblin. His scenes are flooded with sensation and feeling, but he subordinates all the elements to the service of the story. Most important, even his most grotesque murders are staged as artfully as anything in cinema: it's slaughter as

Jessica Harper as Suzy in a scene from *Suspiria* (1977).

performance art. The crimes resonate because they stimulate many emotions—not merely fright, but helplessness, alienation, confusion, and doubt. Like Clouzot before him, Argento is a master manipulator on celluloid.

Even in public scenes set in broad daylight, Argento conveys a sense of dread. Underneath the everyday banter there is something fundamentally wrong with not only people, but the structure of reality itself. The killers are part of a grim psychic ecosystem, manifesting themselves in order to undo the spell of normalcy and reveal the evil and chaos beneath the surface of ordinary life. The worldview of *giallo* is never less than cynical, and often outright nihilistic.

Best Giallo

Blood and Black Lace (1964)
Hatchet for the Honeymoon (1970)
The Bird with the Crystal Plumage (1970)
A Lizard in a Woman's Skin (1971)
A Bay of Blood (1971)
Don't Torture a Duckling (1972)
Deep Red (1975)
The House with Laughing Windows (1976)
Suspiria (1977)
Tenebrae (1982)

Argento hit his pinnacle in two consecutive films, *Deep Red* (1975) and *Suspiria* (1977). In the first, he establishes a supernatural tone immediately. In a lecture hall draped with blood-red velvet curtains, a female psychic spasms, claiming to feel the presence of a killer. Later, that killer slaughters her in her home, in sight of a pianist across the way, Marcus (David Hemmings), who has a nagging suspicion he saw something vital later missing from the crime scene.

With sweeping pans and dolly shots, Argento floats his characters through beautifully balanced widescreen compositions to their dooms, even as our protagonist is sucked into a living nightmare of constantly shifting suspicions. Marcus has a doppelganger, a friend and rival pianist, the self-hating homosexual Carlo. Female characters trigger disquiet. The misogyny is palpable.

And, instead of the art world just being a milieu in which the murders occur, here such things as snatches of music, photos, and artwork become clues used to solve the mystery. Marcus hunts for hidden evidence and finds it, only to see it vanish again and again. Nothing can be proven. The only way he can confront the monster is to place himself in its path.

In *Suspiria*, the supernatural element is even more pronounced. Jessica Harper plays Suzy, a young ballet student joining a dance academy in Germany that is not what it seems. Disappearances, deaths, and odd phenomena plague the school. Suzy is a proactive heroine, and investigates. (The academy harbors a powerful "Black Queen" and her coven.) The gory sequences almost seem unrelated to the narrative of the unveiling of menace, which is here an organized conspiracy, a society within and below "normal" society. It's a death dream more than a story, with Harper as a waiflike heroine on a quest.

"What do witches do?" Suzy asks a local scholar.

The professor answers, "They are malefic, negative, and destructive. Their knowledge and the art of the occult gives them tremendous

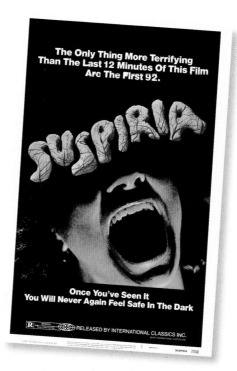

Suspiria (1977) poster.

powers. They can change the course of events and people's lives, but only to harm. Skepticism is the natural reaction of people nowadays, but magic is ever present."

In a perverse way, *Suspiria* is an affirmation of the existence of a spiritual world—and, thus, a positive film. It delineates a concrete, negative entity at work in the world, but it also gives us a female knight, a champion who stares relentlessly into the darkness and defeats it, against all odds. (Argento eventually made *Suspiria* the first part of his "Three Mothers" trilogy, including *Inferno*, 1980, and *The Mother of Tears*, 2007, which postulates three evil supernatural Ladies of Sorrow—Sighs, Tears, and Darkness—who manipulate the world through dark magic.)

By the end of the 1970s, *giallo*'s influence had reached America, helping to give rise to the slasher film. Watching John Carpenter's *Halloween* (1978), Brian De Palma's films, such as *Dressed to Kill* (1980) and *Blow Out* (1981), and the endless run of *Friday the 13th* (1980) and its derivatives, it's impossible to deny the influence of the Italians.

Meanwhile, the growing boldness in graphic violence and raw sexuality found in Italian horror, triggered itself by the game-changing success of Hitchcock's *Psycho*, meant that gory, transgressive horror was on the upswing.

ALL HELL BREAKS LOOSE, 1960-1975

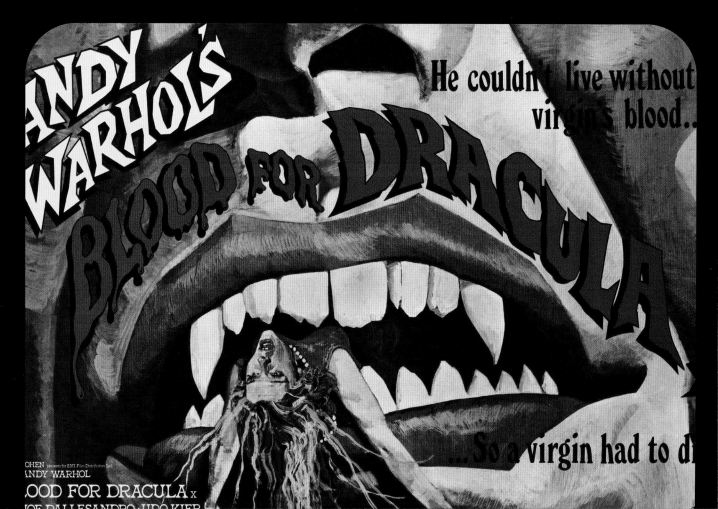

Psycho was the hinge on which horror film turned. Its phenomenal success signaled a sea change in horror-film production. In addition to the prevailing stream of sci-fi type horror, Hammer's Gothic revival output, and the work of Roger Corman and allies at AIP, various factors meant that American viewers now had an embarrassment of gory riches from which to choose. The first taboo to fall in American horror was the showing of graphic violence against women—and the younger and more attractive the victim, the better.

First, the censorship system broke down. Inroads were made by non-horror films such as Sidney Lumet's *The Pawnbroker* (1964), Mike Nichols's *Who's Afraid of Virginia Woolf?* (1966), and Arthur Penn's *Bonnie and Clyde* (1967). The Hays Office of movie censors closed in despair in 1966. On November 1, 1968, the Motion Picture Association of America instituted its voluntary film-ratings system. The sky was now the limit, and the rudest appetites of the masses were now to be indulged. Sex, violence, drugs, gore, the bizarre, and "antiestablishment" values were the rage—and the film industry fed the demands. The "R" rating, restricted to those seventeen and over, was a sought-for, profitable designation. Once again, the sign of society's disapproval became a tacit recommendation. And R-rated films were easy for kids to sneak into.

Second, independent producers became the new engines of production. It was now entrepreneurs, not studios, who put together creative teams and financing, who made distribution deals. Exhibitors were more opportunistic as well, and soon alternative venues, such as drive-ins and "grindhouses," the latter dingy urban cinemas where continuous sleazy films of every kind were shown, or ground out, 24/7, sought new content as well—and they weren't picky.

Third, the deterioration of American barriers against international films was complete. Foreign films sold tickets. All kinds of new, strange-genre films, most of them badly dubbed into English, could be seen in funky downtown cinemas, as part of museum or library programs, and even on late-night local television. Cross-cultural influences sprouted and intertwined.

The independent producers most capable of producing homespun horror were those with the most experience of making movies cheaply and quickly—namely, in this era, pornographers. Non-mainstream film, sometimes termed "paracinema," included that staple of bachelor parties, crudely made "stag" films or "smokers," enjoyed by male-only audiences. This kind of guerilla filmmaking experience made excellent training for wannabe horror auteurs.

Horror film resembles pornography in that it is cheap to produce and relies on the revelation of the forbidden. Their common stock-in-trade is transgression.

Some Z-grade movies, including misogynistic "roughies," hodgepodges of sex and violence, bear the now-familiar names of both the "world's worst director," Ed Wood (*Plan 9 from Outer Space*, 1957), and the now-lauded "Pope of Trash," John Waters; after all, what is Divine in *Multiple Maniacs* (1970) but Godzilla in drag? Other

OPPOSITE: *Blood for Dracula* (1974) poster.

John Waters discusses *Multiple Maniacs* (1970) at AOL HQ in New York in 2016.

hacks such as Joseph P. Mawra (*Olga's House of Shame*, 1964), David F. Friedman (*The Defilers*, 1965), Doris Wishman (*Bad Girls Go to Hell*, 1965), Michael and Roberta Findlay (*The Touch of Her Flesh*, 1967), Andy Milligan (*The Ghastly Ones*, 1968), Ted V. Mikels (*The Corpse Grinders*, 1971), and William Girdler (*Three on a Meathook*, 1973) all provided material for the fleapits.

The two most distinctive American horror impresarios of the early 1960s were alike in some ways. Neither had pretensions to aesthetic superiority. For them, film was a means to an end: profit. But, while one was a master huckster who never ran out of gimmicks, the other was a purist who became the "Godfather of Gore."

William Castle was a genuine auteur. He saw Lugosi in the original Broadway stage production of *Dracula*, and left school at fifteen to become the show's assistant stage manager. He became a masterful promoter at Columbia Pictures and picked up the craft of filmmaking as he went—producing, directing, and writing.

Being inclined to horror temperamentally, and seeing its financial potential in the wake of the phenomenal success of Clouzot's 1955 *Les Diaboliques*, he chose to specialize in that genre. (Interestingly, Castle's low-budget, black-and-white early successes would, in turn, inspire Hitchcock to make *Psycho*.)

For Castle, the movie itself wasn't such a big deal—it was a loss-leader, a gimmick, an excuse for the staging of promotional events. It was the "gaff" (referring to a magician's secret equipment, then to manufactured freaks of

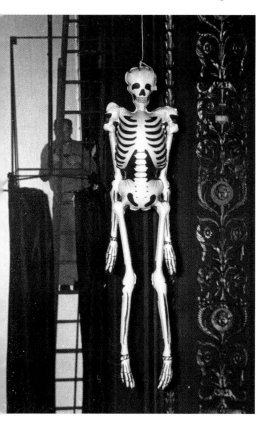

During screenings of *The House on Haunted Hill* (1959), director William Castle arranged for a skeleton to fly out over the audience during a climactic moment, a process called "Emergo." Here, a man stands on a ladder in the background as he prepares to send the skeleton out over a movie theatre audience in the late 1950s or early 1960s.

the sideshow) that mattered. Castle's first big hit *Macabre* (1958) was a snoozer, but he offered every patron a $1,000 life-insurance policy in case of death from fright, stationed nurses in the theater lobbies, and parked hearses outside. Crowds flocked to it.

In *House on Haunted Hill* (1959), five people are dared to spend the night in a haunted house. This quintessential Castle film is a pedestrian murder-thriller, enlivened by a snarky lead performance from Vincent Price. It also had "Emergo," a plastic skeleton on a string that flew into the auditorium on cue at the film's climax. Boo. Kids in the audience grabbed it and pulled it apart.

The Tingler (1959) had buzzers under the auditorium seats the exhibitors could set off to inspire uneasy shrieks. The film itself is pure exploitation. A scientist (Price) discovers a centipede-like human parasite that feeds on fear. The only way to shrink it is to scream. What would happen if you scared someone who couldn't scream? (It's also the first movie to show the use and supposed effects of LSD . . . crazy, Daddy-o!) Castle would pass away shortly after his greatest triumph, his work as producer of the rather more legit Roman Polanski's *Rosemary's Baby* (1968).

Herschell Gordon Lewis left a career in advertising to become a successful film pornographer. *Blood Feast* (1963) was his direct reaction to *Psycho*. Lewis thought that Hitchcock had "cheated" by cutting around the graphic violence in the film, and that a paying audience deserved the whole megillah, as it were. The film features an Egyptian caterer who needs to collect female body parts in order to resurrect the goddess Ishtar. The result is the first-ever "splatter," or "gore," film, devoted to a vivid depiction of graphic violence against the human body. "Oh, I bet there was never a party like this!" "Ah but there was, Mrs. Fremont—5,000 years ago."

There's no sense of redemption in Lewis; everything serves as a mechanism to get the viewer from one sadistic set piece to another. The special effects in *Blood Feast* are over-the-top and ludicrous to look at today, though still deeply disturbing. Lewis has the same fascination for "grossing out" his viewers as a small boy might, one contemplating an afternoon of burning ants with a magnifying glass.

Unintentionally, the most disturbing thing today about Lewis's films are their pristine mid-'60s Florida settings. The suburban, Caucasian homes he filmed in look like furniture showrooms, sterile and sad. The fuzzy, warm pastel tones everyone and everything seem to be clad in lend a jarring note of cognitive dissonance to the grisly proceedings.

Lewis, too, thrived on gimmicks. *Blood Feast*'s producer, David Friedman, got an injunction against showing the film in Sarasota, Florida, making it immediately a censorship cause célèbre and making it more bookable elsewhere . . . a brilliant marketing move. Later in life, Lewis became one of the leading direct-mail advertisers of all time (itself another horrifying yet effective form of communication). His eight horror films, down to the final self-parody of *The Gore Gore Girls* (1972), represent a catalogue of perverse wish-fulfillment, harbingers of a disturbing trend that was soon to hop like a toad into the mainstream.

In America, narrative radio was dead (it would persist and evolve in Britain, where audio drama is thriving even now), but a whole new generation was finding horror normalized on TV. Hitchcock's film crew for *Psycho* were recruited by and large from the crew for his immensely popular weekly anthology series, *Alfred Hitchcock Presents* and *The Alfred Hitchcock Hour* (1955–65)—and Hitchcock-branded horror- and mystery-story collections and magazines littered Baby Boomer shelves. Boris Karloff hosted his own anthology series *Thriller* (1960–62); and there were Rod Serling's *Twilight*

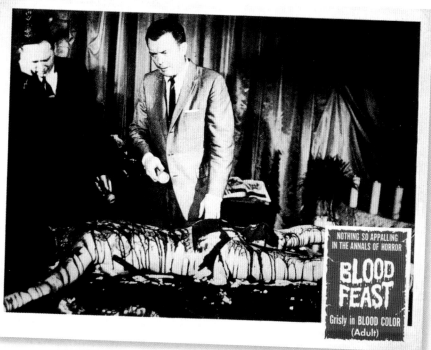

Blood Feast (1963) lobby card.

Zone (1959–64), Leslie Stevens's *The Outer Limits* (1963–65), *Science Fiction Theatre* (1955–57), and the underrated *One Step Beyond* (1959–61). All featured self-contained stories, many of which included elements of horror and the uncanny, not to mention an ironic last-minute twist.

At the same time, TV replayed the early history of horror film in heavy rotation. Television gobbled up original content; old movies were vital for filling programming slots. The *Shock Theater* package of fifty-two pre-1948 horror films entered TV syndication in October of 1957, and was snapped up in every major market. Good, bad, and indifferent, they played for enthusiastic fans, frightened children, and bored teens for nearly twenty years at odd time slots late at night and on weekend mornings, giving the broadest general audience a deep background in the archetypes and norms of classic horror cinema.

The local hosts of these broadcasts became cult figures and household words: Zacherley, Vampira, Ghoulardi, Chilly Billy, and Sinister Seymour all were wisecracking, film-interrupting purveyors of black, and extremely corny, humor. (This tradition stemmed from American radio,

LEFT: Group portrait of the cast of *The Addams Family* TV series (1964–1966), ca. 1964; RIGHT: A publicity photo of the cast of *The Munsters* (1964–1966).

Creatures Who Stopped Living and Became Mixed-Up Zombies!!? (1964) has the distinction of being the first monster musical (beating *The Horror of Party Beach* to release by six weeks). *Incredibly* also boasted two of Hollywood's great future cinematographers, Vilmos Zsigmond and Laszlo Kovacs, as camera operator and assistant camera, respectively. There were Western/ horror hybrids (William Beaudine's *Billy the Kid vs. Dracula* and *Jesse James Meets Frankenstein's Daughter*, both 1966). Satanist/hippie cult films, inspired by the Manson family crimes of the day, flowered evilly (*I Drink Your Blood*, 1970; *Deathmaster*, 1972).

I Drink Your Blood is one of the great so-bad-it's-good exploitation films, about a gang of hippies who are actually Satanists (of course). When they terrorize a small town, the citizens take revenge by infecting the transgressors with rabies. Complications ensue.

There were two memorably awful two-headed transplant films: *The Incredible 2-Headed*

where horror found a comfortable niche early on. The best-known radio horror host was the mordantly tongue-in-cheek host Raymond Edward Johnson, punning madly, who debuted on *Inner Sanctum* in 1941.) EC Comics burst forth in 1950 with a torrent of graphic, hair-raising horror titles such as *Tales from the Crypt*, *The Vault of Horror*, and *The Haunt of Fear*, until 1954, when censorship shut them down. They featured similarly sardonic narrators such as the Old Witch and the Crypt-Keeper.

Monster-themed TV situation comedies such as *The Addams Family* and *The Munsters* (both 1964–1966) spoofed horror conventions. Even the soap opera was not immune, as producer Dan Curtis proved with his immensely popular daytime TV soap-opera series *Dark Shadows* (1966–1971), which had more monsters than you could shake a stick at—and all of them, of course, had severe, complex, and long-lasting personal problems. (Curtis had a great horror touch, as can be seen in his TV movie shockers *The Night Stalker*, 1972; *Trilogy of Terror*, 1975; and his underrated 1976 theatrical feature *Burnt Offerings*.)

A slog through the period's exploitation bin is largely unrewarding. *The Incredibly Strange*

Ganja and Hess (1972) poster.

Transplant (1971) and *The Thing with Two Heads* (1972). For old-school rubber-monster fans, there was 1971's *Octaman*, featuring the endearingly un-frightening debut of future master makeup and special- effects artist Rick Baker, fresh off an apprenticeship with Art Clokey—the latter the acid-gobbling creator of the stop-motion cartoon hero Gumby.

The recently sprouted Blaxploitation genre picked up on the horror trend and produced cross-pollinations such as *Blacula* (1972), *Blackenstein* (1973), the zombie dramas *The House on Skull Mountain* (1974) and *Sugar Hill* (1974), and the *Exorcist* rip-off *Abby* (also 1974).

At the other end of the African American horror spectrum is the intense and innovative beauty of Bill Gunn's treatise on Black vampirism and voodoo, *Ganja & Hess* (1973). In it, an attack with a ceremonial dagger turns an anthropologist into a vampire. The collision of African culture with Black Christianity is explored in a meditative, surreal style that is absolutely unique.

Hitchcock's success prompted other "name" directors to dabble in horror. Modern-art superstar Andy Warhol produced the perverse *Flesh for Frankenstein* (1973) and *Blood for Dracula* (1974), both directed by Paul Morrissey and featuring Udo Kier, who would become a contemporary Peter Lorre, a master of quietly perverse roles.

In 1962, action director Robert Aldrich picked a strange modern Gothic thriller to film, managed to hire Joan Crawford and Bette Davis to costar in it, and created the disturbing *What Ever Happened to Baby Jane?*, the story of two aging sisters, both former Hollywood stars, one of whom is crazy. The tattered tale of guilt and torment sparked a cycle of "hagsploitation," aka "psychobiddy," horror/slasher films inhabited by older actresses, creepy sources of income for late-career actresses such as Crawford, Davis, Tallulah Bankhead, Olivia de Havilland, Shelley Winters, and Agnes Moorehead.

There were exceptions to all these trends, individual horror films that stood out.

Carnival of Souls (1962) poster.

Herk Harvey's *Carnival of Souls* (1962) is an independent passion project that harkens back to the expressiveness of silent cinema. In it, a young organist seems caught between the worlds of life and death when she survives a car wreck. She leaves her hometown abruptly, but finds no peace at a new parish. She is haunted by a white-faced man (director Harvey). In her hands, organ hymns twist into demonic improvisations. She phases in and out of the everyday. "There's no place in this world for me," she laments.

Harvey's gorgeous black-and-white cinematography turns America's mid- and mountain West into a ghostly landscape. The flat, unaffected style of the local amateur actors Harvey uses gives the film a documentary feel. It's a threadbare, evocative meditation on death.

Robert Wise's *The Haunting* (1963) manipulates the viewer expertly. Based on Shirley Jackson's 1959 novel *The Haunting of Hill House*, it follows a quartet of paranormal investigators as they examine a haunted house. But are the phenomena they witness coming from the house, or are they manifesting them from within themselves?

Wise got his start as a director with the famed horror producer Val Lewton, making atmospheric and suggestive horror in the 1940s. *The Haunting* is his tribute to his horror roots, a fright film that sends shocks through implication alone.

Under Wise's direction, production designer Elliot Scott created dark, ornate, and cluttered interiors, filled with angles subtly off the square and topped with oppressively low ceilings. Odd, canting shots and the use of curved lenses add

The Birds (1963) poster.

to the viewer's disorientation and discomfort. By altering the ground rules of traditional filming, Wise manufactures apprehension.

Hitchcock followed *Psycho* with *The Birds* (1963), launching the "when-nature-attacks" eco-horror subgenre. John Frankenheimer's *Seconds* (1966) is ostensibly a science-fiction film, the third in the director's "paranoia trilogy" (following *The Manchurian Candidate*, 1962, and *Seven Days in May*, 1964), but it's really a penetrating modern-day Faust legend. A middle-aged businessman (John Randolph) wants to start over in life and gets to, in the form of Rock Hudson. He finds the bargain's not all it's cracked up to be. Ironically, the film featured several actors who were blacklisted during Hollywood's Red

Scare of the previous decade; Frankenheimer gives them a "second life" here.

Another key year for American horror was 1968. The two most resonant horror films of that year came from opposite ends of the spectrum. Roman Polanksi's *Rosemary's Baby* (much more on this film later on) was a well-budgeted, mainstream hit that reveled in ambiguity and suspense. George A. Romero's arguably more influential *Night of the Living Dead* was its exact opposite.

Shot cheaply and in black-and-white, *Dead* was the epitome of DIY filmmaking: simple, linear, graphic, and effective, it became one of the most popular independent films ever made.

Its story was cobbled from ideas set down in Richard Matheson's 1954 novel *I Am Legend*, and took a lot of its look from the first film adaptation of the book, 1964's *The Last Man on Earth*. A falling satellite's worldwide radiation emission reanimates the recently deceased and gives them an appetite for human flesh as well. Romero changed the nemeses from vampires to the flesh-hungry, slow-moving undead. In doing

Zombies from *Night of the Living Dead* (1968).

so, he single-handedly revived and redefined the zombie-horror subgenre. All the gore-goods are delivered in *Dead*, but there's something else pulsing along underneath all that: a precise and perceptive examination of the behavior of normal people in extreme circumstances.

Norms are subverted throughout. The heroine is catatonic; the hero is Black and unapologetically smarter and more proactive than anyone else in sight. The characters dally, waver, make bad choices, and reverse themselves. Monsters outside, idiots within—no wonder *Dead* was so popular.

Dead's low-grade, black-and-white footage gave the film a gritty documentary-like feel (and Romero's previous film experience was exclusively with documentaries). Romero turned over the film's exposition to scattered, overheard, and glimpsed news broadcasts, keeping the audience just as in the dark as the characters, and adding a touch of satire to the proceedings as well. (Of the ghouls, the local sheriff interviewed on TV says, "They're dead— they're all messed up.") Ironically, the solution to the zombie problem consists of redneck posses roaming the countryside, shooting people in the head (and killing our hero by mistake in the process). As his body is added to the bonfire with the others in a series of stills, the grim truth seems to be that, in this particular horror universe at least, Murphy's Law is ascendant.

The pressure of transgression kept building. Things got bloodier. What was going on here? The country was coming apart at the seams. Families could view bodies every night on the broadcast news, scattered from Vietnam to Memphis. It took more to glut the jaded viewer. The jolts had to be bigger. The mid-1970s represent a bottoming-out of popular taste, as though it was necessary to take film shock as far as possible.

Equinox (1970) was shot by Jack Woods with uncredited but key help from Dennis Muren and Mark Thomas McGee; Muren would later become a key player at special-effects giant Industrial Light & Magic. It's another no-budget film that transcends its limitations. Its imaginative and well-wrought stop- motion and cel animation effects are the missing link between the old-school work of Ray Harryhausen and future, computerized digital work. And its plot hook of a forbidden book that opens a gateway to an evil parallel universe has its roots in Lovecraft but would later be adopted by Sam Raimi for his *Evil Dead* films.

George A. Romero proved he wasn't a one-trick pony with *The Crazies* (1973). Everything you need to know about how people felt about their government in 1973 is here. Romero displays his gift for satire and social commentary, as he delineates what happens when a military bioweapon is accidentally unleashed on a typical American small town. The infected either die or are transformed into homicidal maniacs, and our protagonists are caught between the "crazies" and the infantry assigned to cover up the incident by killing everyone on sight.

Wes Craven was raised in a strict Baptist family, then went from being a high school English teacher to editing and producing industrial films and then to making hardcore porn. He decided to push the genre as far as it could go when he made *The Last House on the Left* (1972). It's a direct assault on the senses, a cross between a revenge tragedy and an orgy of gore. The film is ostensibly a remake of Ingmar Bergman's 1960 *The Virgin Spring*.

In *Last House*, two young women are kidnapped, humiliated, tortured, raped, and murdered; the parents of one of the victims take revenge on the psychopathic perpetrators.

Personal Best

George Romero

***Night of the Living Dead* (1968)**

***The Crazies* (1973)**

***Martin* (1976)**

***Dawn of the Dead* (1978)**

***Creepshow* (1982)**

The Texas Chain Saw Massacre (1974) poster.

(Craven wanted unsimulated sex and more graphic violence, but was reined in.) The camera lingers over the scenes of gruesomeness, save for the comic-relief scenes, in which law enforcement is portrayed as less than useful. There is maximum pain and zero redemption.

Ironically, Craven stated he was being altruistic; he said he made the movie in order to revolt and provoke the audience, and to make it question its complicity with the violence onscreen. That didn't happen. Instead, it was a big hit. (Another big transgressive hit of 1972 was John Boorman's *Deliverance*, about a canoe trip gone savagely wrong in the Appalachian backwoods. Unlike *Last House on the Left*, it was critically acclaimed and is thought of as a thriller rather than as a horror film.)

The defining split between terror and horror lies here. Karloff notably remarked, "Horror means something revolting. Anybody can show you a pail-full of innards. But the object of the roles I played is not to turn your stomach— but merely to make your hair stand on end. . . . Shocks . . . should not be forced into a film without excuse."[1] (Interestingly, director Peter Bogdanovich's first film, *Targets,* 1968, features

The Last House on the Left (1972) poster.

Karloff in his last great role as an old horror star whose majestic presence contrasts with the squalid "modern-day" horror of a deranged sniper randomly killing the viewers at a drive-in.)

Including exploitation film in the horror equation means that we are going to have to admit that somewhere at the bottom of the common psyche, clanking its chains and gnashing its incisors, is an attraction to sheer cruelty. There is a deep-seated, largely unacknowledged desire to sometimes hurt and destroy, to act without regard for God or man, to foster death and chaos—or wouldn't we have created heaven on Earth by now? The twentieth century proved that on a near-daily basis.

This kind of graphic thrill was much more pathological than the teenage "are-you-chicken?" rite-of-passage needs that earlier horror films served. Exploitation films were vicarious enactments of transgressive acts made to provide perverse gratification. The bloody, random pornography of violence and death was on the table, raw and ready to be served.

The avenging father in *The Last House on the Left* dispatches the villain with a chainsaw; that yard tool would soon show up front and center in Tobe Hooper's *The Texas Chain Saw Massacre* (1974). It's brutally effective, a lesson in stripped-down movie mechanics that delivers the goods.

In this virtuoso tour of madness and death, the typical nuclear American family is one that has you over for dinner by having you for dinner. Somehow, this evocation of America as a refuge for crazed murderers plays out with matter-of-fact bluntness.

Hooper's filmmaking skills are top-notch. His deadpan camera makes the horror seem inevitable. He turns a simple foot chase into a seemingly endless, futile nightmare. He made some sly points about the nuclear family and the American way, but ultimately *Chain Saw* is about the efficient mechanics of hunter and hunted. In Hooper's film universe, man is either monster or meat.

The ultimate manifestation of the mainstream/exploitation intersection is the wildly popular, controversial, and much-awarded *The Exorcist* (1973). The smash-hit film about a young girl possessed graphically by Satan is a no-holds-barred assault on the senses and the sensibilities. The graphic, blasphemous, disturbing vision, aided immensely by the special effects of Dick Smith, is, like *Rosemary's Baby*, a tale of Satan set in the upper-middle classes. It transforms its possessed twelve-year-old girl into a raging, horrifying demon. In a way, *The Exorcist* affirms faith as much as it abuses it; without such powerful demons to battle, how could there be such dramatic acts of sacrifice and redemption?

The Exorcist triggered a slew of knockoffs such as *The Antichrist* (1974), *Enter the Devil* (1974), *Exorcismo* (1975), and *The Devil Inside Her* (1977). The gross-outs and shocks from

henceforward would be matters only of degree, not of difference. There was not a hell of a lot further to go, short of the "mondo" subgenre of films that purported to show "the real thing" (that is, mayhem and torture) and morphed into the despicable curiosities of the pseudo-documentary *Faces of Death* series (1978–1990)—a step shy of the rumored and infamous "snuff" films that purported to show recorded murders.

Meanwhile, more restrained, effective horror films were made. Paul Wendkos's *The Mephisto Waltz* (1971) is a roundelay of diabolical body-switching, subtle and menacing. In it, Satanism is simply the most practical way to maintain a cozy, satisfying lifestyle—for eternity. There was the bizarre, wacked-out, near-John Waters-style artistry of *The Baby* (1973). Penned by the immortal Abe Polsky (*Rebel Rousers*), and directed by the uneven Ted Post (*Go Tell the Spartans*, but also *Beneath the Planet of the Apes*), it's just so offhandedly perverse that it shakes you to the core. A woman and her daughters keep their son/brother, now a grown man, in a state of absolute infancy. A concerned social worker seeks to interfere. Yikes.

A new era, more traditionally minded and with an eye on the creation of new horror franchises, was coming. Wes Craven had already made his mark. Soon he'd be joined by three other crucial horror innovators: Bob Clark, John Carpenter, and David Cronenberg.

Actor Linda Blair (left) listens to director William Friedkin on the set of *The Exorcist* (1973).

The Exorcist (1973) poster.

BLOODY ENGLAND
HAMMER'S COMPETITORS

uccess breeds imitators. Hammer Studios' bold reinvention of classic horror film's icons led to a boom in British fright flicks. Initially, Hammer had the field to itself. The only other outstanding British effort from that early period came from director and horror vet Jacques Tourneur. His earlier work for Val Lewton made him the perfect choice to make another "unseen monster" film, *Night of the Demon*, aka *Curse of the Demon* (1957), aided by masterful screenwriter Charles Bennett. Unfortunately, producer Hal E. Chester made the executive decision to show the monster at the beginning and end of the film, utilizing the talents of model-maker/animator Ray Harryhausen. This studio interference crushed the bracing blast of chilly ambiguity out of the project.

Swinging London of the 1960s was a cultural epicenter in many ways, and British film at the time was strong and influential. While Hammer dominated the horror market, there were plenty of competing studios out there. Amicus, Tigon, Anglo-Amalgamated, and Tempean all turned out notable horror films, one of them perfecting the art of the horror anthology film.

British horror output of the 1960s differed from contemporary American horror output in significant ways. First, there was a kind of inverse economy of scale. The compact creative world of English filmmaking could be claustrophobic, but it was also much more tightly knit, and jobs and resources were spread about evenly. People knew each other and worked together frequently, developing relationships that bolstered standards, ensured consistency, and made the end products better.

English production values, up and down the spectrum, were on the whole higher than American ones. A big-budget Hollywood film looks great, but low-budget American films are truly primitive-looking. British movies may start to look the same after a while, but they all have a deliberate look to them, never fall below a certain level of quality, and tend to do a better job of suspending disbelief.

The British Board of Film Censors was still in command, which meant that the outright gore and sex trending in American film was still a no-no in England. This led to more inventive plotting, and the surreptitious planting of levels of meaning that could slip past the guardians of acceptability. Censorship, to the creative artist, is an obstacle, not a deterrent. Such mischievousness can be found in bulk in British horror. In British horror there also seems to be a greater compulsion to maintain the internal logic of a plot, which is inherently more involving than the random transgressions going on in American horror at the time. The stories were better.

A look at the roster of actors in English horror films of the period includes nearly every significant player of the time, of both screen and stage. Of course, Hammer stars Christopher Lee and Peter Cushing were also in many of the non-Hammer horror films of the time, as were other horror regulars, among them Barbara Shelley, Anton Diffring, Herbert Lom, Donald Pleasence, Hazel Court, Patrick Magee, Barbara Steele, Michael Ripper, and Charles Gray.

If you scan English horror of the period, you'll also find highly talented up-and-coming

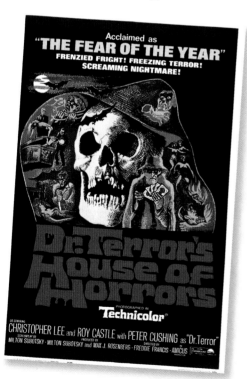

OPPOSITE: *Night of the Demon* (1957) poster.

Dr. Terror's House of Horrors (1965) poster.

The cast of *Mumsy, Nanny, Sonny, and Girly* (1970).

thespians of the day, including Donald Sutherland, John Hurt, Stephanie Beacham, Pamela Franklin, David Warner, and Robert Powell, as well as surprising appearances by respected stars of the previous generation such as Ralph Richardson, Ann Todd, Elisabeth Bergner, Deborah Kerr, and Robert Stephens. These weren't people to sleepwalk through appearances; they gave their professional all (even in, tsk tsk, a horror film). Even Laurence Olivier broke down and played Van Helsing to Frank Langella's *Dracula* (1979). (Langella got his "big break" by playing the thirsty count in a 1977 Broadway remounting of the *Dracula* stage play that made Lugosi's career.)

Finally, in contrast with America's let-it-all-hang-out ethos, England's cultural vibe is buttoned up: stratified, self-serious, repressed, polite, and deadpan—underneath which boils psychotic rage. The contrast is a lot of fun to play with.

Many Hammer writers and directors did work outside that company as well. Roy Ward Baker, Freddie Francis, Jimmy Sangster, and

The Blood Beast Terror (1968) poster.

Anthony Hinds all pursued numerous horror projects hither and thither. Techniques and approaches were shared across English studios.

(Francis's 1970 *Mumsy, Nanny, Sonny, and Girly*, in which a grifter stumbles into history's most dysfunctional family, is a very strange must-see. It is so very close to being horror, but also bears resemblance to similar films made about the same time, a microgenre about a pan-sexual seducer who destroys a family in Pasolini's *Teorema*, 1968, and Radley Metzger's *The Lickerish Quartet*, 1970.)

English horror was bleakly whimsical. In *It!*, aka *Anger of the Golem* or *Curse of the Golem* (1967), Roddy McDowall's creature survives a tactical nuclear strike. *The Blood Beast Terror* (1968) features a "were-moth." *The Asphyx* (1972), despite the terrible title, is ridiculously entertaining, sporting features such as personalized Grim Reapers and an immortal guinea pig.

Hammer's first significant competitor, Amalgamated Productions, released a couple of thoughtful horror films with Boris Karloff, *Corridors of Blood* and *The Haunted Strangler*

(1958). Monty Berman and Robert S. Baker formed Tempean Films, cranking out some nice period horror flicks, culminating with *The Flesh and the Fiends*, aka *Mania* (John Gilling, 1960), a drama on the same topic as Val Lewton's 1945 *Body Snatcher* that features top-notch performances from Cushing, Donald Pleasence, George Rose, and Billie Whitelaw.

"Is the feeding of worms more sacred than the pursuit of truth?" says Peter Cushing at his ruthless, arrogant best in the film as the real-life Dr. Robert Knox. It was he who, in 1828 Edinburgh, paid "resurrectionists" Burke and Hare to dig up and supply him with bodies for dissection, leading to the murders of at least sixteen people. It's a grim and greasy survey of early nineteenth-century horrors.

Decorous English horror films were still made, but their quotient of shocks and gore was slowly ratcheting up. Anglo-Amalgamated Film Distributors was responsible for the transgressive work of the so-called "Sadean trilogy": *Horrors of the Black Museum*, *Circus of Horrors*, and Powell's *Peeping Tom*. All three films featured a major shift in British horror in that they featured aggressive attacks on beautiful women.

Horrors of the Black Museum (1959) opens with a jolt—a gift of binoculars with spikes that poke out a victim's eyes. The opening of this film in "Hypno-vision" makes no bones about upping the ante and presenting graphic cruelty onscreen (the crimes were said to be taken from the real-life ones on display in Scotland Yard's Black Museum). The crisp, acerbic actor Michael Gough (pronounced Goff), an expert at playing annoyed and impatient evildoers, outdoes himself here as a writer who kills people in order to write about murder more accurately.

Anglo-Amalgamated's *Circus of Horrors* (1960) features Anton Diffring, everyone's favorite film Nazi, who here plays a plastic surgeon with a difference. Hiding out in a circus (of course?) he makes disfigured women beautiful, but when they try to leave him, they . . . die. It's deliciously daffy, and as far as I can tell is the only film in which Donald Pleasence is eaten by a bear.

An evil-children film, *Village of the Damned* (1960), has had surprising staying power, spawning a sequel, *Children of the Damned* (1962). (Other bad-kid films of the era include *These Are the Damned,* 1963; *Who Can Kill a Child?,* 1976; and David Cronenberg's *The Brood,* 1979.)

It! (1966) poster.

There is nothing creepier than silent, stone-faced children. In *Village of the Damned*, a whole village of women becomes pregnant spontaneously and gives birth to blonde-haired, glowing-eyed, telepathic tykes that threaten the planet. The film features the urbane George Sanders in one of his last strong roles. In horror film as in real life, distrust of the youthful generation would only grow more pronounced.

In 1962, American producers Milton Subotsky and Max J. Rosenberg set up shop in London as Amicus Productions. They quickly moved into the horror market, making a splash and reestablishing the "portmanteau," or episodic, horror anthology film with *Dr. Terror's House of Horrors*, directed with darkly comic flair by Hammer's Freddie Francis, in 1965.

Producer Subotsky was a screenwriter and worked on the TV version of the long-running American radio horror series, *Lights Out*. It has been suggested that he cribbed a lot of his horror-vignette ideas from the pulp magazines and shock radio shows of that era for his films. Amicus did extensively use the talents of a

prolific protégé of Lovecraft, screenwriter Robert Bloch, the author of *Psycho*.

Dr. Terror is the first and best of a new and numerous crop of English-language horror anthology films. Five doomed men in a railway carriage have their fortunes told by Dr. Schreck (Peter Cushing), with the help of a deadly tarot deck. The entertaining, self-contained horror vignettes are light on graphic scares and heavy on dark humor. No fewer than seven of these Amicus anthologies hit the screen, most of them witty excursions into short-form frights.

Tigon British Film Productions leapt into the fray with the extremely young Michael Reeves's Karloff vehicle *The Sorcerers* in 1967. Reeves was a prodigy consciously seeking to remake the horror film, but he overdosed in 1969 at twenty-five after completing *Witchfinder General* with Vincent Price.

His replacement on his uncompleted *The Oblong Box*, Gordon Hessler, proved to be a solid horror director in his own right, turning out, with Price in the lead, *Cry of the Banshee* and *Scream and Scream Again* (both 1970).

Cry of the Banshee is a rare Elizabethan-era horror tale, featuring a classic Vincent Price performance as the patriarch of a family cursed by witches. It also features one of the great stage actresses of the twentieth century, Elisabeth Bergner, as the leader of a coven. Tigon persisted, lensing one of the last significant pairings of Lee and Cushing, 1973's *The Creeping Flesh*.

The only British director to go completely graphic was Pete Walker, yet another pornographic filmmaker who moved on to horror. *The Flesh and Blood Show* (1972)

Circus of Horrors (1960) poster.

is a graphic romp set in a theater; *House of Whipcord* (1974) creates a secret prison. Though gory and transgressive, Walker's films actually grew in technique and thoughtfulness as he progressed. A pointed theme of deep distrust of authority binds these films together, sometimes overcoming their flaws. Finally, in the *House of the Long Shadows* (1983), he united Lee, Cushing, Price, and John Carradine one last time, in a spoofy tribute to the horror masters.

Jack Clayton's *The Innocents* (1961) is one of the best films ever made, let alone one of horror's finest. It's an adaptation of Henry James's 1898 novella *The Turn of the Screw*, dark and evocative as a charcoal sketch. Deborah Kerr is a governess whose two young charges seem to be under the power of a pair of ghostly lovers. This definitive adaptation features Freddie Francis's flawless cinematography, and a perfectly balanced story—are a pair of children possessed, or is their governess going mad? Clayton's absolute refusal to confirm or deny the validity of the heroine's perceptions, and his insistence that the viewer identify with her, still makes for a maddening viewing experience.

Some films have never been accepted into the horror canon, perhaps because the mainstream seems to need to reclassify great horror movies

as something else, something that transcends the ratty genre. Director Ken Russell was the central iconoclast of British cinema in the 1960s, ruthlessly strange and affected in his style, and never shy about putting the most disturbing images he could conceive of on camera. Best known for his musical biographies/fantasies, he set out to film an adaptation of Aldous Huxley's 1952 novel (based on true events) *The Devils of Loudun*, set in seventeenth-century France.

That *The Devils* (1971) is still banned in most of the world is a testament to its unyielding depiction of madness, sadism, and perversion, and to its indictment of the structures that govern human society. It calls into question every figure of authority of the day. Here, the king of France is a hermaphroditic demigod, his cardinal a ruthless schemer.

When a proud, licentious priest (Oliver Reed) attempts to maintain the self-government of the city of Loudun, the powers that be contrive to bring him down. Not for the religious-minded, it features a sexual assault on a crucifix. By nuns. This is all in the name of pointing up the follies of religion, but still. Like Elem Klimov's graphic,

Burn (1964), *Eye of the Devil* (1966), *Witchfinder General* (1968), *The Ballad of Tam Lin* (1970), and *The Blood on Satan's Claw* (1971). Some were period pieces, and in some the ancient gods crept into contemporary life.

In Robin Hardy's *The Wicker Man* (1973), the folk horror theme is ingeniously worked up into a masterful mystery capped with a horrifying conclusion: a tragic clash of cultures.

Vanessa Redgrave in *The Devils* (1971).

INSET: *The Devils* (1971) poster.

repulsive antiwar film *Come and See* (1985), it's a film worth seeing, but only once.

One British film by an American director, Richard Fleischer, is classified as a crime drama about one of England's most notorious serial killers, but it contains one of the most chilling portrayals of mundane evil ever depicted and deserves a mention. In *10 Rillington Place* (1971) famed actor/director Richard Attenborough (much better remembered today as the founder of *Jurassic Park*) gives the performance of a lifetime as the dodgy little serial killer John Christie, who murdered at least eight people during and after World War II. Director Fleischer had an up-and-down career, but here he really nails the horror-in-plain-sight film with impassive ruthlessness.

One small fad gave birth to one of horror's best films. "Folk horror"—the idea that paganism still holds sway in the subbasement of the British psyche—can be found in films of the time such as *Night of the Eagle*, aka *Burn, Witch,*

A girl is reported missing on a Hebridean isle, and the religious and repressed Sergeant Howie investigates. It turns out the inhabitants are pagans, who routinely provide human sacrifice in order to ensure a good harvest. It features Christopher Lee in one of his best roles as Lord Summerisle (a role he enjoyed so much he performed for free). Anthony Shaffer's meticulously researched script creates an entirely believable, and deadly, society.

The masterful cinematographer Nicolas Roeg became an evocative director with a Cubistic approach. Roeg's *Don't Look Now* (1973), in jumbled sequence, takes a couple (Donald Sutherland and Julie Christie) grieving for their child and plunges them into a world of menace and premonition. The film is grounded in the occult thriller subgenre, but it opens out into a wider disquisition on memory and loss. It's an intricately edited, poetic puzzle.

Most British horror fare was just as outrageous and silly as could be. In Gary Sherman's *Death Line*, aka *Raw Meat* (1972), subway workers trapped for generations below ground subsist on human flesh . . . donated by unwary commuters. The film actually features great performances by Hugh Armstrong as the monster and Donald Pleasence as a police inspector, and features a beautiful Wil Malone score. Robert Hartford-Davis's *The Fiend*, aka *Beware My Brethren* (also 1972), features older English starlet Ann Todd as a whacked-out Holy Roller with a serial killer for a son; the church in her home celebrates with full musical production numbers, and Patrick Magee plays its unblinking, sibilant, maniacal, and malignant minister.

By the mid-1970s, the British horror boom was over. The British Isles continued to produce a steady stream of fright flicks, but a backlash against explicit content would put a damper on their wild, shocking, and original creations.

The climax of Robin Hardy's *The Wicker Man* (1973).

13

THE SLEEP OF REASON

HORROR IN SPANISH

In 1799, the brilliant, rebellious, and troubled Spanish artist Francisco Goya printed an album of eighty aquatinted etchings, dark, cynical, and forbidding, titled *Los Caprichos* (*The Caprices*), in the sense of amusements. After only twenty-seven copies were sold, he withdrew it from the market. Four years later, he offered up the prints and plates to the affable, dim-witted Spanish king Carlos IV. The forty-third etching is one of horror's most powerful images. It shows a slumbering artist at his desk, overtaken by nightmare creatures. The etching's title is: "The sleep of reason produces monsters."

Horror in the Spanish-speaking world did not feature strongly in its literature, as it did in other cultures. Mexico and Spain were late to horror-film production, just as England and Italy were. As in those countries, they struggled with censorship early on, but then moved quickly and fiercely into forbidden territory.

Mexico's horror films were more conservative, included primarily in a peculiar subgenre featuring the heroic exploits of masked wrestlers. Spain's horror movies were far more transgressive, dark, and bizarre, leading to multiple, many-named, mutilated versions edited with or without varying degrees of graphic sex and gore.

During the early age of the talkies, Hollywood sometimes created foreign-language versions of their feature films. Substitute casts shot on the same sets at night, or polylingual actors repeated themselves for the foreign versions. Laurel and Hardy recorded some of their films in other languages by reading them phonetically off moveable blackboards—proto-cue cards.

The notable Spanish-language *Dracula* was filmed concurrently, at night, on the same sets as Lugosi/Browning's in 1931. Directed by George Melford and starring a moony, Lugosi-ish Carlos Villarias, it actually received more critical praise than the American version. Pablo Alvarez Rubio plays the Iberian Renfield with panache and intensity, much more maniacally than Dwight Frye in the English-language version.

The first true Mexican horror film was 1933's *La Llorona* by Ramón Peón, based on the Mexican legend of the "crying woman" ghost of the title who, seeking her lost children, causes harm to those who encounter her. Director and screenwriter Juan Bustillo Oro followed with *The Phantom of the Convent* and *Two Monks* (1934) and *The Mystery of the Ghastly Face* (1935). Oro's style is evocative, but his treatment of the material is very gentle and unchallenging, much more of a "spooky" experience than anything else.

Mexico didn't have a movie industry that was under the thumb of a fascist government, as was the case in Spain, Argentina, and elsewhere. Without hindrance, the industry's production facilities grew and improved, and experience sharpened expertise. By 1940, Mexico had entered its Golden Age of cinema.

Carlos Villarias (left) as Count Dracula and Pablo Alvarez Rubio as Renfield in the Spanish-language *Dracula* (1931).

OPPOSITE: *The sleep of reason produces monsters* (No. 43), from *Los Caprichos*, by Francisco Goya, 1799 etching.

El Vampiro (1957) poster.

Director/screenwriter/actor Chano Urueta (best remembered for playing the philosophical old Don Jose in Sam Peckinpah's 1969 *The Wild Bunch*), who helmed an amazing 117 films in forty years, dabbled in horror during the '30s (*Desecration*, 1933; *The Sign of Death*, 1939). It was Urueta who made *The Magnificent Beast* (1952), one of the first Mexican films to feature masked wrestlers (*luchadores*), which proved insanely popular. In the following year, working with producer/actor Abel Salazar, Urueta made the first truly modern Mexican horror film, *The Resuscitated Monster*, a Frankenstein rehash.

Salazar hopped on the horror bandwagon, and soon produced and appeared in *El Vampiro*, directed by Fernando Méndez, in 1957. Twenty-six years after the Spanish *Dracula*, it ignited the horror boom in Mexico. The vampire, here Count Karol de Lavud, was played by Germán Robles, who would go on to make a "Nostradamus"

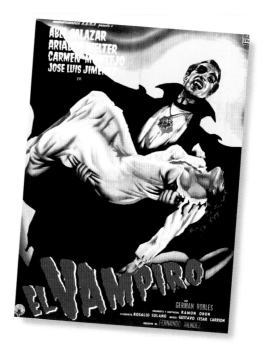

Director, screenwriter, and actor Chano Ureta made the first modern Mexican horror movie, 1953's *El monstruo resuscitado*.

vampire movie serial and reprise his signature role from time to time, though he was never typecast as restrictively as Bela Lugosi was.

Soon the Urueta/Salazar team would be making horror films such as *The Witch's Mirror* and *The Brainiac*, both in 1962—the latter wildly popular, and featuring a mind-controlling baron and sorcerer who can change into a demon who can suck out his victims' brains with his long, forked tongue.

Méndez was joined by others such as Federico Curiel (*The Vengeance of the Women Vampire*, 1970) and Rafael Baledón (*The She-Wolf*, 1965). These were all low-budget efforts, but they shared a strong rancho-Gothic flavor that went over well. (Mendez's *The Black Pit of Dr. M*, 1959, contains compelling imagery and good makeup work.)

In Alfonso Corona Blake's wacky *The World of the Vampires* (1961), not only does our hero know a musical composition that kills vampires, but the head vampire, who seeks revenge for something that's never really specified, has a home cavern conveniently equipped with a pipe organ (evidently jerry-built out of human bones). The vampire, who has it made in the shade, as it were, enjoys the assistance of bat-masked minions and sexy slave vampire women.

Blue Demon and
Mil Mascaras
check out *The
Mummies of
Guanajuato*
(1972).

(drip-dry turtleneck short-sleeves?), slacks, and full-face masks.

They fight monsters, gangsters, and anyone else available. The plot takes a break with the awkward insertion of a genuine wrestling bout (or two, or three). (The similarity to the wrestling monsters of Japan's *kaiju* movies is instructive. The world's collective unconscious at the time seemed to need to see enormous things grapple on the big screen.) And, of course, every ending in the *luchador* film is happy.

Santo became, and still is, a national hero. He and other *luchadores* such as Blue Demon, Mil Mascaras ("Thousand Masks"), and Tinieblas ("Darkness") lit up the screens with their battles against mighty enemies such as mummies (Aztec or Mayan, not Egyptian), monsters, zombies, vampires, wolfmen, and mad scientists. The series' high point financially was the triple threat of Santo, Blue Demon, and Mil Mascaras in Curiel's 1972 *The Mummies of Guanajuato*.

Mexican horror began to catch on in America, too, thanks to the machinations of the independent film producer K. Gordon Murray. Murray started out as a bingo-parlor operator, and rose to the position of carnival manager. He helped find little people for the cast of 1939's *The Wizard of Oz*, and later helped to promote Cecil B. DeMille's 1952 circus epic *The Greatest Show on Earth*. Murray then started dubbing foreign children's films into English and booking them around the US, earning him the title of "The King of the Kiddie Matinee." Soon he was dubbing *luchador* films into English and booking them as well. He released an impressive sixty films in just fifteen years, but ran afoul of the Internal Revenue Service, which confiscated his ragtag, overdubbed output. He died in mid-litigation with the government in 1979 at age fifty-seven.

The overwhelming popularity of these unthreatening, kid-friendly *luchador* films meant that not a lot of different horror work was done in

Luchadores and movie monsters were flung together by producer Guillermo Calderon Stell in 1962's *Santo contra los mujeres vampiros* (*Santo vs. the Vampire Women*). The protagonist is played by professional wrestler Rodolfo Guzmán Huerta, aka El Santo, "The Saint." From 1942 on, Santo hid his face under a distinctive silver mask. During the 1950s, Santo starred in a series of photo-based comic-style novels, or "fumetti," that pitted him against villains both realistic and otherworldly. This paved the way for his success in a series of low-budget films.

The template for these *luchador* films is unvarying. First, whether at work, rest, or play, the heroes do everything in their masks. Usually, they are called up by a government seeking aid as they lounge around their dens in sport shirts

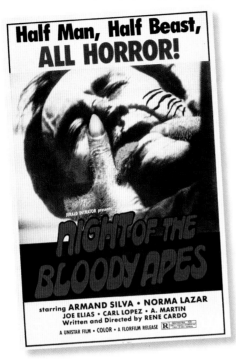

Half Man, Half Beast,
ALL HORROR!

JERALD INTRATOR presents...

**NIGHT OF THE
BLOODY APES**

starring **ARMAND SILVA** • **NORMA LAZAR**
JOE ELIAS • CARL LOPEZ • A. MARTIN
Written and Directed by **RENE CARDO**
A UNISTAR FILM • COLOR • A FLORFILM RELEASE ℝ

the country at the time. The first Mexican horror film in color, Rene Cardona's 1969 *Night of the Bloody Apes*, was a remake of his 1962 *Wrestling Women vs. the Killer Doctor*, supplemented with Technicolor gore and nudity. Its alternate title is brutally honest: *Sexo y Horror*. One dedicated horror screenwriter, Carlos Enrique Taboada, graduated to directing and turned out a trio of restrained, atmospheric, and effective ghostly tales: *Even the Wind is Afraid* (1968*)*, *The Book of Stone* (1969), and *Blacker Than Night* (1975).

The most radical horror director of the time was Juan López Moctezuma, an early collaborator with the visionary filmmaker Alejandro Jodorowsky (*El Topo*, 1970; *The Holy Mountain*, 1973), some of whose enigmatic style rubbed off on him. Moctezuma only made five films, all horror-related, the best of which is his first, the beautifully composed, compelling allegory *The Mansion of Madness* (1972), loosely based on a Poe story, in which the lunatics literally take over the asylum. It's halfway between horror and avant-garde theater. (His *Alucarda*, 1977, is a must-see for transgressives that combines sex and gore with pointed political and anti-clerical messages.)

It took Spain even longer to get around to making horror films—if you don't count the unsettling surrealisms of Luis Buñuel. Along with other key players, such as artist Salvador Dalí and poet Federico García Lorca, Buñuel founded Spain's twentieth-century avant-garde movement. Buñuel and Dalí's surreal and subversive movie masterpieces, *Un Chien Andalou* (1929) and *L'Age d'Or* (1930), are not horror films, but their nonlinear, nightmarish, dread-filled films influenced the depiction of horror from future filmmakers such as David Lynch and David Cronenberg. Buñuel fought the fascists in Spain, then decamped first to America in 1938 and then to Mexico in 1946, continuing to make bizarre masterpieces wherever he could.

Like Italy's Mussolini, the Spanish dictator Francisco Franco didn't like horror movies, so he banned them as well. In fact, during the whole term of Franco's uncrowned kingship, from 1936 through 1975, he exercised tight control over Spanish cultural life, eliminating anything that might cause "dis- order, panic, or violence" (especially independent thought). In concert with the Catholic hierarchy of the country, Franco tried to dominate the Spanish imagination. (The first Spanish horror film, Edgar Neville's *The Tower of the Seven Hunchbacks*, 1944, is really just a tame ghost story.)

Following World War II, film companies from around the world found Spain to be a congenial, versatile, and cheap filming location for epics, Westerns, biblical films, sword-and-sandal flicks, and the like. Eventually, in 1964, Franco's government gave its blessing to international co-productions and swept in the resulting revenue. The need for trained local workers and improved cinematic resources led to the creation of a strong, homegrown Spanish film industry. A burst of creativity exploded from the new filmmakers. The New Spanish Cinema was born.

As is usual in a culture of censorship, the artists in Franco's Spain subverted the dictator's intentions. They did this through coded language and implication. The psychic buildup in the collective unconscious of Spain was growing profoundly large. When the lid came off, it did so with a vengeance. One hundred and fifty horror titles were produced in Spain between 1968 and 1975; twenty-nine came out in 1973 and 1974 alone.

While other countries' horror films have a touch of playfulness about them, in Spain horror is a grim and deadly business. In Spanish, as in Italian horror film, women are victimized cruelly. However, in Italy's *giallo* films, there is still the sense that violence against women is a crime, and shouldn't be committed. In Spain, it's not only deemed to be not too much of a crime, but it always seems to be what the female victims deserve, especially if they exhibit sexuality, intellect, or assertiveness. In Spanish horror, sin is still real, Hell exists, and retribution is certain, even if only for the existential crime of being born a woman.

Oh, and one more thing: no Spanish horror film of the period, even if obviously filmed in Spain, was allowed to be set in Spain. The censors didn't allow it for, you see, such terrible things could never happen in fascist Spain. The underlying tone of Spanish horror, mirrored in its convoluted, impoverished style, is the loud buzz of mental and emotional denial.

Spanish horror really began with one of cinema's most intriguing and frustrating characters—namely, another Franco. Director/ screenwriter/editor/composer/actor Jesús Franco . . . aka Jess Franco, Jess Frank, Pablo Villa, Clifford Brown, Terry de Corsia, Joan Almirall, Dave Tough, David Khune, J. P. Johnson, P. Querut, Raymond Dubois, Dennis Farnon, Juan G. Cabral, et al. This madly fertile and many-monikered filmmaker made more than 200 films between 1957 and 2013, in a career that ramped rapidly downward from mainstream horror

The Awful Dr. Orlof (1962) poster.

to the margins of hardcore porn. Perhaps only an unstable innovator like Franco could have broken the taboos that needed breaking, and figured out a way to make transgressive films that could be screened in Spain.

He was an up-and-coming director when he got his producers to watch Hammer's *The Brides of Dracula* and convinced them he could work up something similar (and similarly profitable). Mimicking the feel of that movie, throwing in the sex and violence of *Psycho*, and stealing much of his plot from Franju's *Eyes Without a Face*, Franco cobbled together a convincingly scary, stark tale. *The Awful Dr. Orlof* (1962) turned out to be an international hit.

It features Howard Vernon, part of Franco's stock company of actors, as a mad doctor

Scene from *The Sadistic Baron Von Klaus* (1962).

whose blind assistant, Morpho, kidnaps women so that Orlof can use their flesh to heal his scarred daughter. Stylistically, it set a low bar. Contemporary scenes alternate with Gothic ones.

Shoddiness would plague Spanish horror films of the period. Many times, a pedestrian sense of pace and/or weird, uncinematic settings undercut the efforts. There always seems to be a castle handy—right next door to a hotel, or a disco, or a laundromat. The lighting of Spanish horror films was consistently awful, and their soundtracks were the worst kind of Eurojazz hodgepodge.

But Franco's camerawork is inventive, and he maintains the viewers' interest no matter how bad the script—or the acting—or the lighting—is. More important, he establishes the tone of the genre in Spain. Franco's horror-film world is sadistic and perverse, filled with a kind of adolescent, deadpan nihilism that defies the Big Brother, all-is-well stance of official Spanish culture. Franco captures the morbidity of his time perfectly.

In order to get *Orlof* made at all, Franco needed to mount it as an international co-production, a way of doing business that would pull him away from Spain eventually and in entirety. Franco wanted to show graphic violence and nudity, and wanted his films to play in Spain as well, but these were a mutually exclusive set of goals. So, he did what many enterprising filmmakers of the time were already doing—he made two versions, a "family" cut for the restrictive British and Spanish censors, and an "adult" cut for the rest of Europe, sophisticated and tolerant.

Franco had a loyal, if not necessarily gifted, bench of actors—among them the aforementioned Vernon, Jack Taylor, Paul Muller, and Rosalba Neri—which he supplemented when he could with bigger names such as Dennis Price, Klaus Kinski, Herbert Lom, and Christopher Lee.

Franco was prolific, and pushed the envelope of acceptability every time. In *The Sadistic Baron Von Klaus* (1962), there's the whipping of a nearly

One
soul
hungered
to
touch
another!

99 WOMEN
...behind bars—without men!

Maria
SCHELL · Mercedes
McCAMBRIDGE · Luciana
PALUZZI · Herbert
LOM

COLOR

Maria Rohm in
Jess Franco's
*The Blood of Fu
Manchu* (1968).

INSET: *99 Women*
(1968) poster.

enjoy. The wire-crossing of the sexual and homicidal impulses is fundamental to Spanish horror film.

In Franco's sequel, *Dr. Orloff's Monster* (1964), the plot engine is lifted directly from Clouzot's *Les Diaboliques*. What's really unique about the film is that much of it is spent in Spanish hipster territory— a kind *of La dolce vita* that features drugs, sex, and rock 'n' roll. The real thrill to be found in the movie is not the monster, but in these everyday transgressions of the flesh, condemned by El Caudillo and the Mother Church. At the end of the movie, Morpho, the monstrous servant, gains a measure of pathos, destroying his evil master and then succumbing gently to a bullet in the back of the head. A tear runs down his cheek as he says, "Thank you." *Blam!*

Franco had a trio of muses in actresses Maria Rohm, Soledad Miranda, and Lina Romay, each corresponding to a different, and progressively less-effective, period. As he continued through his career, Franco made more and more explicit films, and his aesthetic sense started to fall apart as well. By 1968, he had moved into color, and kickstarted the women-in-prison genre to boot, with *99 Women*. He directed the last two of the five-film series of Christopher Lee's *Fu Manchu* films. (Technically these are crime/ adventure films, but these tales of the nefarious mastermind are fun, ingenious, and strange, and contain some horrific elements.)

However, after his 1970 adaptation *Count Dracula* with Lee (awkwardly staged but probably the most faithful to Stoker's novel that Lee ever starred in), Franco got lost. He spent the rest of his career concocting inane, plotless fantasies of sex and death that are the work of a

naked woman, who's then suspended on a hook and disemboweled. You might call this tasteful in that the shot of the disemboweling focuses on the legs of the actors; when stabbed, one of the victim's legs cocks up coyly behind her, the Hollywood cliché usually used when panning away from a passionate kiss not acceptable to censors. The dark implication being that this is just the kind of thing the murder victim would

Count Dracula
(1970) poster.

pornographer, his gaze finally, inevitably, resting on the pubic triangle. Franco continued to be an iconoclast, but no one cared save for those who shared his perverse obsessions.

Other Spanish horror directors started to make films with sex and gore levels tailored to different markets. One cut generated another cut, depending on the specific restrictions imposed by the censors of the country involved. Movies deteriorated or got lost, and already fragmentary narratives became incomprehensible. Spanish horror films would be released and rereleased under different titles: Jorge Grau's 1974 *Let Sleeping Corpses Lie* screened under no fewer than sixteen different titles. It is a researcher's nightmare to comb through the tangled versions and pseudonyms plaguing these films, to try to obtain a coherent sense of what certain directors were trying to accomplish.

There was more sober talent to be found than Franco. José María Elorrieta, an old hand at spaghetti Westerns, turned to horror at the end

of his career (*The Curse of the Vampyr* and *Feast of Satan*, both 1971). Jorge Grau made an impact with entries such as *The Legend of Blood Castle* in 1972, and two years later, the aforementioned *Let Sleeping Corpses Lie*—an intelligent, more politically pointed, and well-done take on Romero's *Night of the Living Dead*. In *Corpses*, an electronic device designed to kill insects is given a field trial by the Ministry of Agriculture. Result: carnivorous zombies. It's fun, it's fast-paced, and of course the police think the protagonists are hippie-cult killers.

Eloy de la Iglesia made a few thoughtful, complex, provocative, and sometimes outright bonkers horror films on his way to becoming a leading maker of *quinqui* (juvenile delinquent) films, and films dealing boldly with themes of homosexuality, after the death of General Franco in 1975. In horror movies such as *The Glass Ceiling* (1971), *The Cannibal Man* (1972), *No One Heard the Scream*, and *Murder in a Blue World* (both 1973), he played with *giallo* and Hitchcockian styles, making potent allegories and sly commentaries about life under a dictatorship.

Narciso Ibáñez Serrador proved to be one of Spain's most innovative horror writer/directors, although he made only two feature horror films. The first, *The House that Screamed* (1969), is a Gothic, girls' school mystery that anticipates the body-horror subgenre, as well as Lucky McKee's disturbing 2002 *May*. His *Who Can Kill a Child?* gives us an island full of preteen murderers. Much more disturbing than any other kids-as-monsters film, the cognitive dissonance created by happy, smiling children who kill off any and all adults around them is almost unbearable, and very thought-provoking. (Serrador went on to create the classic Spanish horror TV series, *Stories to Keep You Awake*.)

Other good individual efforts included Eugenio Martín's 1973 *A Candle for the Devil*, in which two disapproving, middle-aged, psychotically homicidal sisters kill "sluts" who stay at their charming hotel, and Claudio Guerin Hill's *The Bell from Hell*, from the same year, an extremely effective and beautifully shot vengeance story studded with anticlerical feeling. (Church bell as murder weapon, anyone?) Notoriously, the director died on the last day of shooting, when he fell, or was pushed, or jumped, from the bell tower used in the film. Vicente Aranda's interesting *The Blood-Spattered Bride* (1972) explores lesbian vampirism through Sheridan Le Fanu's *Carmilla* character.

In eight films over a span of six years, Amando de Ossorio made a major impact on the Spanish horror film, creating a memorable franchise. His first horror film, *Fangs of the Living Dead* (1969), is a psychological thriller— nervous producers recut and supplemented it to make its heroine Malenka (Anita Ekberg) an actual, not imagined, vampire. *Fangs* is a well-done imitation of the Corman/Bava Gothic horror-film style that indulges a Spanish predilection for inescapably prominent bosoms.

Much of Spanish horror is steeped in ghost stories and Gothic romance, even when these elements clash with the go-go boots and miniskirts of the period's wayward female victims. Ossorio expertly excavated the Gothic

vibe with his next creation, *Tombs of the Blind Dead*, aka *The Night of Blind Terror*, in 1972. It's the first in a series of four films about a cursed band of mummified, blind, Satanic Knights Templar who rise from the grave to feast on human flesh.

For inspiration, he reached back into the fabulous tales of gloomy nineteenth-century Spanish literary success Gustavo Aldolfo Bécquer. Bécquer's 1861 story "El monte de las animas" describes a convocation of dead and cursed Knights Templar from the time of the Crusades, who were accused of heresy and slaughtered to a man by the order of the pope on Friday the 13th of October, 1307. In the story, they rise from the grave, pursuing bloody vengeance against some hapless would-be lovers.

Ossorio reset the story in the present day, and put transgressive youth in danger, prefiguring the American slasher movies of the 1980s. Here, the wandering young hipsters confront the reanimated mummies of the Knights Templar, a blood-drinking, virgin-sacrificing sect of warrior monks (we get a flashback scene of the virgin-torturing, of course). Ossorio was very firm about the Blind Dead (so-called because their exhibited corpses had their eyes pecked out) being mummies, not zombies, but their lust for human flesh allies them closely with Romero's Living Dead.

Above all, Ossorio knew how to shoot his monsters evocatively. *The Blind Dead* rise and gather in slow-motion, seemingly evadable but ultimately inescapable, marching together or riding on ghostly horses, swords brandished. Shot from low angles, they seem punishing— reactionary figures from the Spanish Inquisition, ready to devour the beliefless living. Tombs of the Blind Dead does not end on an optimistic note, as the hapless heroine leads the threat out into the world at large.

Blind Dead was so popular that it triggered three increasingly unbelievable sequels, including one with the threatening of glamorous models on a cruise ship (*The Ghost Galleon*, 1974) and a seaside romp (*Night of the Seagulls*, 1975).

The House that Screamed (1969) poster.

The Blind Dead return for the fourth time in *The Night of the Seagulls* (1975).

Ossorio did additional excellent work on horror projects all completed in short order—*The Loreley's Grasp*, *Night of the Sorcerers* (voodoo! beheadings! interpretive dance!), and *Demon Witch Child*, another *Exorcist* knockoff. Ossorio wrapped up his filmmaking career soon after, and wound up making a living painting and selling portraits of his *Blind Dead* creations.

Given their low budgets, horrible lighting, strange color values that rapidly decayed, scratchy and fragmentary prints, and jumbled storylines, many Spanish horror movies are technical horrors themselves. Bizarre effects, random bursts of sex and gore, and tedious subplots all blend and blur together in them.

Nowhere is this look more present than in the films of Paul Naschy, aka Jacinto Molina Álvarez, a legend known (primarily in Spain) as the "king of Spanish horror" and "the Spanish Lon Chaney." Inspired by his childhood viewing of Hollywood's *Frankenstein Meets the Wolf Man*, the short but powerfully built professional weightlifter yearned to be a horror star—not just a horror star, but the greatest and most versatile of them all. He

wound up as one of the most prolific. Over the course of almost 100 horror films, he surpassed Lon Chaney Sr. in the number of horror characters played. He rivaled the stony pathos of Lon Chaney Jr. as the werewolf Waldemar Daninsky.

The Mark of the Wolfman, aka *Frankenstein's Bloody Terror*, *Hell's Creatures: Dracula and The Werewolf*, or *The Nights of Satan* (1968) marks the beginning of Naschy's reign. Naschy was already thirty-four when he wrote the screenplay for *The Mark of the Wolfman* in 1968¸ and producers asked him to try playing the lead role as well. The result was known in America as *Frankenstein's Bloody Terror*. (There are no Frankensteins in the film; an awkward prologue tacked on for American viewing explains that all the Frankenstein monsters had evolved into werewolves— so there you go.) The film was pooh-poohed by Spanish critics but was a hit at the box office. It was the first of twelve Daninsky movies, and marked the birth of Naschy's prolific career. By the time of the fourth entry in the series, Naschy's *Wolfman* was a pan-European hit.

Each film in the series follows the same pattern. Daninsky is a virtuous gentleman who, through various Satanic or supernatural machinations, is bitten by a werewolf and becomes one himself. He rages against all manner of enemies, mostly monsters of comparable status, but he is primarily a force for good. He always falls in love with a "pure" woman who puts him out of his misery by killing him by the film's end.

The Werewolf vs. the Vampire Woman, aka *Walpurgis Night* or *Werewolf Shadow* (1971), is the most exuberant of the Daninsky films, combining the usual formula with the addition of sexy, partially clad vampire ladies. And in 3D no less (in select theaters)!

You just wish the victims had seen more horror movies. There are so, so many bad choices made here—silver bullets removed from a werewolf, the dead molested, blood dripped onto a witch's corpse . . .

Internal logic be damned, this wonderfully bad film wears its heart, literally, on its sleeve.

Squat Naschy looks much like a young Napoleon, with a tall, broad forehead and large, wedge-shaped nose. He can't really act; he is a "personality" film actor in the sense that he imposes his unchanging persona onto the characters he portrays, much as Gary Cooper or Clark Gable did.

He is stolid and unemotional, save for when he goes into spasms of agony or sadism. In fact, Naschy is made for silent film; it pays to watch him with the sound off. (The English dubbing of his films is a lot of claptrap that tries convolutedly to convey some kind of plot.) Naschy at rest was serious and earnest, a perfect doomed Romantic hero possessed of tragic dignity, and that resonated with viewers.

Naschy was absolutely determined. He would not be deterred from playing these parts, well- or ill-suited for them as he might be. And it's this amazing force of self-belief that sustains the viewer's interest in him on screen, no matter how preposterous his milieu. He played

not only a werewolf, but vampires (in *Count Dracula's Great Love*, 1973—he's so macho he stakes himself!), the Mummy, Mr. Hyde, Jack the Ripper, hunchbacks, warlocks, a "zombie master," psychos, serial killers, and Satan. Even in the hands of talented horror directors such as León Klimovsky and Carlos Aured, the results with Naschy are largely the same.

Many people watch Naschy through the lens of condescension, but it's difficult to think of another filmmaker who set such a specific challenge for themselves and fulfilled it so splendidly. (Naschy cultivated his legend carefully, especially among critical writers, which has gradually expanded his reputation—in Europe, at least.)

In the end, Naschy knew what the public wanted—formulaic thrills—and he delivered them. He even gave Waldemar Daninsky a happy ending. In *Curse of the Beast* (1975), he not only fights (and defeats) the Abominable Snowman, but he's freed of the werewolf curse, and trudges away from the camera happily through the faux-Tibetan snow with his beloved, just like Charlie Chaplin and Paulette Goddard at the end of 1936's *Modern Times*. You can't help but applaud.

Paul Naschy in *The Mark of the Wolfman* (1968).

GODZILLA
& CO.

FAR EAST HORROR IN TRANSITION

The horror-film boom kept building, roaring around the world during the 1960s and 1970s. In addition to the bumper crop of fright flicks churned out in America, England, Italy, Mexico, and Spain, many other countries, most notably Japan, joined in.

Japanese culture long harbored room for horror. Shinto belief invests nearly everything with a distinct spirit. In early Japanese horror, ancient ghosts (*mononoke*), demons (*oni*), and monsters (*yokai*) abounded beneath the stereotypically calm, reserved, and highly mannered surface of society, fertile ground for terror. Successive waves of Buddhism and Christianity added layers of afterlife to dread—elaborate hells and purgatories.

Two influential writers shaped the future of Japanese horror. In a way, they were mirror images of each other. Lafcadio Hearn (1850–1904), officially born in Greece, but a British subject with an Irish father, was a globe-trotting journalist and writer who lived in Japan for the last fourteen years of his life. Taking the name Yakumo Koizumi, he collected and

expanded on (and some say ripped off) Japanese legends, folk tales, and ghost stories, to great success. In contrast, Taro Hirai (1894–1965), equally influential, took up the pen name Edogawa Rampo, in honor of Edgar Allan Poe, and founded Japanese mystery and detective fiction, his work shading into *ero guro nansenso*—erotic, grotesque, and disturbingly irrational adventures.

"Ghost films" appeared in Japan as early as 1898, following the template of the traditional *bakeneko* ("changed cat") folk tale. In these, the vengeful spirit of a murdered person is "lapped up" by a cat that drinks their blood; the cat then becomes a demon enacting revenge. Salvador Murguía estimates at least twenty-nine of these stories were filmed during the silent era.[1] Between 1937 and 1940, director Shigeru Mokudo made six of them, all starring actress Sumiko Suzuki, making her the first "queen of *kaidan*" (ghost stories).

Japan's military state outlawed horror film during World War II (again, as in Italy, Spain, and elsewhere at the time, despots despised the genre). After the war ended, the film industry gradually recovered and *kaidan* films were made again. Director Arai Ryoeh began with *Ghost of Saga Mansion* in 1953, starring Takako Irie. She had been a silent-era star, and now enjoyed a second round of fame as the second great "queen of *kaidan*," appearing in almost thirty of them between 1953 and 1959.

Also in 1953, director Kenji Mizoguchi released *Ugetsu*, a perpetual rider on the top-film lists of all time. Ghosts and horror play a prominent part in the double story, but it's generally classified not as a horror film but as a romantic fantasy (a rather grim one at that) or a period drama (*jidaigeki*). The lure of excitement and profit drag two men away from their wives, as all are swept up in the fury of war. Finally, a potter is seduced by an evil spirit. The dead hunger for the living. Its climax, full of dread revelations, is harrowing. Its evocative style would become an example for Japanese *yokai* (monster) stories to follow.

OPPOSITE: *Godzilla* (1954) poster.

Greek-born writer Lafcadio Hearn (1850-1904) worked as a journalist in Cincinnati and New Orleans. He moved to Japan in 1890 to become a Japanese citizen and continue his career as a novelist under the pen name Koizumi Yakumo.

Toho Studios and director Ishiro Honda concocted the now-iconic monster—the green, scaly spined, two-legged tower of a prehistoric dino-lizard Godzilla in 1954. As the only nation, hopefully ever, to suffer atomic attack, Japan's deep-seated terror of the Bomb fed into Godzilla's sway over its imagination. In his origin story, he is a prehistoric undersea behemoth triggered back to life by hydrogen-bomb testing. The message is clear: the Atomic Age, like Goya's "sleep of reason," produced its own unique set of monsters. Godzilla is destroyed at the end of the first film, but his popularity entitled him to repeated resurrections and reconfigurations. He triggered a domino-fall of sequels, an entire subgenre (*tokusatsu*, or live-action special-effects-laden fantasy, sci-fi, and horror films), and within that, further division into *kaiju* (giant monster) and *kaijin* (humanoid supervillain) movies. To date, Godzilla has hit the screen no less than thirty-seven times.

Godzilla's name was a portmanteau of the Japanese words for "gorilla" and "whale"; likewise,

Godzilla was a fascinating hybrid of monster and superhero. In addition to his power to crush miniature cities, Godzilla had a devastating "atomic heat beam" that issued from his mouth. As the films continued, his powers grew.

Part of the fun of these *kaiju* ("strange beast") films came from a new approach to creature animation. Instead of stop-motion miniature figures blown up optically and cut together with live actors, the new monsters were enacted by sweating, creature-wearing performers. The first man inside the Godzilla suit, Haruo Nakajima, was a black belt in karate, and his athleticism informed the role. Nonetheless, Godzilla's emotional range was extremely limited. He could help mankind, or petulantly turn against humanity; he was highly susceptible to alien mind control as well. You never really knew where you stood with him.

Audiences loved Godzilla, and demand spawned a battling menagerie of rubber-suited creatures. Toho produced twenty-eight of these monster movies in just twenty-one years. It wasn't long before the King of the Monsters morphed into a hero in these films, and the horror deteriorated into bouts of stagy combat not unlike those in the Mexican *luchador* films of the time. By Godzilla's fifth appearance, he had begun the slow transition from mindless force of destruction to rogue champion of those in distress, and eventually to the status of national symbol and friendly mascot.

Godzilla developed a roster of enemies and allies. There was the caterpillar/moth Mothra, who was worshipped by a South Seas tribe and enjoyed the company of two tiny, singing fairies; King Ghidorah, the evil three-headed monster; the Pteranodon Rodan; Gigan, with hook arms and buzzsaw torso; Baragon; Megalon;

Godzilla stomps through a city and eats a commuter train in a scene from *Godzilla, King of the Monsters!* (1956).

The titular monster in *Mothra* (1961).

Mechagodzilla; and on and on. The list of reboots continues, but to this date, no reboot of the Godzilla franchise has proved as popular as the original version of the King of the Monsters.

Studios such as Toho (also the home studio of Akira Kurosawa—*Godzilla* opened the same year as *Seven Samurai*), Tsuburaya (home of superhero Ultraman), P Productions, and Toei created highly successful film and TV franchises based on *kaiju* and *kaijin*.

Designated American stars were grafted onto Japanese monster movies. Raymond Burr was edited into *Godzilla* for its 1956 American release, Nick Adams was used as a lead player in *Frankenstein Conquers the World* and *Invasion of Astro-Monster* (both 1965), and Russ Tamblyn played a heroic doctor in *The War of the Gargantuas* (1966).

The talent of Toho's special-effects wizard Eiji Tsuburaya allowed the studio to branch into other non-rubber-monster sci-fi/horror outings, the so-called *henshin ningen* films, beginning with *The Invisible Man*, aka *The Invisible Avenger*, in 1954, continuing with the A-bomb transformations of *The H-Man* in 1958, *The Human Vapor* in 1960, and Honda's *Matango*, aka *Attack of the Mushroom People*, in 1963.

Mushroom People is artful and accomplished, a fitting culmination of the cycle; dark, despairing, claustrophobic, it manifests fears about mutation, assimilation, and addiction as it plays out in a foggy, dank landscape encrusted with pale, slimy, fleshy flora, and, eventually, fauna.

In *Mushroom People*, a cross section of upper-middle-class types is stranded on an uncharted island by a storm. They find themselves in a mycological heaven—vast forests of spongy, colorless growths are the island's only life forms, and food source. Soon, the castaways turn on each other. As supplies dwindle, more and more of them succumb to the new and highly addictive diet.

Gradually, the survivors turn into the fungal folk of the title, becoming tranquil and blissed out, like the *Odyssey*'s legendary lotus-eaters. Eating the 'shrooms for the first time gives one character erotic hallucinations (a cheesy montage of Dutch angles and contortionist showgirls). Shot in deep mist with far better production values than the wacky story deserves, and acted with conviction, it's a movie that

Frankenstein Conquers The World (1965) poster.

thinks hard about the seductions and costs of conformity.

The master of the *kaidan* subgenre was Nobuo Nakagawa, who created beautifully filmed, well-acted, and crisply edited versions of the familiar tales. The Yotsuya Kaidan is Japan's most popular vengeful-ghost story, and has been adapted for film more than thirty times. Nakagawa's 1959 version, *The Ghost of Yotsuya*, is the definitive take on the story. (He was aided immensely by his writing partner Yoshihiro Ishikawa, who scripted many of these films and directed a fair entry himself, *The Ghost Cat of Otama Pond*, in 1960.) In it, a ne'er-do-well murders his wife in order to marry a rich woman; her ghost destroys all those around him, then swoops in for the kill. The beautifully balanced widescreen compositions belie the blood-freezing material.

When Nakagawa broke away from the conventions of the horror genre, he did so with a vengeance. 1960's *Jigoku*, his final horror film, is as far away from his stylish period *kaidan* stories as you can get. He set this film in the present day, and its protagonist, Shiro, is a theology student with a dark and bitter double, his frenemy Tamura.

Shiro's weakness of character leads to his culpability in the death of many. His visit to a retirement community run by his parents reveals a society in miniature riddled with corruption, venality, sin, and murderous intent. All the inhabitants die and are sent to one of the most graphic and disturbing hells ever depicted. It's a bleak, bloody place of endless torture where every soul is ground down to its most tormented state.

Whenever he can, Nakagawa suspends his scenes in pools of in-studio blackness. Against this he pins his performers in blazing spotlights. The effect is isolative, disorienting, and alienating. The last time we see Shiro, he is frozen in mid-struggle on the Wheel of Karma, an image that is the epitome of despair. There's but a glimpse of redemption in the final seconds of *Jigoku*, but it's fleeting and not very convincing.

A more traditional approach produced one of

the most beautiful color horror films ever made, Masaki Kobayashi's *Kwaidan* (1964), a four-story anthology developed from Lafcadio Hearn tales. The film is three engaging hours of majestic camerawork and sumptuous art direction.

The year 1964 saw yet another approach by Kaneto Shindo, who produced the savage, lo-fi, black-and-white demon/ghost drama, *Onibaba*. Set in a dog-eat-dog universe, two women murder traveling samurai and sell their weapons and armor for food. A man returns and begins an affair with the younger woman, causing the older one (a great Nobuko Otowa) to concoct a demonic vengeance. The harsh lighting and bitter struggles of the central characters are horrifying enough, then an otherworldly element pushes the film over the edge—an approach that Shindo would repeat in his similar 1968 *Kuroneko*.

The most idiosyncratic attempt at original Japanese horror came from the Shochiku Studio, which released four horror films in the space of two years. *The X from Outer Space* (1967) is the ultimate bad rubber-monster movie, and the winningly titled *Genocide* (1968) is another early entry in the eco-horror subgenre, concerning a global insect onslaught. *The Living Skeleton* (1968) is a pallid imitation of the Euro-horror of the time, but it has a weird poetry, and pop score, of its own. (Michio Yamamoto's "Bloodthirsty" trilogy—*The Vampire Doll*, 1970; *Lake of Dracula*, 1971; and *Evil of Dracula*, 1974, awash with Christian imagery—represented another attempt to make Japanese horror in the European style.)

And Hajime Sato's 1968 *Goke, Body Snatcher from Hell*, is the most unique Shochiku offering of all. It's a bizarre, vibrant, demented concoction of vampires, alien beings, social commentary, and life forms oozing in and out of people's split foreheads. It's closer in spirit to the transgressive perversity of contemporary Kinji Fukasaku (*Black Lizard*, *The Green Slime*) and the even more troubling Yasuzo Masamura and Teruo Ishii, who led the charge toward explicitly sadomasochistic, deviant, nihilistic fare in films such as *Blind Beast* and *Horrors of Malformed Men* (1969), both early entries in the Rampo-inspired *ero guro* films. (*Ero guro* is a style that emphasizes the erotic wedded to the grotesque.)

In *Goke*, we get a hijacking, a mad bomber, and a jetliner crash—all before the opening credits. As in *Matango*, *Goke* strands a cross-section of society together and watches it all come apart. The trigger for the dog-eat-dog tactics of the dwindling party of survivors is (of course) an alien invasion. Soon, Day-Glo fluids are slurping themselves into human's heads, turning their hosts into vampires that attack with tedious tenacity. It's an exuberant and crazy mishmash of frights that exemplifies the exuberant spirit of the short-lived studio.

The horror cinema of Japan is far more pessimistic than many, chained to absolute despair about mankind's future, and firmly suspicious of society. As the 1970s played out, it subsided into exploitation fare. It would take twenty years for Japanese horror to leap to the forefront again.

Korea's early horror output was small and timid. The very first Korean horror film, Kim Ki-young's *The Housemaid* (1960), is a classic au-pair-destroys-family film, but a contrived happy ending mars

it and many other early Korean fright films. It almost seems in bad taste to intend anyone serious harm in the Korean films of the period.

China was also late to the game. Its first horror film, Ma-Xu Weibang 1937's *Song at Midnight*, is a *Phantom of the Opera* adaptation. Weibang followed with the fright flicks *Walking Corpse in an Old House* and *The Lonely Soul* in 1938.

The turmoil of World War II and the revolution meant that most of the filmmaking industry moved to the freer and more stable capitalist confines of Hong Kong, China. A huge amount of film issued from there after World War II, but little of it was horror. The only glimmer of horror in China was a strong vein of *jiangshi* ("hopping vampires"—i.e., reanimated corpses) movies, based on folk tales. Fused with comedy and action genres, these films were destined to become big hits in the 1980s.

In terms of international impact, Asian horror was dormant for decades. It wasn't until the late 1990s that horror would boom again in Japan when the country mapped out its own highly imitated "J-horror."

Scene from *The Green Slime* (1968).

15

POLANSKI, COFFIN JOÉ, AND OTHERS

ROMAN POLA

avec

CATHERINE DEN

YVONNE FURN

IAN HE

JOHN FR

The most influential European horror director of the period was someone never classified as one. However, five of the eight films Roman Polanski made between 1965 and 1976 were horror-themed, starting with his so-called "apartment trilogy," *Repulsion* (1965), *Rosemary's Baby* (1968), and *The Tenant* (1976); as well as his malevolent, stomach-churning adaptation of *Macbeth* (1971) and his horror comedy *The Fearless Vampire Killers; or: Pardon Me, But Your Teeth Are in My Neck* (1967).

Polanski is a polarizing figure. His tragic childhood was spent evading extermination in the Holocaust. The brutal murder of his wife and unborn child by the Manson Family in 1969, and his conviction and continuing avoidance of punishment for child sexual abuse, both informs his work and obscures it.

The #MeToo movement has finally, and justly, exposed various creative achievers as reprehensible individuals. Should we throw out consideration of Polanski's work because he's a criminal? I say no. Though his work doesn't excuse his criminal behavior, his films are part of the history of horror. However, we must factor that information into our analysis. Polanski, a victim of horror, is evidently a perpetrator as well.

Polanski's horror is the kind that takes place in everyday life, subtle terrors that no one besides the victim seems to notice. It's an embodiment of the theory of the twentieth century's "banality of evil," the passive willingness of people to assist in perpetrating or ignoring atrocities against others, proposed by historian and philosopher Hannah Arendt (1906–1975) in response to the Holocaust. Arendt's searing analyses such as *The Origins of Totalitarianism* and *Eichmann in Jerusalem* are sobering dissections of the social mechanics that enabled this modern tragedy. They are essential reading for those who would temper their enthusiasm for pretend horror with a mature understanding of reality's real-life terrors.

In a perfect world, there would be no horrors at all, would there? So—are we complicit? Isn't it our demand for new shocks that drives these entertainments of evil? As Michael Powell showed us in the staggering *Peeping Tom*, we must negotiate our relation to the transgressive. The market was, is, and ever shall be value-neutral. It will give you what you want. That's why cultural output is a mirror of its time.

Polanski takes horror seriously, and makes it reveal much more about human nature than any other director of the period. Whatever else he is, he is exquisitely high-strung, full of sympathy for his cursed, tragic protagonists. In contrast to the increasingly graphic and sloppy horror filmmaking of the period, Polanski keeps a tight grip on the story and production values. And he is so dark, soaked in sadness, relentless. There is no escape. There are no reliable narrators in Polanski; is it the protagonist that's crazy, or everyone else? Or is it the viewer?

Polanski's horror-trilogy protagonists are alienated, uncertain moderns who rapidly become disconnected from reality. The beautiful Catherine Deneuve in *Repulsion* is repressed and homicidal, but she keeps it all wrapped in a mousiness that is belied by her sexual nightmares. She becomes a killing machine because she can't function as a sexual object.

OPPOSITE:
Repulsion (1965) poster.

Catherine Deneuve behind the scenes on *Repulsion* (1965).

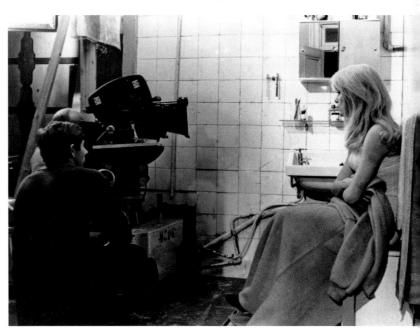

John Cassavetes (left) and Mia Farrow in *Rosemary's Baby* (1968).

In *Rosemary's Baby*, the mother of the title is an unassertive Mia Farrow. She is one half of an aspiring young couple who find a great apartment in Manhattan—the only catch is, unbeknownst to her the coven that lives there needs her to bear Satan's baby. The movie's clear understanding of the fears of and mistakes made by expectant parents lets it leverage a level of believability without which it would have fallen flat. All manner of deep and primitive fears attend the states of pregnancy and childbirth, something the film plays on. The fact, too, that Rosemary slips into a kind of psychic darkness in broad daylight is especially harrowing.

In *Rosemary*, as in Mark Robson's 1943 *The Seventh Victim*, Satan worshippers are really a mundane bunch, convincingly dull. Who would ever suspect this daffy bunch of bringing the Antichrist to Earth? Evil in the guise of cute old

Rosemary's Baby (1968) poster.

people. Polanski is an expert at creating and maintaining unease, as a seemingly placid and innocent existence is gradually revealed to be sitting in the mouth of Hell.

In *The Tenant*, the director himself plays a man either slipping into madness or finally seeing the true, Kafkaesque nature of reality. He's an apartment-dweller who begins to take on the attributes of the previous, female, tenant—who committed suicide. By film's end, he has replicated his predecessor to a T, dressing in drag and throwing himself out the window.

The Fearless Vampire Killers captures Polanski at his brightest, and the film is a loving, color-saturated spoof. The director himself plays Alfred, the assistant to the resolute but bumbling Van Helsing-wannabe Professor Abronsius (played by the comic master Jack MacGowran). And he sneaks in the best vampire joke ever. A victim thrusts a crucifix at one monster—but the bloodsucker is (was?) Jewish. "Hev you got de wronk vempeyer!" he chuckles, advancing heedless.

In the Soviet Union, horror film was simply not permitted to be made. The state had no use for it. Russia's sole significant horror entry from the period, greenlit because of its status as the adaptation of a classic, is the outstanding *Viy* (1967) codirected by Konstantin Yershov and

Georgi Kropachyov. It's a vivid, fanciful, and bold story, taken from Gogol, about a student priest who battles a witch over the course of three harrowing nights.

Soviet Bloc countries came closest to horror film in satires; Czech animator Jiří Trnka, the "Walt Disney of Eastern Europe," made several short- and long-form masterpieces. His *The Cybernetic Grandma* (1962) and *The Hand* (1965) contain subtle horrors and serve as allegories about dehumanization and the loss of individualism.

Czech director Juraj Herz's disorienting live-action *The Cremator* (1969) pushes bureaucratic logic and brotherly feeling to its absurd conclusion, as its protagonist decides that his mission is to free the vexed souls of the living by killing them; Jaromil Jires's *Valerie and Her Week of Wonders* (1970) is a surreal meditation on female sexuality as much as it is a folk tale about witchy things; Karel Kachnya's *The Ear* (1970), about an ambitious couple who may be under government surveillance, is a mix of confessional drama and paranoid fright flick.

Czech animator Jan Svankmajer picked up where Trnka left off, manufacturing melancholy

and evocative stop-motion animation that incorporated texts from Poe and legends. He created harsh, dysfunctional dreamscapes in rusting half-light; film such as *The Pendulum, the Pit and Hope* (1983), *Little Otik* (2000), and *Lunacy* (2005).

Belgium's Harry Kumel produced a pair of weirdly scary films: the mysterious puzzle *Malpertuis* and the more successful *Daughters of Darkness* (both 1971), both production-designed to within an inch of their existences. In the latter, the legendary, bloodthirsty Countess Bathory (a fine performance from Delphine Seyrig) befriends a young couple, with intentions both sexual and murderous. It's heady, stylish, and erotic.

Germany was averse to horror after World War II, but became fond of its *krimi* films. These were mystery stories set in England, most based on the works of writer Edgar Wallace (1875–1932). These atmospheric whodunits featured future horror standout Klaus Kinski in various suspicious roles. The best of these is Alfred Vohrer's 1962 *The Inn on the River*.

The Tenant (1976) poster.

Roman Polanski in *The Fearless Vampire Killers* (1967).

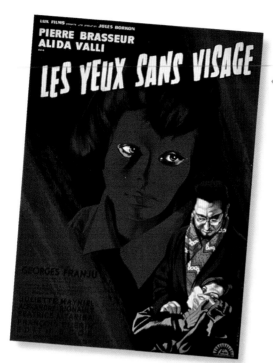

Eyes Without a Face (1960) poster.

German horror film of the period was derivative, at once explicit and oddly pedestrian. *Mark of the Devil* (1970), "rated V for violence," featured Herbert Lom in a typical late-career role of menace, along with scar-faced villain Reggie Nalder, and spooky Eurovillain Udo Kier—the last as the hero, for once. Its sequel proudly announced that it was banned in nineteen countries.

In France, too, horror was moribund. The single exception was *Eyes Without a Face* (1960). The Mad Doctor movie steps forward into more graphic territory here, but Georges Franju's soulful direction gives heft and mythic weight to the story of a father who kills beautiful women to transplant their features onto those of his scarred daughter. A remarkable number of later horror films borrowed from this source.

The single French filmmaker to take horror to heart was Jean Rollin, another writer/director/producer in the mold of Spain's Jesus Franco, with the same obsessions of extreme violence and explicit sex. A typical product is his *Caged Virgins* (1971), in which two attractive young girls find a castle, make love all over it, get bitten by bats, and fight vampires—not necessarily in that order.

In South America, Coffin Joe held sway. José Mojica Marins was a young, short, pug-nosed, balding Brazilian horror enthusiast who created one of the strangest demonic figures in film.

Jose Mojica Marins during the 2001 Sundance Film Festival.

His Coffin Joe (in Portuguese, Zé do Caixão) is a villain sporting a top hat, cape, and long curly fingernails, sometimes puffing away on a pipe. A mocker of religion, he seeks a "perfect woman" to bear his unholy man-child, and beginning in 1964 with *At Midnight I'll Take Your Soul*, this one-man band created a no-budget series of popular films. (When not busy with horror, his production company created exploitation films, porn, and Westerns.)

Was Coffin Joe scary? No. But as a kind of minor-league freethinker/killer—a nerdy, confident Raskolnikov—he inspires affection. The only other significant maker of horror films on the continent at the time was Argentinian Emilio Vieyra, another follower of the template of sex and gore in such fare as *Feast of Flesh* (1967) and *The Curious Dr. Hummp* (1969).

Another interesting source of cheap horror was the Philippines, home of non-union film workers and lax safety regulations. Beginning with *Terror Is a Man* in 1959, directors such as Gerardo de Leon and Eddie Romero churned

out many formulaic fright shows. These primitive shoots became a training ground for aspiring actors—Blaxploitation queen Pam Grier has an early role in Romero's 1972 *The Twilight People* (a Dr. Moreau rip-off) as Ayesha, the Panther Woman.

Horror was primarily low-end fare around the world, but Hitchcock's influence legitimized the genre for art-film directors as well. Sweden's Ingmar Bergman came close to horror in his evocative *Hour of the Wolf* (1968), about an artist who fractures his relationship to reality and succumbs to his own demons. And, lest we forget, his brutal drama *The Virgin Spring* had a strong influence on Wes Craven's *The Last House on the Left*. European directors Federico Fellini, Roger Vadim, and Louis Malle created a three-part *Spirits of the Dead* horror anthology as well; only Fellini's "Toby Dammit" sequence holds up well today. In it, a burnt-out actor (Terence Stamp) pursues visions of death.

By the mid-1970s, restraint was gone. The benchmark of offensiveness is a movie so disturbing it's rarely capable of being screened, Pier Paolo Pasolini's *Saló, or, the 120 Days of Sodom* (1975), which combines the sadomasochism of the Marquis de Sade with a disquisition on fascism. It's an unflinching look at corruption and the abuse of power, played out in graphic scenes of torture and sexual abuse, a nightmare on film that one is well-advised not to watch without warning.

The idea for the film begins with de Sade's perverted 1785 novel *The 120 Days of Sodom*, but transferred its story to fascist Italy in 1944. De Sade (from whom we derive the words "sadist" and "sadism") was an unrepentant sensualist who wrote feverishly of mingling sexual feeling with violence, torture, cruelty, and blasphemy. In Pasolini's *Saló*, four wealthy authority figures—the Duke, the Bishop, the Judge, and the President—with absolute power and no limitations, kidnap nine young men and nine young women and subject them to graphic debasement, sexual assault, and torture.

It's still one of the most widely banned films of all time. It equates fascism with perversion and sadism, and then puts that theory through its paces with nauseating literalness. It's a deeply troubling examination of the negative potentialities of humankind. Like Ken Russell's *The Devils*, it's an obscene indictment of the status quo.

The rebellious and prolific Pasolini had gone from neorealism to adaptations of classic literature such as *The Decameron* (1971), *The Canterbury Tales* (1972), and *The Thousand and One Nights* (1974) to this final shocking turn (Pasolini was murdered three weeks before the film was released, presumably because of his homosexuality, his leftist activism, or both).

The onscreen perversions and torments are realistically simulated. The horror in *Saló* is that there is no redemption or deliverance. The terror continues until all the victims are slain. The absolute despair, the resolute nihilism of the story paint humanity as, perpetually and unredeemingly, morally inches away from indulging in the creation of a hell on earth.

Saló and other transgressive films of the period—*The Last House on the Left, The Texas Chain Saw Massacre, The Exorcist*, and *The Devils*—seemingly pushed the genre as far as it could go. Where to next? From North America, the answer came in the form of four vital, intelligent, and audacious horror filmmakers.

16

CLARK, CRAVEN, CARPENTER, AND CRONENBERG

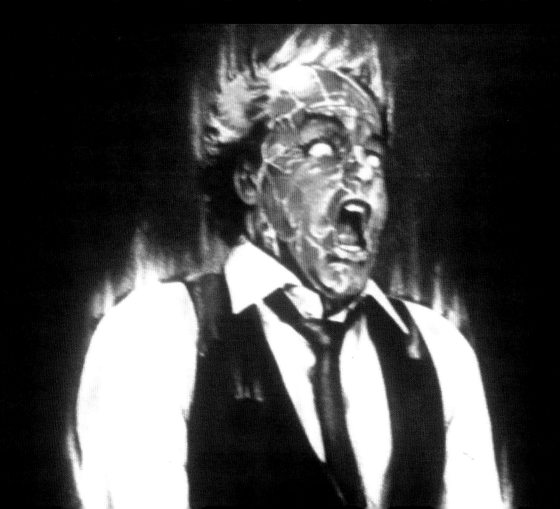

The horror films of the 1960s and 1970s churned up a lot of material from the collective unconscious, only some of it compelling. Many of the boundaries that were being broken were those of taste. A new batch of exceptional horror filmmakers came along at just the right time. They were led by George A. Romero (*Night of the Living Dead*, 1968), Wes Craven (*The Last House on the Left*, 1972), Bob Clark (*Children Shouldn't Play with Dead Things*, 1972), and Tobe Hooper (*The Texas Chain Saw Massacre*, 1974), and were soon joined by heavyweight genre artists John Carpenter and David Cronenberg. These writers and directors were ready to inject horror with fresh life.

Many factors fed into the success of horror film during a phase that sputtered to life in the 1970s and exploded in the 1980s. The general psychic turmoil caused by the graphic intrusion of the horrors of Vietnam, and domestic crime and upheaval, via television, lowered the resistance of the American audience to graphic shock. By the ignominious end of the Nixon administration, the American dream had begun to sour and curl at the edges, and it was hard not to be caught up in a feeling of hopelessness and ennui.

On a more practical level, there was a new crop of teenagers to frighten. The 1970s saw the coming of age of the last of the Baby Boomers—the final generation of American middle-class teens to experience material well-being and economic abundance. Additionally, advances in movie technology in terms of makeup, prosthetics, and effects (pre-computer-generated imagery, or CGI) made it possible to stage more ambitious and convincing scenes of horror.

Finally, the time was right—to question everything. Whatever cultural, political, or psychosocial reasons are given for their popularity, horror films from this period represent a powerful and influential Silver Age of American horror.

The short-lived but transformative American New Wave in film ended with a return to formulaic blockbusters such as *Star Wars* (1977) and *Raiders of the Lost Ark* (1981). In between, it

triggered a decade of innovative and challenging (and sometimes self-indulgent) fare, movies such as *Easy Rider* (1969), *The Godfather* (1972), and *Nashville* (1975). Young filmmakers were given money to make movies that were independent and idiosyncratic. The old Hollywood formulas weren't working—and studios were willing to take chances.

The French auteur theory, promoting the concept of director as the auteur or primary creative artist of a film, spread and gained acceptance, even in America. Film was finally accepted as an art form, and schools of film studies, both theoretical and practical, began to emerge in universities. You could now learn filmmaking in an academic environment instead of on a studio lot.

The improved academic atmosphere meant also that film was being taken seriously (sometimes way too seriously) as an art form. Genre film, looked down upon for decades as filler for light-minded individuals—in contrast with the large-scale, dramatic, and "serious" offerings Hollywood prided itself on and crafted for Oscar season—started to be valued in and of itself, and mined for meaning. Ambitious

Richard Towers in *The Last House on the Left* (1972).

OPPOSITE: *Scanners* (1981) poster.

young filmmakers didn't see anything wrong with diving into genre filmmaking. They could manipulate those genre rules to their own subversive ends. The end of the studio system finished many careers, but it also made entering the film industry, in some ways, easier. And horror was still one of the cheapest genres of film to produce.

Horror filmmaking demanded a demonstrable competence, in contrast with the sometimes self-indulgent dramas of many New Wave Hollywood mavericks. To create a sense of suspense, and then terrify, is a very quantifiable, practical concern. But in a time when gratuitous gore and gross-outs ruled the roost, how could a horror director win back a mainstream audience?

The answer was to return to basics. This included an ambition to mine the mythic, solid plotting, memorable characters, and technical quality—and, if possible, the inclusion of a boatload of provocative and disturbing ideas. In the hands of a few key directors, American horror film would rapidly become more interesting and profound.

This was a generation of filmmakers who had a common cultural diet. They grew up during the sci-fi/horror age of the 1950s, catching a blast of

that on the big screen (remakes of those films crop up throughout the Silver Age) as well as absorbing the older, classic Hollywood horror films through the widespread distribution of the *Shock Theater* syndication package and sci-fi programs such as *The Twilight Zone* on television. The horror canon inhabited and enlivened their extremely aware, intelligent, and playful imaginations.

Wes Craven's *The Last House on the Left* was a pioneer of the new, savage style. Craven insisted on sharing the victims' perspectives, the perpetrators' perspectives, and the revengers' perspectives, in gruesome, relentless color. The flip side of America's repressed, God-fearing Puritan heritage is an equally strong, wild, dark impulse to transgress against everything, punish the guilty, and wreak general havoc. *Last House* struck a nerve because it let the viewers participate vicariously both in the crime and in its vengeance.

In response to shock concerning the graphic rape and murder in the film, John Wooley quotes Craven as saying, "That was the only way to get that message about the demeaning nature of violence across. So I deliberately dragged some of the most frightening skeletons I could find out of my closet. And, second, because I didn't think there was any way anybody I knew would ever see it."[1] *Last House* cost $87,000 to make, and it grossed $3 million. The success of it and Tobe Hooper's *The Texas Chain Saw Massacre* opened the floodgates.

Larry Cohen was a producer and screenwriter who got his start in TV (he created the 1960s-era sci-fi series *The Invaders*). He soon found success as an independent filmmaker with 1974's *It's Alive*, about a corporate-negligence-created monster baby and his conflicted parents, shot in a serious and gritty New York style. His quirky, thought-provoking, and fun horror-filled takes on religion (*God Told Me To*, 1976), New Yorkers' love/hate of their city (*Q, the Winged Serpent*, 1982), and consumerism (*The Stuff*, 1985) showed that you could be conceptually outrageous, fiscally prudent, and still enthrall the viewer. *The*

Director and screenwriter Tobe Hooper.

In the film, a sadistic community-theater director takes his cast out to an island cemetery for the criminally insane and jokingly attempts to revive the corpses. He succeeds, and panic ensues. Co-writer and lead actor Alan Ormsby's pants should have won Best Supporting Oscar that year.

Clark's *Deathdream* takes the zombie/vampire paradigm and applies it to the horrors of war. Andy is reported dead in Vietnam, but arrives home to his family. He is wan and distant, and people start dying . . .

The idea that dead soldiers return in one destructive way or another is a complex and sophisticated idea to pull off. Clark knew the film could take it, and the conceit works brilliantly, not least due to the performance of the great John Marley as Andy's distraught father.

Clark's outstanding horror achievement, the innovative and influential *Black Christmas* (also 1974), reads like a string of clichés today—but they all started with this film. This template for the slasher film involves sorority sisters who are bumped off by a psychotic killer hiding in their attic.

Stuff, in particular, hits the nail on the head with a darkly comic fable about consumer culture—a delicious, calorie-free substance oozes out of the ground, addicting those who taste it and turning them into zombies. Cohen would remain a stubborn independent throughout his career.

Bob Clark was an American transplant to Canada, who made some of the worst movies ever produced (*Rhinestone*, 1984; *Baby Geniuses*, 1999); some of the most profitable (he created the *Porky's* teen sex comedy franchise, and executive-produced the source for the unlikely US TV hit *The Dukes of Hazzard*, 1979–1985); and perceptive work in many different genres (*Murder by Decree*, 1979*; A Christmas Story*, 1983), including horror.

Clark was an exuberant pulp artist who never saw a script he didn't like. A regional filmmaker, he originally worked out of Florida, making his first two horror films, *Children Shouldn't Play with Dead Things* and *Dead of Night*, aka *Deathdream* (1974), there back-to-back. *Dead Things* is innovative in that it combines grisly gore and comedy, setting the tone for future horror-comedy directors such as Sam Raimi, Peter Jackson, Joe Dante, Barry Sonnenfeld, and Bob Zemeckis.

Clark never shows us the killer. We hear his demented voice over the phone; as in Powell's *Peeping Tom*, we are forced to share the maniac's point of view. Everyone's a suspect; anyone can die. It's the first significant "the call is coming from inside the house" film, and one of the first holiday-themed horror movies as well. This also triggered Canada's first big cultural export—a glut of such horror movies, later dubbed "Canuxploitation."

Roy Moore's script is a brilliant blueprint, combining graphic moments of shock with the clues and suspects of a whodunit; a callback to the approach of the "old dark house" horror comedies of the 1920s and '30s. Clark's strong shot selection and brisk pacing inform *Christmas*; he keeps the audience guessing and gleefully toys with expectations. It's Clark who first clearly ties together humor and horror in the modern era. All of his horror films are populated with believable, appealing, funny characters. . . who just happen to get brutally murdered. It's meta—there simply isn't anyone in the film intelligent or perceptive enough to survive.

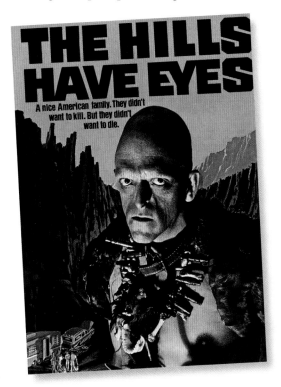

The Hills Have Eyes (1977) poster.

Those who live by the film cliché die by the film cliché. Suddenly it was OK to have a laugh at a horror movie, to be in on the joke, and to be a connoisseur of the genre's ins and outs.

The subgenre of Christmas-themed horror was launched earlier in the TV movie *Home for the Holidays* (1972), the "And All Through the House" segment of the British horror anthology *Tales from the Crypt* from the same year, and *Silent Night, Bloody Night* (1972). The Xmas-ploitation microgenre grew to include such immortal titles as *Christmas Evil* (1980), *Santa's Slay* (2005), and *Better Watch Out* (2016). Horror seems a natural corrective to the overly cheery vibe of Yuletide. In fact, the successful Christmas release of *The Exorcist* in 1973 led to the traditional release of a horror title or two on Christmas Day for filmgoers looking for something different than the usual family-friendly or Oscar-contending films dominating the cinemas at the end of the year.

In 1977, Wes Craven proved his initial success was not a fluke with his second horror film, *The Hills Have Eyes*. His camerawork is an order of magnitude better, and the performances in the film are uniformly good. It's a gruesome exploitation film, to be sure, but it's a witty, thought-provoking, and pointedly satirical one.

The film tells the story of two dysfunctional nuclear families, pitted against each other in the bombing-range wasteland of Nevada. In what could be called the Worst Vacation Ever, the Carter extended family gets stranded out in the desert and is hunted down and attacked by a clan of feral cannibals, led by Papa Jupiter. As is their wont.

The structure and behavior of Papa's clan is as appropriate to its desolate environment as the crass, blasé, weak, and prosperous Carters is to theirs—a fragile suburban environment that, in the form of their comfy trailer, they tow around with them. It, like their assumptions, is easily penetrated.

While the murders, rapes, and tortures multiply, a savage battle of values takes place, and it seems Papa Jupiter's are ascendant. He lectures the Carter patriarch's corpse as he and his wife and children eat him for dinner: "You come out here and stick your life in my face? Stick your fingers in my pie? That was a bad mistake. I thought you was smart and tough. You're stupid! You're nothing I'll see the wind blow your dried-up seeds away! I'll eat the heart of your stinkin' memory." The quasi-biblical language placed in the mouth of an insane killer seems to sanctify the anarchic impulse to kill, devour, destroy, and subjugate. In Craven's cinematic universe, that impulse is on the surface, and very powerful.

The Carters have to ratchet up their aggression and smack down their compassion in order to survive—a grim and subversive message to send in the middle of the complacent, "Have a Nice Day" 1970s. Horror had carried a subtext before, usually unconsciously. Craven and his contemporaries realized the power the horror genre had to provide a window for outright social commentary, satire, even philosophy. In David Cronenberg's hands, it would develop even further.

Craven would then craft the first of his two seminal horror-film series. In 1984, he came up with *A Nightmare on Elm Street*, using the

(from left to right) Nick Corri, Amanda Wyss, Johnny Depp, and Heather Langenkamp in *A Nightmare On Elm Street* (1984).

IF NANCY DOESN'T WAKE UP SCREAMING SHE WON'T WAKE UP AT ALL

WES CRAVEN'S
A Nightmare ON ELM STREET

A Nightmare on Elm Street (1984) poster.

novel premise of a vengeful killer who attacks his victims only in their dreams. This is Freddy Krueger, a child murderer who was burned to death by an angry mob of parents. He returns years later to continue his killing spree, manifesting during a victim's sleep. The teen protagonists are alone in their battle against the monster; the adults want to forget the past, and they are resolutely clueless when faced with danger, which only makes things worse.

The constant switching between dream and reality in the *Nightmare on Elm Street* movies made for a looser, more ambitious style that audiences responded to. The increasingly

Halloween (1978) poster.

humorous and darkly endearing nature of the blade-fingered, fire-scarred Freddy, as played by the irreplaceable Robert Englund, created a legion of fans. This triggered a long list of sequels, including a crossover featuring *Freddy vs. Jason* (2003)—both of whom were so well known by now that no further explanation of the title was necessary.

John Carpenter was another game-changer. He is a "regular guy" who can direct with energy, power, and efficiency, just like his Golden Age Hollywood heroes Howard Hawks and John Ford. Carpenter is a master movie craftsman. Like most of the heroes and antiheroes of his films, he's both genial and cynical, wielding a hip, dark, quintessentially American sensibility that pervades everything he does. He doesn't waste the viewer's time, and he has confidence in their intelligence. His *Halloween* screenplay with Debra Hill takes all those elements of urban legends, cautionary tales, and older "mad killer" films and ties them together, creating a new and very resonant myth. The last place in which you'd expect chaos and death to break out—the safe and wholesome typical American suburb— becomes the perfect setting for it. No place is safe.

Six-year-old Michael Myers kills his teenage sister after she has sex. Fifteen years later, he

escapes from the mental asylum and goes home, where he promptly and randomly starts killing all the teenagers in his old neighborhood, most of whom are having sex—all except for Laurie (Jamie Lee Curtis), the intelligent town virgin and film's most famous "Final Girl." Donald Pleasence gets a memorable supporting role as a harbinger of doom, the psychiatrist Dr. Loomis. Carpenter passed the franchise off to less talented hands.

Carpenter's not content with merely providing scares. He invests the Michael Myers character with supernatural, nonhuman qualities, such that even Dr. Loomis describes him as pure, soulless evil. *Halloween*'s open, unresolved ending would later become a signature of horror moviemakers seeking to squeeze out a sequel, but here it was still fresh—a chilling coda that destroys the payoff of resolution, keeping the audience

Jamie Lee Curtis in a scene from *Halloween* (1978).

Jamie Lee Curtis

Daughter of actor Tony Curtis and *Psycho* scream queen Janet Leigh, Jamie Lee Curtis got her start in movies with her role as Laurie Strode, the "final girl" in John Carpenter's original *Halloween* in 1978. She followed this film debut with other horror roles in *The Fog*, *Prom Night*, and *Terror Train*. She then appeared in *Halloween II* in 1981, but soon found mainstream stardom after appearing in *Trading Places*. She stayed away from the horror genre for some time, but later returned in her iconic role in *Halloween H2O: 20 Years Later* (1998), *Halloween: Resurrection* (2002), *Halloween* (2018), *Halloween Kills* (2021), and *Halloween Ends* (2022).

Jamie Lee Curtis arrives at the premiere of *Halloween* (2018) in Los Angeles.

looking over its collective shoulder long after the lights go up.

Carpenter's deep suspicions about society, its systems of belief, and the flimsy nature of consensual reality remain at the fore, but he never forgets to be entertaining. He doesn't mind being a genre director, which seems to free him to make horror films with unequaled gusto. His 1980 *The Fog* is a jolly, bloody ghost story. Later, *They Live* (1988) served as Carpenter's ultimate paranoid sci-fi/horror fantasy. In it, aliens have co-opted the planet with the aid of craven human collaborators, and the people of the world are hypnotized into obeying, conforming, reproducing, and consuming like a herd of cattle. Carpenter's disgust at commercialism and Reaganomics could not be clearer.

Carpenter brilliantly mines metaphors of colonialism and capitalism. Only drifter Nada (wrestling star "Rowdy" Roddy Piper), who finds sunglasses that reveal the truth to the wearer, can save the world from the outer-space parasites. And it features cinema history's longest fistfight to date, between Piper and Keith David.

With his self-titled "apocalypse trilogy" of *The Thing* (1982), *Prince of Darkness* (1987), and *In the Mouth of Madness* (1994), Carpenter moves beyond satire and social commentary, creating superlative horror films that call into question the norms of reality itself. Orrin Grey's superb analyses of the three films identifies Carpenter's overarching concerns in them with the "cosmic horror" of Lovecraft, in which human life, measured against the scope of the universe, is meaningless and insignificant.[2] In fact, the three

Personal Best

John Carpenter

Halloween (1978)

The Thing (1982)

Prince of Darkness (1987)

They Live (1988)

In the Mouth of Madness (1994)

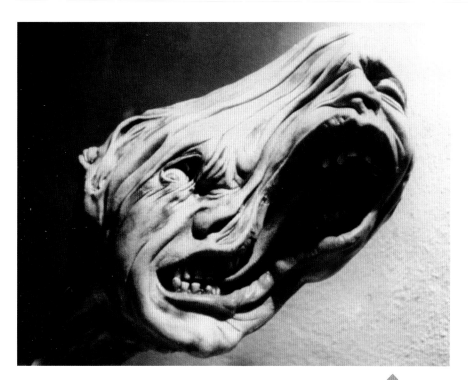

Creature design from *The Thing* (1982).

collapses on the subatomic level into ghosts and shadows."

Finally, in *In the Mouth of Madness*, those who read a popular horror novelist's new book help to manifest a worldwide Lovecraftian invasion of monsters and the extinction of mankind, and are driven mad in the bargain. An insurance investigator played by Sam Neill seeks the elusive author, driving into the landscape of the writer's dark imagination and watching the everyday world fly to pieces.

Everything in *Mouth* is a manifestation of the fictional author Sutter Cane's mind: everyone's fate is prewritten, and the universe becomes an inescapable nightmare that folds in on itself, repeating endlessly. In Carpenter's horror films, the permanent dominion of evil is only a flip of perception or an accident of fate away from manifestation in the world. Carpenter demonstrates how thin the membrane between sanity and chaos can be.

A Canadian director, Toronto's David Cronenberg, has shaped the most visionary horror career yet. In nine out of his first thirteen feature films, Cronenberg uses horror as an opportunity to create mind-bending meditations on identity, evolution, love, and humanity's place in the universe.

"My films are *sui generis*," Cronenberg says to Chris Rodley in his magisterial book-length set of interviews with the filmmaker, *Cronenberg on Cronenberg*.[3] Cronenberg, who was strongly influenced by the paranoid and surreal literary fantasies of twentieth-century avant-garde writers such as William S. Burroughs, Vladimir Nabokov, and Henry Miller, possesses a clear and complete vision, a novelistic density that can only be communicated through film, and that seems particularly congenial to horror.

Cronenberg's horror is rooted in the human body, which in his films is not only immensely

films refute in turn the idea of consensual reality, the value of the spiritual, and the worth of the individual.

The Thing is a remake of Howard Hawks's seminal 1951 *The Thing from Another World*, but it is vastly more graphic, suspenseful, dark, and paranoid. At an all-male research station in the Antarctic, a ruthless, murderous, advanced alien life form is found, one that can take any shape and is almost undetectable. It's a mystery in which the suspect changes constantly, with nauseatingly fatal consequences for the unwary. Kurt Russell, Carpenter's go-to leading man, is snarlingly efficient as antihero MacReady, who, as his name suggests, is prepared to exterminate his infected coworkers instantly. The film features an Ennio Morricone score, as well as outstanding pre-CGI special effects by Rob Bottin and Stan Winston. It's stomach-churningly graphic, and plotted as tautly as a piano string.

In *Prince of Darkness*, the forces of science and religion unite, at great cost, to defeat an "anti-God" who seeks to destroy the universe by entering it. "Say goodbye to classical reality," says a physicist in the film. "Because our logic vulnerable, but easily and casually torn, spindled, and mutilated. With unerring regularity, every year or two from 1975 to 1999, he put out a horror film, moving deeper into his obsessions and insights.

His list of subjects progresses from the sex-as-plague visions of *Shivers* (1975) and *Rabid* (1977) to the nightmarish portrayal of psychoanalytics in 1979's *The Brood*. In that film, an experimental "psychoplasmics" makes rage and distress manifest themselves physically, and a divorced woman uses it to create angry, feral hate-children who kill her enemies.

Here Cronenberg unites his disturbing view of human relationships with his initial mastery of his trademark graphic-surrealist style. Standout performances from Oliver Reed and Samantha Eggar ground this unlikely story. It also happens to be one of the great films about divorce, and it features the strong musical scoring of Howard Shore, who would go on to compose for nearly all of Cronenberg's films.

Cronenberg moved on to the renegade thought-wars of *Scanners* (1981), then the horrorshow entertainment vortex of *Videodrome* (1983). The director's examination of the links between entertainment, violence, conformity,

repression, and voyeurism rapidly takes flight into surreal fantasy as protagonist TV exec Max Renn (James Woods) finds out he is only a foot soldier in the struggle of two factions for control of consensual reality.

Renn is a bottom-feeder—a network hustler looking for forbidden thrills for his exploitation TV channel. He gets turned on to a toxic live torture and murder broadcast that he thinks will revolutionize the industry. His search for Videodrome reveals an embattled landscape in which a conspiracy seeks to infect, mutate, and mentally enslave the world through its addiction to voyeurism. Cronenberg asserts that we allow ourselves to be colonized, physically and mentally, by evil; we program ourselves to do its bidding. *Videodrome* is disturbing, transgressive, and remains ahead of its time. In the midst of the mundane, the most horrible nightmares writhe.

He circled back to sexual horror in *Dead Ringers* (1988). One of the few legitimately gripping horror films to be based on a true story, Cronenberg's tale of twin gynecologists, both played rivetingly by Jeremy Irons, who share addiction and women, disturbs deeply, declining into a miasma of double destruction.

Irons is a master Jekyll/Hyde. His precisely calculated performance as identical twins—the cynical and manipulative Elliot and the shy and

A head explodes in *Scanners* (1981).

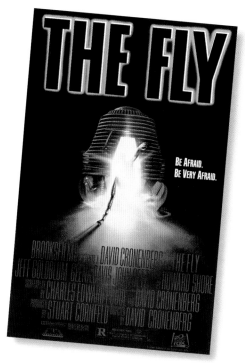

The Fly (1986) poster.

weak-minded Beverly—is award-worthy. The psychosexual complexities of the doppelganger are dissected in excruciating close-up.

Finally, the virtual digital wastelands of 1999's *eXistenZ* contribute to an eerily prescient adventure between alternative realities.

Among all these original works he made one of the finest Stephen King film adaptations (*The Dead Zone*, 1983), plus a profoundly superior 1986 remake of 1958's *The Fly*. At the center of the latter film is the tragic romance of the ambitious scientist (Jeff Goldblum) and a science journalist (Geena Davis). As in the original, the fusion of man and housefly takes place, but here the mutation is gradual, allowing Cronenberg to isolate and examine defining human traits. Some think his greatest achievement was adapting William S. Burroughs's surreal, transgressive, and "unadaptable" 1959 novel *Naked Lunch*, magnificently, for the screen in 1991.

Cronenberg is unimpressed with humanity's grand conceptions of itself, and its institutions in his universe seem contrived, malignant, false, and impotent. His seemingly dispassionate gaze puts mankind on the same level with all the other species, and sometimes below them. For Cronenberg, the political is manifested in the physical—through science, medicine, entertainment, and psychology. All infect the

Dawn of the Dead (1978) poster.

individual system and mutate it from within, leading to death and/or a new order of existence. In other words, evolution's a bitch.

His worldview, philosophy, tone, and optics are all powerfully individual, making these efforts much stronger than the genre fare of the time. He is talking about fate and death and the meaning of life, asking many more questions than he answers and dealing with uncomfortable truths with the frankness that horror provides. This makes Cronenberg the most auteurist of horror filmmakers, and the one whose work will stand on its own as a coherent body of work in the future. Though his last pure horror effort was *eXistenZ*, he has moved on to making more mainstream yet no less gripping and affecting films. (His son Brandon made his first film, a horror outing, *Antiviral*, in 2012.)

Meanwhile, Hooper, Craven, and Romero were turning out a steady stream of fright. After a stunning TV adaptation of Stephen King's *Salem's Lot* (1979), Hooper made the haunted-house specials-effects extravaganza *Poltergeist* (1982), which bears the heavy stylistic hand of producer Steven Spielberg. After his fun space-vampire

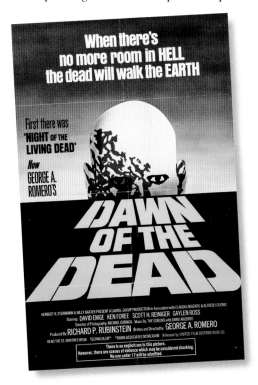

Scream (1996) poster.

romp *Lifeforce* in 1985, Hooper settled into a more mainstream, workaday mode.

George A. Romero stayed with the genre while also staying as independent as possible. His *Martin* (1976) is a downbeat, low-key examination of the life of a would-be vampire. By treating a vampire story in the style of psychological realism, Romero plays relentlessly with the expectations of all the characters, and those of the audience as well. *Dawn of the Dead* (1978) and other zombie-film sequels mine the vein of social satire. Romero's films may not look polished, but they have their own appealing, warm, lo-fi aesthetic, featuring surprisingly strong performances from casts of unknowns. *Dawn* tackles consumer culture; *Day of the Dead* (1985) attacks the military mindset.

One of the most significant contemporary American directors, David Lynch made his feature film debut in 1977 with *Eraserhead*, a deeply discomfiting surreal fantasy that is nothing if not a horror film. Lynch would also plow his own furrow with a series of films full of strangeness and transgression, steeped in his own sensibilities, but none after *Eraserhead* would bear the outright label of a horror film.

The cleverest and most enthusiastic horror director, however, continued to be Wes Craven. His relentless experimentation led to some duds, but it also produced top-notch work such as

the voodoo drama *The Serpent and the Rainbow* (1988) and the energetic and funny *The People Under the Stairs* (1991).

Craven's most playful fright fest, *Stairs*, takes the shape of a fable about a brave boy who dares to overcome evil. At the center is the ultimate haunted house, inhabited by a comically bizarre brother-sister married couple who keep their chastised, mutated offspring in the basement, where they've turned into feral cannibals. Of course.

Craven continued to innovate, creating the definitive postmodern horror film, *Scream* (1996), full of horror references, jokes, homages, and games played with genre rules. Both that film and *I Know What You Did Last Summer* (1997) were written by Kevin Williamson, an expert horror screenwriter who also wrote such horror titles as *Scream 2* (1997), *The Faculty* (1998), *Cursed* (2005), *Scream 4* (2011), as well as TV's *The Vampire Diaries* (2009–17).

In fact, *Nightmare on Elm Street*, *Scream*, *Halloween*, *Friday the 13th*, and many other now socially acceptable, multi-sequelized horror film franchises would rule the roost for years to come. Horror was leaving the drive-in and the grindhouse, and entering the multiplex.

17

MAINSTREAM HORROR OR: BRING THE KIDS!

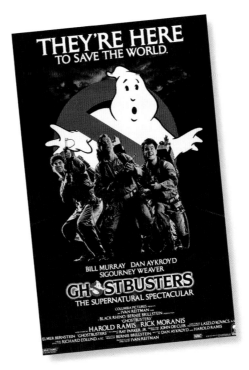

Ghostbusters
(1984) poster.

Steven Spielberg's shark-attack thriller *Jaws* premiered on June 20, 1975. June was not noted for big moviegoing crowds at the time, but people flocked to this film, and it became the first summer blockbuster. It also signaled an increased popular appetite for thrills on screen that would make the horror genre resurgent, and above all make it acceptable for mainstream viewing.

The plot of *Jaws* is pure horror template: a monster from beyond, or in this case beneath, attacks humanity and must be battled. When a giant man-eating shark terrorizes a summer vacation getaway, the local sheriff unites with a brainy oceanographer and a crusty, vengeful old salt to destroy it.

Spielberg, just like his contemporaries Carpenter, Hooper, and Craven, grew up on and loved sci-fi, horror, and other cheesy fun just as much as he did "great" cinema. Like them (and the rest of us), he read his copies of *Famous Monsters of Filmland* horror fan magazine (1958–1983) faithfully. Its wonderfully pulpy monthly contents were curated by Los Angeles horror guru, historian, editor, publisher, and collector Forrest J. Ackerman, aka the Ackermonster. Like us, Spielberg put together one, some, or all of the Aurora monster model kits (1961–1966), based on the classic Universal monsters.

Spielberg's blazingly clear, purely filmic way of thinking enlivened and expanded familiar material, as with his career-making 1971, Richard Matheson-penned TV-movie gem *Duel*, about an innocent traveler menaced by an unseen nemesis in a tanker truck.

Jaws, adapted from Peter Benchley's popular 1974 novel, is firmly in the line of the eco-horror subgenre. It came on the heels of the successful trend begun by other animals-gone-amok films of the time such as *Willard* (1971) and *Frogs* (1972), the latter featuring Ray Milland in his typical late-career role of grouchy old industrialist hoisted by his own petard. And though *Jaws* widens out into a classic adventure story (it resonates with echoes of Henrik Ibsen's 1882 play *An Enemy of the People* and Herman Melville's classic 1851 novel *Moby Dick*), it is, in both structure and tone, a horror film.

Spielberg's forward momentum in films is generated through the units of taut and springy suspense-and-payoff, stimuli-and-reward sequences that he sets up, a very horror-centric way of thinking. The result is that there are plenty of bravura sequences in his films—memorable, stand-alone episodes that parallel the direct-reflex responses and rewards of early video game scenarios. This influence would soon permeate the film industry.

Now films were crafted specifically to bring in summer audiences. The major players decided to haul horror films out of the genre wilderness and give them the attention and support of big-budget "A" films.

Star Wars and *Raiders of the Lost Ark* are, essentially, genre films blown up to A-budget proportions. The same logic applied itself to horror. After the experiments, personal statements, and intense questionings of other 1970s films, the market returned to a reliance on familiarity and formula. It wanted spectacle, it wanted unreflecting action, usually leavened with comedy, as with the phenomenally successful horror-comedy *Ghostbusters* in 1984 (directed by Ivan Reitman, who had earlier made the pioneering Canuxploitation film, *Cannibal Girls*, in 1973).

OPPOSITE:
Jaws (1975) poster.

Richard Matheson

Richard Matheson is a vital figure in the history of American film horror. He wrote the landmark horror novel *I Am Legend*, which has been filmed three times: *The Last Man on Earth* (1964), *The Omega Man* (1971), and *I Am Legend* (2007). Other of his works to be adapted include *The Shrinking Man*, *Hell House*, and *A Stir of Echoes*. He wrote no fewer than 16 episodes of the series *The Twilight Zone*. He wrote the story and the screenplay for the classic suspense film *Duel*. He wrote the teleplays for *The Night Stalker* (1972) and *Trilogy of Terror* (1975). On top of all this, he adapted *The Devil Rides Out* (1968) for Hammer, and several Poe works for Roger Corman: *House of Usher* (1960), *The Pit and the Pendulum* (1961), *Tales of Terror* (1962), and *The Raven* (1963).

Richard Matheson in France in 2000.

The market went for "high-concept" films—that is, films with strong, simple premises with the widest possible appeal. Mainstream films in the 1980s were plus-sized, candy-colored, and overproduced. It was the time of violent adventures featuring pun-spouting beefcake-heroes such as Sylvester Stallone, Arnold Schwarzenegger, Chuck Norris, Steven Seagal, and Jean-Claude Van Damme. Immensely profitable franchises and sequel factories sprang to life. Horror followed suit.

The demand for cinematic product was enormous. Old picture palaces were torn down and replaced, or subdivided, into film complexes with many smaller auditoriums, each with its own screen—the multiplex. The innovation increased profits for exhibitors, but now they needed more movies to fill their expanding number of screens.

In addition, the creation of the VHS taping and playback system meant that videotapes of films could be purchased and rented by individuals for home viewing via hookup to their televisions. This led to the creation of the video store, a great advance for film enthusiasts but also an invitation for independent, low-budget production companies to crank out films that never even lit up a movie screen and instead went "straight-to-video." Many of these were horror films.

(The trend was so prevalent, even this author knew several people in mid-continental America, as far as possible from traditional, coastal US filmmaking centers, who contributed to viable regionally produced outings such as *Mindkiller* (1987), about a librarian who develops psychic powers, and *Destroyer* (1988), a slasher film starring former football defensive lineman Lyle Alzado.)

Last but not least, the "midnight movie" phenomenon leaned heavily on horror. The midnight screenings began in December 1970 at the Elgin Theater in New York City with Alejandro Jodorowsky's surreal "acid Western" *El Topo*. The idea of showing oddball, taboo fare for the drugged-out counterculture was encouraged by Elgin attendee John Lennon, and the practice spread. Soon transgressive or distasteful horror fare such as *Night of the Living Dead* and *Equinox* joined *Harold and Maude* (1971), *Pink Flamingos* (1972), *King of Hearts* (1966), *Eraserhead* (1977), *Liquid Sky* (1982), *Reefer Madness* (1936), and *The Harder They Come* (1972) on the midnight bills.

It was the astounding late-night popularity of Jim Sharman's 1975 *The Rocky Horror Picture Show* that made the midnight movie a standard offering at many venues for decades. Based on Richard O'Brien's 1973 stage musical, *The Rocky Horror Show*, it's *Frankenstein* crossed with Fellini's *Satyricon* (1969) and a Busby Berkeley musical.

The monster metaphor for society's then-hidden and oppressed LGBT culture proved particularly apt and resonant. It mixes high camp with polyandrous hijinks and campy jokes, infused with references to nearly every significant Golden Age sci-fi and horror-film icon and cliché. The screenings encouraged audience participation. This came in two forms: audience members armed with multiple props, gesturing from their seats, blurting sarcastic, timed responses to onscreen lines, and a suite of fans/actors who dressed as the

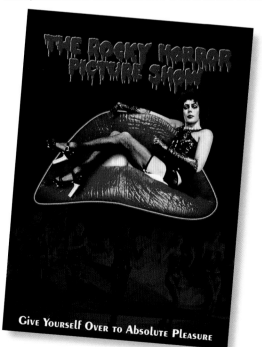

GIVE YOURSELF OVER TO ABSOLUTE PLEASURE

Longest-Running Horror Franchises

The *Amityville* movies (23 movies)

Witchcraft (16)

Puppet Master franchise (14)

Friday the 13th (12)

Halloween (12)

George Romero *Dead* films (11)

Hellraiser (10)

Children of the Corn (9)

A Nightmare on Elm Street (9)

Saw (9)

film's characters and acted the film out at the base of the screen as it played.

At the height of the boom in 1987, nearly 100 horror films were released in America alone.[1] Every original horror film aspired to launch sequels. The horror sequels of the 1930s and 1940s were cobbled together on the fly, but horror projects in the 1980s were designed deliberately to be open-ended, establish a "brand," and encourage as many reiterations as possible. The term "sequel" isn't accurate either. In few cases did a horror sequel advance a storyline or expand its narrative. It merely repeated the initial premise, using fresh actors to replace the characters slaughtered in the movie before. It was a mass-production deal.

A cursory search reveals the creation of nearly four dozen horror franchises born between 1975 and 2000—from *Halloween* (eleven films, 1978–present), *Friday the 13th* (twelve films, 1980–2009), and *Nightmare on Elm Street* (nine films, 1984–2010) to the more questionable delights of the *Leprechaun* (eight films, 1993–2014). The current record-holder is the *Amityville* series (1979–present), which consists of no fewer than twenty-three entries to date.

It was no longer shameful or weird, but cool and hip, to be a horror aficionado. Horror movies were "fun," and now acceptable for the family to see. The amount of casual violence in all kinds

The Rocky Horror Picture Show (1975) poster.

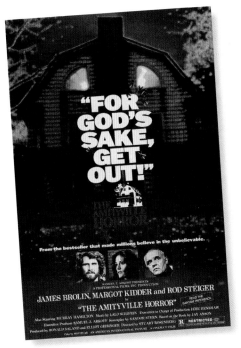

The Amityville Horror (1979) poster.

of American films during this period ramped up dramatically, and the "R" rating was still required for any movie's success, especially a horror film. (In Mickey Rose's excellent 1981 teen-horror spoof *Student Bodies*, the film grinds to a halt in the middle so that a sedate announcer can calmly spout a profane suggestion in order to earn the coveted "R" rating.)

The quotient of sex in these films stayed low, and, of course, sexual transgression in them was always punished. However, violence against women in horror films became more aggressive, explicit, and casual than ever. It was a time when America's religious right resurged. It's as though the mad Puritan soul of the country, enraged by the excesses of the prior two decades, came out swinging a reactionary axe.

At the same time, a second generation of memorable TV horror anthologies sprang up, starting with *Twilight Zone* creator Rod Serling's gutty *Night Gallery* (1969–1973) and later to include *Tales of the Unexpected* (1979–1988), *Tales from the Darkside* (1983–1988), *The Ray Bradbury Theater* (1985–1992), *Friday the 13th: The Series* (1987–1990), *Monsters* (1988–1991), and *Tales from the Crypt* (1989–1996). There was the overlooked but well-done Spielberg-generated *Amazing Stories* (1985–1987), chock-full of wonderful work from multiple directors, including horror directors Tobe Hooper, Bob

The Crypt Keeper in *Tales from the Crypt* (1989).

Clark, Tom Holland, and Joe Dante—and, eventually, along came even reboots of the iconic *Twilight Zone* (1985–1989), *Alfred Hitchcock Presents* (1985–1989), and *The Outer Limits* (1995–2002).

Even the spoofy, sarcastic TV horror host returned to life, thanks to comedian and actress Cassandra Peterson. In the persona of the Goth, deep-cleavaged, wisecracking Elvira, Mistress of the Dark, she ruled over the highly popular syndicated *Movie Macabre* from 1981 through 1985. There was a whole new generation of bad horror films to mock, and so like her predecessors Zacherley, Ghoulardi, and Chilly Billy, she interrupted the cheesiness with double entendres.

There's a highly schematic feel about the bulk of the horror films of this period. Strangely, while most of these films themselves are unmemorable, more lasting horror-film icons were created during this time than at any other since the 1930s.

Let's see, there was . . . Leatherface from *The Texas Chain Saw Massacre*, Michael Myers from *Halloween*, Freddy Krueger from *Nightmare on Elm Street*, hockey-masked Jason Voorhees from *Friday the 13th*, the Tall Man from *Phantasm* (1979), Chucky the demonic doll from *Child's*

Play (1988), porcupine-noggined Pinhead from *Hellraiser* (1987), the titular *Alien*, the *Predator* (1987), and more—all of whom romped across the screen in sequels, prequels, crossovers, and reboots of ever-decreasing quality.

Sean S. Cunningham's *Friday the 13th* is a perfect example of basic, industrial-strength horror. The formula of teen transgression being punished with death and dismemberment, in manners rigorous and graphic, is a winner. Victor Miller's by-the-numbers script is an effective genre vehicle that seemingly tolerates infinite repetition.

Friday's power relies on its roots in folk mythology, in all those campfire stories we all told each other on summer nights in an effort to freak each other out. Watch out, Camp Crystal Lakers! Jason Voorhees drowned out here one summer twenty years ago, and now mysterious murders keep racking up quite a total of horny teenagers.

(Spoiler alert: In the original *Friday the 13th*, Jason is not the killer. Providentially, makeup man Tom Savini suggested leaving Jason's fate at the film's conclusion open-ended. How could he know he was helping to create an immortal monster?)

Don Coscarelli showed in *Phantasm* that a small independent horror filmmaker could break through. It took Coscarelli a year to make this no-budget tale of two brothers fighting a grim undertaker who enslaves the souls of the

Scariest Monsters of Horror

The Thing from *The Thing* (1982)

The Alien from the *Alien* film franchise

Pennywise the Clown from *It* (1990, 2017, 2019)

The Monster, *Possession* (1981)

The Gwoemul, *The Host* (2006)

The Pale Man, *Pan's Labyrinth* (2006)

Cenobites, from the *Hellraiser* film franchise

Freddy Krueger, the *Nightmare on Elm Street* films

Sadako from *Ringu* (1998)

The alien invaders in *Society* (1989)

Betsy Palmer as Mrs. Voorhees, cinema's most dedicated mother, in *Friday the 13th* (1980).

dead and turns them into his dwarf minions. Coscarelli's audacious visuals ornament a film that contains surprising feeling and mythic depth. The success of *Phantasm* allowed Coscarelli to craft more installments in the series, as well as comedy-horror masterpieces like *Bubba Ho-Tep* (2002) and *John Dies at the End* (2012).

Most of these 1980s-era monster roles did not require a performer with a sense of charisma or menace to enact them. Hidden behind masks, or voicing "puppetronic" monsters, only a few '80s iconic horror actors established themselves in the public consciousness.

Jeffrey Combs became director Stuart Gordon's antihero Doctor Herbert West in *Re-Animator* and other Lovecraftian features. Robert Englund had his claim to fame as Freddy Krueger in the *Nightmare* series. Brad Dourif earned horror fame as the voice of the demonic doll Chucky for the *Child's Play* franchise.

Jamie Lee Curtis of *Halloween* became the era's most famous "scream queen." She was joined by others such as Dee Wallace (*The Hills Have Eyes*, 1977; *The Howling*, 1981; *Cujo*, 1983; *Critters*, 1986; *Alligator II: The Mutation*, 1991 . . .); Linnea Quigley (*The Return of the Living Dead*, 1985), Brinke Stevens (*Sorority Babes in the Slimeball*

Bowl-O-Rama, 1988), and Michelle Bauer (*Hollywood Chainsaw Hookers*, 1988). Quigley even had her own Horror Workout videotape— "the scariest exercise video ever made!"

The special effects of the period overpowered both the narratives and performers. It's not the technicians' fault; technology kept advancing, and the SFX departments' skills increased with each challenge met.

Alongside the advances crafted by the visual-effects wizardry of visionary *Star Wars* creator George Lucas's Industrial Light & Magic (founded in 1975), a host of extremely talented practical-effects artists were names that prompted hardcore horror fans to pay attention.

The roster included Rick Baker (*The Howling, An American Werewolf in London*), Tom Savini (*Friday the 13th, Dawn of the Dead*), Stan Winston (*Aliens, Predator*), Rob Bottin (*The Thing, Se7en*), Dick Smith (*The Exorcist, Scanners*), Chris Walas (*Gremlins, The Fly*), Stuart Conran (*The Lair of the White Worm, Shaun of the Dead*), Gianetto de Rossi, and Greg Nicotero, Robert Kurtzman, and Howard Bergman's KNB Effects (*The People Under the Stairs, In the Mouth of Madness, Scream*) and Screaming Mad George, aka Joji

Tani (*Predator, Society*). (CGI, which was cheaper, more versatile, and increasingly convincing, would begin to take over in 1995.)

The augmented ability to render gore onscreen led to what George A. Romero dubbed the "splatter" film—officially begun by Herschell Gordon Lewis with his *Blood Feast*—which leaned heavily on graphic violence, often to absurd lengths. The exhibition of these were battled in many places, resulting in a notable 1984 British list of "video nasties" (which gave fans a convenient shopping list).

Oddly, the director of the time most infused with a horror sensibility only intermittently made outright horror movies. Tim Burton was an animator who started his career with short films, most notably *Vincent* (1982), a darkly comic, six-minute, stop-motion animation about a boy who fantasizes that he is Vincent Price (and Burton even got Price to do the narration).

Burton casts his exaggerated, visually wild style into everything he works on, veering closer to horror in dark fantasies such as *Beetlejuice* (1988), *Edward Scissorhands* (1990), *The Nightmare Before Christmas* (1993, conceived and produced by Burton but directed by Henry Selick), *Ed Wood* (1994), *Sleepy Hollow* (1999), *Corpse Bride* (2005), and *Sweeney Todd: The Demon Barber of Fleet Street* (2007). Frequently using his versatile go-to leading man, Johnny Depp, Burton explores with gloomy, campy relish the ins and outs of the American Gothic tradition.

Another enormous phenomenon was the rise to prominence of America's most gifted horror writer since Poe, Stephen King. The enterprising and prolific novelist continues to produce a steady stream of work that includes classics such as *Carrie, The Shining, The Dead Zone, Misery*, and more. More than seventy, and sometimes seemingly

The werewolf transformation in *An American Werewolf in London* (1981).

many, many more, of his works have been adapted for film or television (Hooper's 1979 miniseries *Salem's Lot* and Tommy Lee Wallace's 1990 miniseries *It* both stand up alongside the best film adaptations of King's work).

Some of the best horror directors helmed a Stephen King film: Cronenberg made *The Dead Zone* (1983), Carpenter made *Christine* (also 1983), and Romero made *Creepshow* (1982) and *The Dark Half* (1993).

And there were many awful directors who made Stephen King movies as well—hell, even Stephen King made a Stephen King film (1986's horror-comedy *Maximum Overdrive*). This has led to burnout for many save the most faithful King fans, but the great storyteller does continue to produce work that generates highly anticipated adaptations more than forty years after his first success.

Contemporary audiences hooked into the appropriate horror archetypes to meet their particular psychic needs. In our time, the traditional, old-school monsters have been supplanted by the serial killer and the zombie. King's dominance on screen was surpassed only by the universal prevalence of the serial killer or slasher film, which forms an immense body of largely unvarying work.

The myth of the serial killer grew rapidly in Western culture. The triggering event was the five unsolved murders committed by Jack the Ripper in London in 1888. The fact that the murderer

From Scream Queens to Final Girls

Sandra Peabody (left) in *The Last House on the Left* (1972).

Scream queens were originally written to serve as damsels in distress, captured by the monster and rescued by the hero. Such was the case with the very first scream queen, Mary Philbin, in *The Phantom of the Opera* (1925). The most popular scream queen of the classic era was Fay Wray (*King Kong*, 1933). Later in the century, Janet Leigh would be noted as one for her appearance in *Psycho* (1960).

The concept of the "final girl" came along in the 1970s, the idea that a horror film's female protagonist could take action to save herself and others from evil. Soon, certain actresses found themselves in a number of horror films, from great to awful

Below are some contemporary scream queens/final girls and their most notable horror roles:

Barbara Steele: *Black Sunday* (1960)
Sandra Peabody: *The Last House on the Left* (1972)
Linda Blair: *The Exorcist* (1973)
Olivia Hussey: *Black Christmas* (1974)
Marilyn Burns: *The Texas Chain Saw Massacre* (1974)
Daria Nicolodi: *Deep Red* (1975)
Dee Wallace: *The Hills Have Eyes* (1977)
Jamie Lee Curtis: *Halloween* (1978)
Heather Langenkamp: *A Nightmare on Elm Street* (1984)
Linnea Quigley: *The Return of the Living Dead* (1985)

was never identified, much less caught, created a huge nexus of fear in the urban population.

Cities were places of mass and activity, filled with people who were uprooted, mobile (upwardly and downwardly), and unknown. As Peter Ackroyd put it so succinctly in his *London: The Biography*, "The isolation and anonymity of strangers passing through the city leave them peculiarly defenceless to the depredations of an urban killer."[2] Here was a monster who could not be detected, who could kill without fearing capture. The perpetrator could have been anyone.

Since then, others have imitated those murderous pursuits, giving us a litany of evil names to conjure with: Manson, Bundy, Dahmer, Gacy, Gein, the Zodiac Killer, the Son of Sam, the Boston Strangler. They roll off the tongue far too easily. As Darryl Jones put it so aptly, "The serial killer is our great modern demon."[3] The power of this randomized terror permeates the modern consciousness.

At the same time, we are fascinated with the killers. The lives of these compulsive criminals are documented thoroughly, and sometimes romanticized. What attracts us to their stories? Transgression is seductive, and those who break taboos gain acolytes.

My Bloody Valentine (1981) poster.

Holliday Horror

Silent Night, Bloody Night (1972)
Black Christmas (1974)
Halloween (1978)
New Year's Evil (1980)
My Bloody Valentine (1981)
April Fool's Day (1986)
Resurrection (1999)
ThanksKilling (2009)

The slasher film is rigorously schematic, like a Greek tragedy. The plot is triggered by a tragic action in the past that transforms the victim into a monstrous killer that seeks revenge. The killer's attacks are triggered by an anniversary of the tragedy's date, and the victims are primarily sexually active teens. The cast is whittled down to the Final Girl, usually virginal, who outwits and defeats the killer . . . who may have survived . . .

The idea of a commemorative date or anniversary that prompts onscreen mayhem was so prevalent that there is now a "holiday horror" slasher film subgenre (and we've already touched on the rich legacy of Christmas horror movies, which proliferate like mogwai). You could program a year-round viewing calendar with selections such as *New Year's Evil* (1980), *My Bloody Valentine* (1981), and *ThanksKilling* (2009).

Between 1978 and 1984, more than 100 slasher films were made in America alone. They flowed in from everywhere, including Canada (more Canuxploitation) and Australia (labeled as "Ozploitation"). A turn in the national mood was palpable. We weren't identifying with the victims anymore—we were identifying with the remorseless killers, the infinitely renewable, seemingly immortal murderers. We wanted to see what kinds of mayhem they could conjure. We were becoming connoisseurs of brutality.

Some horror escaped under the imprint of the thriller. The best American thriller director of the period was Brian De Palma, whose career stretched far beyond horror but who helmed the first successful Stephen King film adaptation, *Carrie*, in 1976. De Palma was strongly influenced by Italian *giallo* as well as Hitchcock, and films such as *Dressed to Kill* (1980), *Blow Out* (1981), and *Body Double* (1984) all adhere to those aesthetics.

Other subgenres ground along inexorably. For the continuing stampede of eco-horror, you had dozens of angry critters to choose from—films such as *Grizzly* (1976), Joe Dante's *Piranha* (1978), and *Alligator* (1980). *Piranha* and *Alligator* feature witty screenplays by up-and-coming film auteur John Sayles. There were also hilarious duds like 1977's *The Day of the Animals*, in which Leslie Nielsen fights a bear in a rainstorm with his shirt off—Nielsen's, that is—and 1972's *Night of the Lepus*, with giant carnivorous bunnies. There were unexpected gems like *Jaws* and like 1978's *Long Weekend*, the latter an excellent and subtle exercise in eco-horror thrills from Australian Colin Eggleston. The spoof *Attack of the Killer Tomatoes!* (1978) takes the premise to its comic, logical extreme. (Spoiler alert: the evil *Solanum lycopersium* are deathly allergic to the insipid pop ballad "Puberty Love.")

There was a revival of horror anthology in films such as *Creepshow*, *Deadtime Stories* (1986), *Body Bags* (Carpenter and Hooper, 1993), and *Tales from the Hood* (1995). Zombie films persisted, cropping up here and there. American

Top Ten Horror Films of the 1980s

Friday the 13th (1980)

The Shining (1980)

The Howling (1981)

The Thing (1982)

Videodrome (1983)

A Nightmare on Elm Street (1984)

Aliens (1986)

Evil Dead 2: Dead by Dawn (1987)

Near Dark (1987)

They Live (1988)

International Pictures, home of Roger Corman, churned out more low-budget horror, including a trilogy of extremely loose and cheesy H. G. Wells adaptations (*The Food of the Gods*, 1976, and *The Empire of the Ants*, 1977, were both directed by Bert I. Gordon of *The Amazing Colossal Man* fame; *The Island of Dr. Moreau*, 1977, was helmed by actor-turned-director Don Taylor), causing no serious damage.

There were new horror specialists as well. Stuart Gordon and Brian Yuzna created gripping horror films together and apart. They concocted the grimly funny body-horror splatterfest *Re-Animator* in 1985, based on the work of H. P. Lovecraft, and the decidedly lighter Disney hit and franchise *Honey, I Shrunk the Kids* (1989), which leans heavily on '50s sci-fi/horror tropes.

Yuzna's greatest achievement is his gross-out classic *Society* (1989), an extremely pointed satire of the relationship between America's rich and poor. As in Carpenter's *They Live*, *Society*'s rich prey on the lower classes—but here they literally feed on them, melding their bodies with those of their victims and devouring their substance in an obscene parody of a cocktail party crossed with an orgy. The practical effects by Screaming Mad George are incomparably disgusting.

Clive Barker is a prominent British horror novelist and self-taught filmmaker. His *Books of Blood* were bestsellers in the mid-'80s. His displeasure with how his material was adapted to film led him to launch the popular *Hellraiser* series in 1987. As in Lovecraft, there are extradimensional beings at work; in Barker, they are Cenobites, creatures who seek carnal pleasure through the sadomasochistic destruction of living humans. The extreme, graphic story proved popular

Hellraiser (1987) poster.

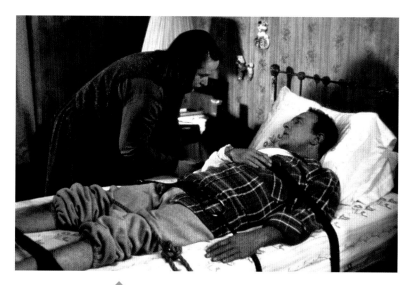

enough to trigger nine sequels to date.

Barker's short story "The Forbidden" was adapted by Bernard Rose into the gripping and powerful *Candyman* in 1992. A grad student researching urban legends finds one that still lives, in the Chicago ghetto. The monster can be summoned by chanting his name in front of a mirror, which, of course, is exactly what our heroine does—on her path to becoming an urban legend herself.

Meanwhile, Abel Ferrara, in traditional East Coast fashion, came to horror film through experience in the porn industry and started his career when he both filmed and starred in *Driller Killer* (1979) before moving on to disturbing and gritty non-horror fare such as *Bad Lieutenant* (1992) (he'd circle back to horror with a drop-dead cool, intellectual study of vampirism, *The Addiction*, in 1995).

Dan O'Bannon got his start with fellow student John Carpenter at the University of Southern California, working with him on what became the cult sci-fi comedy *Dark Star* (1974). He generated all kinds of material, including the source material for the films *Alien*, *Lifeforce*, and *Total Recall* (1990), as well as his own solid independent efforts (the horror-comedy *The Return of the Living Dead*, 1985; *The Resurrected*, 1991).

Indie pioneer Robert Rodriguez came late to the boom, but excelled in horror with his gangsters-vs.-vampire strippers *From Dusk Till Dawn* (1996), aliens-vs.-teenagers *The Faculty* (1998), and *Planet Terror* (2007), a perfect recreation of 1970s-era zombie horror in the megafeature *Grindhouse* (2007). Tom Holland (*Fright Night*, 1985; *Child's Play*, 1988; *Thinner*, 1996) was a dependable horror craftsman as well.

Further down the scale are the efforts of prolific and less-discriminate artists such as

producer/writer/director Charles Band (the *Puppet Master* franchise, 1989–present), Jim Wynorski (*Not of This Earth*, 1988), Kevin S. Tenney (*Night of the Demons*, 1988), and Todd Sheets (*Zombie Bloodbath*, 1993), all of whom were stalwarts of the direct-to-video era.

Meanwhile, in the more privileged neighborhoods of Hollywood, horror was profitable and prestigious. Among the many mainstream horror hits were Richard Donner's *The Omen* (1976), about the rather ominous childhood of the Antichrist; Stuart Rosenberg's *The Amityville Horror* (1979), about the world's worst real-estate deal; Tony Scott's haunting tale of vampires, love, and betrayal across the ages *The Hunger* (1983); and Rob Reiner's *Misery* (1990), the last strong Stephen King adaptation that won a Best Actress Oscar for Kathy Bates as Annie Wilkes, a psychotic romance-novel fan who kidnaps and torments her favorite author.

"Name" directors were still taking cracks at the genre, supported with studio money. The results were, as often as not, stodgy and pretentious failures. There was John Badham's tedious 1979 *Dracula*. Francis Ford Coppola crafted an overwrought *Bram Stoker's Dracula* in 1992. To be fair, it's a more faithful adaptation than many, but it's defeated by wrongheaded casting choices. Rock star and actor Sting played Dr. Frankenstein for Franc Roddam in 1985 (*The*

Bride), while in 1994 Kenneth Branagh played the doctor and directed *Mary Shelley's Frankenstein*, with Robert De Niro playing a unique version of the Monster.

Richard Attenborough directed *Magic* (1978), with Anthony Hopkins as a mad ventriloquist, à la Michael Redgrave in *Dead of Night*. Joel Schumacher had star-studded, lavishly produced horror hits such as *The Lost Boys* (1987), about gnarly Goth vampire punks who infest a coastal California town, and *Flatliners* (1990), in which a troupe of hip young scientists explore the afterlife and discover it contains mostly angry ghosts seeking karmic revenge. Even the urbane director Mike Nichols made a werewolf movie, with Jack Nicholson as an intriguing, aging antihero (*Wolf*, 1994).

There were remakes galore. In addition to Carpenter (*The Thing*), Cronenberg (*The Fly*), and Hooper (*Invaders from Mars*), Philip Kaufman redid *Invasion of the Body Snatchers* in 1978, and Paul Schrader remade *Cat People* in 1982. *The Blob* came to life again in 1988, and ten years after that, Gus van Sant felt possessed of the need to remake Hitchcock's *Psycho*, practically shot for shot.

There was a raft of innovative, independent horror efforts as well, most of which got crushed at the box office at the time of their release by the more familiar pleasures of the 2s, IIIs, Revenges, and Seeds Ofs.

One of them was *The Little Girl Who Lives Down the Lane* (1976). Before the genuinely sweet Martin Sheen played the president on TV's *The West Wing*, he was a prolific and excellent player of villains. He portrayed evil political candidate Greg Stillson in Cronenberg's 1983 film adaptation of *The Dead Zone*. In *Girl*, he is absolutely terrifying as a child molester who has his sights set on the mysteriously solitary and independent Jodie Foster.

Anyone with interest in sound in film and film scoring should get their hands on a copy of *The Shout* (1978). Its premise is that a drifter (Alan Bates) knows an aboriginal technique for issuing a death-summoning roar. His encounter

with a composer and his wife (John Hurt and Susannah York) leads to a game of bewitchment, control, and betrayal that's shot in a breezy yet convincing style, made believable by three great performances.

On the whimsical side, there are entries such as the low-budget but witty and stylish *Fade to Black* (1980), about a film buff who kills people while he's in character as a panoply of horror-film figures. It features a great performance by Dennis Christopher, as well as an early sighting of Mickey Rourke as a goombah.

Motel Hell (1980) is a delightfully funny and subversive satire, about a motel owner, butcher, and farmer (incongruously, played with earnest drollness by former B-movie action star Rory Calhoun) who uses human meat in his recipes. His slogan: "It takes all kinds of critters to make Farmer Vincent's fritters." It features a climatic chainsaw duel.

More serious efforts include *The Entity* (1982), featuring a great performance by Barbara Hershey as a woman being assaulted by a poltergeist; and *Henry: Portrait of a Serial Killer* (1986), a brutal lo-fi effort with a stellar acting job by Michael Rooker at its center. Future Oscar winner Kathryn Bigelow's first great film,

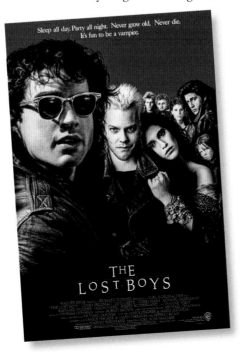

The Lost Boys (1987) poster.

Near Dark (1987), took the vampire trope and moved it to the contemporary American Southwest, revitalizing it immensely.

Other overlooked gems include Frank LaLoggia's low-key, creepy *Lady in White* (1988), Philip Ridley's *The Reflecting Skin* (1990), Richard Stanley's Africa-sited *Dust Devil* (1992), Steve Miner's silly croc saga *Lake Placid* (1999), Antonia Bird's Old West cannibal fest *Ravenous* (1999), and John Fawcett's emocore werewolf film, *Ginger Snaps* (2000).

English directors continued to put their own flamboyant spin on horror. Ken Russell's adaptation of Stoker's *The Lair of the White Worm* (1988) was a romp, and Adrian Lyne's epiphanic *Jacob's Ladder* (1990) was equal parts disturbing and haunting, a terrifying *Pilgrim's Progress*.

Some of the most significant horror films of the period, however, were also the most popular ones. The diabolical conjunction of Dan O'Bannon's script, Ridley Scott's direction, H. R. Giger's techno-Gothic design, and Carlo

Top Ten Horror Films of the 1990s

It (1990)

Misery (1990)

The People Under the Stairs (1991)

The Silence of the Lambs (1991)

Candyman (1992)

In the Mouth of Madness (1994)

Scream (1996)

Cure (1997)

Funny Games (1997)

I Stand Alone (1998)

Rambaldi's creature-making skills added up to 1979's *Alien*.

"In space no one can hear you scream." A commercial space crew answers a distress signal, only to find and bring aboard a deadly, unstoppable alien life form. The inherent exo-terrors of outer space had been touched on in films such as Stanley Kubrick's *2001: A Space Odyssey* (1968) and John Sturges's *Marooned* (1969). To these terrors, Ridley Scott added a grisly, darkened palette, a killing machine, and a cynical narrative about corporate exploitation. That theme is mirrored ironically by the way the Alien monster colonizes and incubates in the bodies of the crew of would-be colonizers it devours, placed in harm's way by a company happy to use them as bait.

It's a grungy movie—dark and nihilistic, relentless in its exploitation of the fear of bodily violation, and its heroine, Ripley, played by Sigourney Weaver, is the first real Final Woman—an autonomous, thinking being instead of a hapless victim who, frankly, can kick monster ass. It triggered a series of sequels, the first of which, the equally stunning 1986 *Aliens*, made the reputation of director James Cameron (*Titanic*, *Avatar*).

Stanley Kubrick's adaptation of Stephen King's *The Shining* in 1980 was not well-received when it was released, but has since risen in estimation to be regarded as one of the best horror films of all time. A slow pace and divergence from the novel still dismay some, but it stands on its own merits. The story of the psychic boy in a hotel full of murderous ghosts is gripping, and Jack Nicholson's performance as the mentally disintegrating, possessed villain is itself a classic.

The first horror film to win the Oscar for Best Picture, *The Silence of the Lambs* (1991), came from a most unlikely source, director Jonathan Demme, who until then had been best known for his goofy romantic comedies. The power and inventiveness of Demme's direction, tied in with top-notch cutting and pacing, and anchored by definitive performances by Jodie Foster and Anthony Hopkins, created a mesmerizing sleeper hit that deeply impacted the public mind.

Hopkins's performance as Hannibal "the Cannibal" Lecter, the erudite, witty, and sensitive

serial killer who aids FBI agent Clarice Starling (Foster) in tracking down the psychotic murderer "Buffalo Bill," made the character the first in quite a while to become a horror icon.

Lecter is a monster, but a kind of superman and also an old-school gentleman. His class and adherence to a peculiar code of honor make the audience ultimately root for what would seem to be an irrevocably repellent person. English actors made the best baddies, and the roster of them grew during this period, including Jeremy Irons (*Dead Ringers*, *Reversal of Fortune*) and Ralph Fiennes (*Schindler's List*, *Spider*).

After a disastrous experience making *Alien³* (1992), director David Fincher bounced back with *Se7en* (1995), ostensibly a police thriller but much more of what the director termed a "meditation on evil." It's a deep, dark, graphic adventure into sin and punishment with an inspired and anonymous killer, John Doe (Kevin Spacey), at its center. Morgan Freeman and Brad Pitt play the police detectives charged with tracking down Doe, who is murdering people in accordance with his conception of the Seven Deadly Sins.

In 1996, Wes Craven's *Scream* closed the circle of horror's self-referentiality. In this, the ultimate postmodern horror film, everything is predicated on the characters and audience being intimately familiar with the unwritten rules and practices of the genre.

Finally, the culture had turned itself inside out—what was once the province of fanboys only now was common currency. It seemed the genre had played itself out once again. From where could a fresh charge of energy come?

It turned out to be Asia's turn.

Se7en (1995) poster.

The Silence of the Lambs (1991) poster.

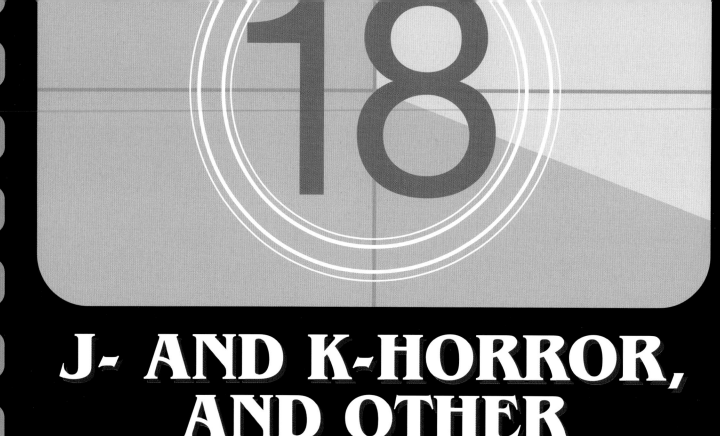

J- AND K-HORROR, AND OTHER ASIAN ENTRIES

Beginning in the late 1980s, and cresting at the turn of the twenty-first century, a new wave of original Japanese horror films achieved success, first at home and then worldwide. This wave spawned sequels, imitations, and remakes, and sparked an explosion in the horror genre elsewhere in Asia, most notably in Korea. These directors of "J-horror," as it came to be termed, revitalized the horror genre, just as Craven, Clark, Cronenberg, and Carpenter had in America the generation before.

Japanese horror developed its own distinct atmosphere and way of engaging the viewer. It stood in stark contrast to American mainstream horror's predictable plots, shocks, and camera angles, the soundtrack that tipped you off or told you what to feel. In the late 1990s, a wide range of Japanese horror films began to share the same grimy, dim, dilapidated settings. The pace of these films is consistently slower, the shocks generated by their edits all obey an unfamiliar, jarring rhythm. Over and over, the characters in a variety of Japanese horror films collapse and suffer in an exhausted, abandoned world.

An important harbinger of the Japanese wave was so odd that it had a lot of influence

Director Nobuhiko Obayashi.

but no successors. Nobuhiko Obayashi's *House* (1977) takes a) the familiar Japanese concepts of the angry ghost, b) the inherent (sometimes malevolent) spirit of places and objects, and c) applies avant-garde techniques to their telling. It's stylized and bizarre, in the spirit of transgressive, non-horror Japanese New Wave directors of the previous generation, among them Kinji Fukasaku (*Black Lizard*, 1968), Nagisa Oshima (*Death by Hanging*, 1968), and Seijun Suzuki (*Branded to Kill*, 1967).

House is a delirious one-of-a-kind cinematic rampage. Seven hopelessly cheery schoolgirl friends, each embodying a stereotypical attribute, visit one of their aunt's homes; it turns out that the hostess is a ghost who devours unmarried girls. Utilizing an array of bizarre effects, the director's mad, kinetic approach would be celebrated after reappraisal decades later.

Shigeru Izumiya's surrealistic cyberpunk no-budget epic *Death Powder* (1986) inspired Shinya Tsukamoto's disturbing body-horror tale *Tetsuo: The Iron Man* (1989). *Iron Man* is a nightmare

OPPOSITE:
Scene from *Ringu* (1998).

Film still from *House* (1977).

Film still from
*Tetsuo: The Iron
Man* (1988).

of dehumanization. In it, a man finds himself turning into a machine in a bizarre and sadistic, lo-fi, black-and-white saga. The film takes body horror to its logical extreme, turning human flesh into mechanisms that deliver pain and death—a terrifying metaphor for the steamroller effect of technology on the individual. (Tsukamoto could create naturalistic horror as well, as seen in his gripping Meji Period piece about doppelgangers, *Gemini*, 1999.)

There are four J-horror masters, though all of them have directed outside the genre as well. In 1989, up-and-coming filmmaker Kiyoshi Kurosawa made his first horror film, *Sweet Home*. Though formulaic (another angry ghost must be supplicated), it demonstrated an attention to story, detailed character development, and a distinct visual code, pace, and mood that would become trademarks of J-horror. *Sweet*

Home skillfully incorporates computer-generated effects into the story, and focuses on the parent-child relationship, a theme that would recur frequently in Asian horror.

Kurosawa's next important horror film, *Cure* (1997), is a classic. In it, people are driven to randomly kill and cannot explain their motives. A detective tracks down the only common denominator, a student of hypnotism who seems to have no personal memories but who

Director Kiyoshi
Kurosawa (left)
and actor Koji
Yakusho at a 2018
press conference
for their movie
Cure (1997).

is capable of getting inside the head of anyone he's been in contact with—except the detective himself. Is evil transmittable, like any virus?

Actor Koji Yakusho is fascinating to watch as a determined detective with secrets of his own, who unravels as forces he doesn't understand begin to control him. Kurosawa's subtle and deliberately paced direction ratchets up the tension to unbearable levels. Kurosawa's settings are dank and dilapidated, and he's a master at pacing and creating a gentle sense of unease. It's primarily conveyed through suggestion and unresolved incongruities, as in Val Lewton's films of the 1940s. Like Hitchcock or the cinematic clown Jacques Tati, Kurosawa plants information inconspicuously all over the screen, forcing the viewer to work to complete the picture. He baffles audiences with misdirection and then slams them with insight.

In Kurosawa's universe, society and life itself are depressingly inescapable, and horror only throws that fundamental despair into sharp relief. His *Pulse* (2001) takes in nothing less than

the end of the world in the same fascinating and visually intriguing manner. People begin to kill themselves and then vanish, leaving only black stains behind. Meanwhile, ghosts invade reality, harassing the living. By not nailing down specifics about what is happening, Kurosawa makes the monstrous dwell in the ambiguity.

Hideo Nakata crafted several competent horror movies before making the one that turned the West on to the J-horror boom, *Ringu*, in 1998. Once again, the ancient Japanese horror story of the *onryo* (angry spirit), the *Yotsuya Kaidan*, is used, but updated to modern times. In *Ringu*, based on the novel by Koji Suzuki, viewing the ghost on a cursed videotape causes the person who views it to die in a week—unless the tape is copied and watched by someone else.

A brilliant premise, treated realistically, makes the film a moral inquiry (whom should I curse?) as well as a scary experience, but there's more to its appeal than that. At its heart, underneath the technological trappings of its gimmick, imagery such as a body down a well and a vengeful ghost with long black hair is straight out of Japanese folklore. The ancient demons can't be suppressed. *Ringu*'s popularity in America would trigger a series of distribution

Director Hideo Nakata (right) on the set of *Ring 2* (2005) with Naomi Watts.

Ringu (1998) poster.

Remakes and Reboots

A Nightmare on Elm Street (2010) poster.

Horror's easily repeatable formulas mean that remakes and reboots are likely, more so than in any other film genre. Some second takes outdo their templates; many others fall far short. Here's a look at some frequently renewed features and film series:

The Phantom of the Opera: 1925, 1943, 1962, and 2004, not to mention the successful musical adaptation that opened on the West End and Broadway in the 1980s.

The Invisible Man: The 1933 movie later became *Hollow Man* (2000) and *The Invisible Man* (2020).

King Kong: The great ape appeared on screens in 1931, 1976, and 2005.

One of the dance scenes from *Suspiria* (2018).

The Thing from Another World (1951) became *The Thing* (1982).

The Fly: Bet you didn't know there was a 1958 version before the 1986 entry!

House of Wax (1953) was remade in 2005.

Invasion of the Body Snatchers (1956) was remade in 1978.

Black Christmas: 1974, 2006, and 2019.

The Texas Chain Saw Massacre: 1974 and 2003.

Suspiria: 1977 and 2018.

Halloween: 1978, 2007 (a reimagining of the original film), and 2018 (a direct sequel to the original, which ignores the decades of sequels in between).

Friday the 13th: 1980 and 2009.

A Nightmare on Elm Street: 1984 and 2010, with Jackie Earle Haley taking over the role of Freddy Krueger in the remake.

Ringu (1998) received an American-made remake in *The Ring* (2002).

Ju-on: The Grudge (2002) was also remade in English as *The Grudge* (2004).

The Eye: 2002 and 2008.

Let the Right One In (2008) was remade in English as *Let Me In* (2010).

deals for J-horror films, and a series of American remakes as well—most of them sorry imitations of the originals. The tag-you're-cursed premise had legs.

Nakata would press on in horror, his other remarkable contribution being the moving and suspenseful *Dark Water* (2002), about mother love and sacrifice. It's based on a story in another Suzuki book, this one about a single mother who moves with her child into a dilapidated apartment building. A leak in the place above leads to the discovery of a child's needy ghost. Filmed without gore or shock effects, the film demonstrates yet again that deep feeling and a strong story create powerful horror.

A masterful stylist, Nakata also crafted *Kaidan* (2007), a beautiful salute to the traditional, period-set ghost stories in the style of earlier decades.

A wilder filmmaker is Takashi Miike, whose prolific career features films filled with extreme violence, sexual perversion, dark humor, and a loud, ludicrous visual style remindful of Ken Russell's. However, his breakthrough horror film, *Audition* (1999), is uncharacteristically constrained. It plays out like a wistful romantic comedy before it abruptly pulls out the rug from

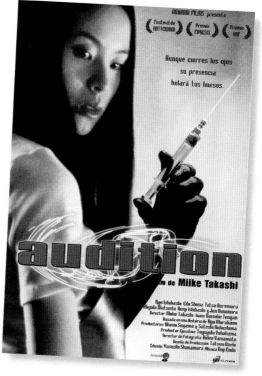

Audition (1999) poster.

under both the protagonist and the audience. A widower seeks a sweet and submissive new wife, and falls for one of the most terrifying females ever put on film. Whether you read the film as a misogynistic statement or as a subversion of patriarchy, the actions and images seen here won't let you be.

Amid his many other projects, Miike would strike horror gold again with *One Missed Call* (2003). By this time, the premise is degraded to: your future self calls you, letting you know you're going to die soon. It makes no sense, but Miike makes it entertaining.

Miike returns periodically to the genre. His more recent work has a more settled style and a sharper satirical wit. *Over Your Dead Body* (2014), for example, tackles the theater-set horror film, as a traditional play about a vengeful spirit who intersects with reality. In *As the Gods Will* (2014) a "revolution started by God" separates the good from the

Director Takashi Miike.

evil by subjecting them to a gauntlet of deadly children's games.

Takashi Shimizu is a director who started off in V-cinema, the Japanese equivalent of direct-to-video films. His astonishing, bone-chilling hit *Ju-on: The Grudge* (2002) was actually his third *Ju-on* film but only his first theatrical release; the whole thing was filmed in only nine days. It has spawned twelve related films to date. Shimizu made more classics such as *Marebito* (2004). In the film, an attempt to understand the nature of fear draws an obsessive cameraman into an underground world. From there, he draws up a young girl, whom he chains in this apartment and feeds on blood. Even stronger is the bizarre, hallucinatory *Tormented* (2011), which features terror in a giant bunny outfit.

Dozens of J-horror titles have emerged since 1998, and there are several journeymen who have turned out more than their fair share of films—Ataru Oikawa, who in 1998 launched the popular series of live-action adaptations of the bestselling

manga *Tomie*, about a self-replicating monster in female form who incites evil. There are others, including Sion Sono (the controversially transgressive *Suicide Club*, 2001; *Strange Circus*, 2005; *Cold Fish*, 2010) and Koji Shiraishi, who specializes in "found footage" horror such as *Noroi: The Curse* (2005), which is in the vein of *The Blair Witch Project* (1999).

The most impactful horror film of the period in Japan came from old avant-garde filmmaker Kinji Fukasaku (who had influenced *House* director Obayashi twenty years earlier): *Battle Royale* (2000), his last completed film. Adapted from Koushun Takami's novel, the film told of a group of school-age teens who are forced to fight to the death in a televised national entertainment. Sound familiar, *Hunger Games* fans? Its tone is vastly more savage and cynical than its imitator's.

Despite the immense popularity of J-horror, not one of the nearly dozen American J-horror remakes had the same feel and heft of the

Battle Royale (2000) poster.

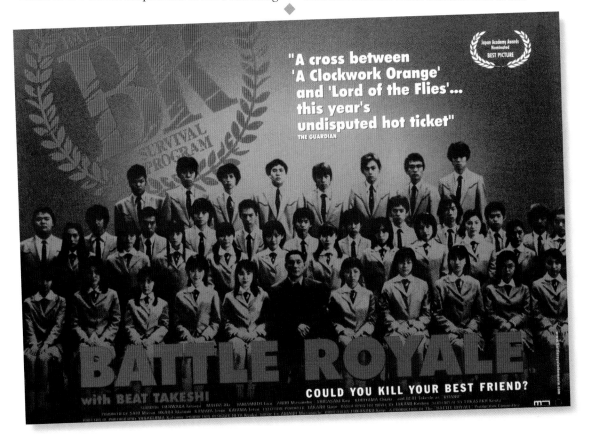

╺╾╾═══ ♦▮▮▮▮▮♦ ═══╾╾╸

Top Ten Horror Films of the 2000s

American Psycho (2000)

Battle Royale (2000)

The Cell (2000)

The Others (2001)

28 Days Later . . . (2002)

May (2002)

Shaun of the Dead (2004)

The Host (2006)

Pan's Labyrinth (2006)

Let the Right One In (2008)

originals. J-horror brought a slower pace, more earnest and heartfelt stories, and a grungy aesthetic to horror, but its general lack of concern with logic and its championing of visual impact over narrative thrust didn't translate well. *The Ring* (2002), *The Grudge* (2004), *Dark Water* (2005), *Pulse* (2006), *One Missed Call* (2008) and other Americanized J-horror copies were relative failures. The same story could be shot, but the same scares couldn't be generated.

Innovations continued. "Higuchinsky," aka Akihiro Higuchi, made the fascinating *Spiral* in 2000, in which the simple repetition of the title pattern subsumes and destroys mankind; Tomoo Haruguchi gave us a Samurai werewolf in *Kibakichi* (2004). In 2016, Koji Shiraishi made *Sadako vs. Kayako*—a modern "monster rally" crossover pitting the nemeses from the *Ring* and *Grudge* franchises against each other.

The South Korean horror wave picked up in 1998, about ten years after Japan's did. It was delayed by strict censorship that smothered filmmakers' creativity, particularly between 1973 and 1979. The boom, when it finally came, was fueled by an influx of foreign investment in the South Korean film industry after the Asian financial crisis of 1997.

The boom was launched by the only real Korean horror auteur to date, Kim Jee-woon. His *The Quiet Family* (1998) is a black horror-comedy about a family whose dream of owning a country inn is complicated by a sudden and exponential explosion of deaths at their establishment. (Takashi Miike remade it as a surreal musical, *The Happiness of the Katakuris*, in 2001.)

The freewheeling, deadpan whimsy found in the absurd tale is significantly different from the downbeat atmosphere of J-horror. "K-horror" is much more open to innovation and cross-genre experiments. It possesses not only an emotional directness but a sly and ready wit.

Jee-woon would move beyond horror, but would return for exceptionally strong outings such as *A Tale of Two Sisters* in 2003, about dysfunctional family dynamics, confused identities, psychosis, and amnesia (this was the first Korean horror film to crack the US market, and it inspired the 2009 remake *The Uninvited*); and *I Saw the Devil*, a demented horror-thriller that takes vengeance to an extremely unnerving extreme, in 2010.

There were dependable horror directors in South Korea such as Ahn Byeong-ki (*Nightmare*, 2000; *Phone*, 2002; *Apt.*, 2006) and Park Ki-hyung (the school-centered *Whispering Corridors* franchise, which launched in 1998). However, a broad spread of filmmakers were making innovative work, including Kong Su-Chang's Vietnam War story *R-Point* (2004), in which a missing combat patrol starts radioing in for help, and a search party is sent. One of the few horror movies to take place amid a wartime setting, it applies the vengeful-ghost concept to the world of combat, folding ideas about national guilt into the mix.

Other Korean gems include the visually sumptuous horror anthology, Jung Sik and Jung Bum-shik's *Epitaph* (2007), Jang Cheol-soo's *Bedevilled* (2010), and Yim Pil-sung's *Hansel and Gretel* (2007), in which a lost salesman stumbles across a helpful girl who brings him to her charming cottage in the forest—only to find there's no escape from it. It's a stylized, brightly colored mindbender that takes Western conceits popular in South Korea, such as fairy tales and Christmas, only to turn them inside out.

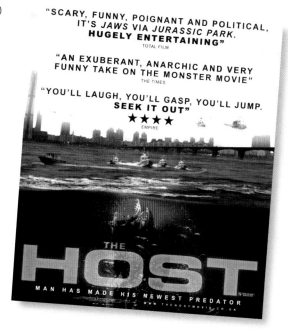

The Host (2006) poster.

In Na Hong-jin's *The Chaser* (2008), a disgraced former policeman fights a ruthless serial killer. Much evil is done on both sides in an effort to prevent worse from happening. In Park Chan-wook's *Thirst* (2009), a priest volunteers to test a new vaccine, which turns him into a vampire. It's a straight-faced examination of conscience. How can a moral man bear the burden of monstrosity? The protagonist is a complex character, doubtful about his vocation and drawn to the pleasures of the flesh. His fatal attraction to his best friend's wife triggers a series of tragedies. It's one of the most thoughtful monster movies made.

The highlight of South Korean horror to date is Bong Joon-ho's *The Host* (2006), a wickedly funny and stylish tour de force. When arrogant Americans force their Korean assistants to dump leftover chemicals into the water supply, they create an insatiable monster that no one in power wants to deal with, honestly.

The film's working-class protagonist must fight both the monster and the government to save his child. On the surface, it's a simple monster movie. However, it's also an astute examination of politics and society as well. Officialdom's efforts to contain the crisis only make things much, much worse. It's the rejects of society who save the day.

Yeon Sang-ho's high-octane, popular zombie/action film, *Train to Busan*, and its anime prequel, *Seoul Station*, both released in 2016, demonstrate that, in Korea at least, the horror boom is not over.

In Hong Kong, the 1997 horror anthology *Troublesome Night*, largely under the direction of Herman Yau, would grow into a nineteen-film series. Brothers Danny Pang Phat and Oxide Pang Chun created the superb *The Eye* in 2002, which, like many other hit Asian horrors, received an inferior American remake. In it, a young woman receives corneal transplants from a psychic suicide victim, and begins to foresee death and disaster. Anchoring a strong story is the riveting central performance from Angelica Lee as the unlucky donatee.

Aside from rare entries such as Rico Chung's intriguing 2011 *Mysterious Island*, set inside a murderous game show, the straight horror output of mainland China tends toward the blasé, formulaic, and derivative. Horror comedies, though, became box-office champs (as explored in the succeeding chapter).

The Indian subcontinent's vast film industry took a long time to get into the horror genre as well. When it did, it did so while in compliance with Bollywood formula, which states that a mainstream Indian film must be a musical, preferably one involving tragic romance, with a comic subplot or two. Surprisingly, India's first horror film *Mahal* (1949) fits all these criteria—but still manages to evoke some scares, though it's really more of a supernatural soap opera. Lovers divided by death scheme to reunite through murder (the premise was used in the 1975 American film *The Reincarnation of Peter Proud*). As with many Indian horror films to follow, it foregrounds ghosts and reincarnation. *Bees Saal Baad*, a spooky adaptation of *The Hound of the Baskervilles*, was a hit when it was released in 1962.

The team that finally kickstarted the Indian horror film was the Ramsinghani family, a father and seven sons who owned a chain of electronics stores in Karachi, Lahore, and Mumbai. They decided to move into film production and did so as the Ramsays. After several unsuccessful efforts that put them deeply in debt, in 1972 they risked making a horror film—*Do Gaz Zameen Ke Neeche*, aka *Two Yards Underground*. In it, a murdered husband returns as a vengeful zombie. The film transcends its bare-bones production values with some genuine scares. It was immensely profitable.

The Ramsays quickly became the kings of Indian horror film, cranking out twenty-six horror titles over the next forty-two years, in addition to much non-horror fare. Films of theirs such as *Purana Mandir*, aka *The Old Temple* (1984), and *Veerana* (1988) are still fondly regarded by many. Since the turn of the twenty-first century, Indian horror film has escaped its early strictures and now delivers a broad variety of standard-gauge horror.

In the Philippines, others followed the horror tradition that was started by Gerardo de Leon and Eddie Romero in the 1960s. It turns out the Philippines has an insane assemblage of mythical and monstrous creatures about which to make films. There are *duwende*, evil dwarfs;

manananggal, winged, half-bodied vampires; *aswang*, blood-sucking monsters disguised as humans; *tiyanak*, vampires disguised as infants; giant, tobacco-smoking tree giants named *kapre*; and many more—all of which figure in Philippine horror film.

The most successful Philippine horror director has been Chito S. Rono, whose *Sukob*, aka *The Wedding Curse* (2006), was a big hit, as was Yam Laranas's *Sigaw* (2004), which he was able to remake in the West as *The Echo* four years later. Beginning in 1984, Peque Gallaga, Lore Reyes, and others have created an ongoing horror anthology series, *Shake, Rattle, and Roll*, which is up to its fifteenth iteration as of this writing.

Indonesia and Malaysia's horror films parallel developments in the Philippines, featuring creatures such as *kuntilanaks* and *pontianaks*, female vampiric ghosts. Thailand's Banjong Pisanthanakun and Parkpoom Wongpoom have teamed up to create several engaging horror films (*Shutter*, 2004; *Alone*, 2007, *4bia*, 2008). Vietnam released its first horror movie in 2007, *Muoi: The Legend of a Portrait*.

The most up-and-down horror-film industry of the region has undoubtedly been Cambodia's.

The healthy beginnings of such were crushed by the dominance of the brutal Khmer Rouge regime in 1975; Vietnam ousted that murderous faction in 1979. The nation's film industry didn't come back to life until 1987. Then, in 1991, Vietnam withdrew from the country, after which Hong Kong and Thai movies flooded the Cambodian film market, crowding out native filmmakers. It took popular demand to restore an indigenous film industry to Cambodia in 2001. The first film made was *The Snake King's Child* . . . a horror film.

Film still from *Train to Busan* (2016).

THE PROBLEM OF TORTURE PORN

How far is too far? How much is too much?

A huge part of the appeal of horror is transgression. Horror shatters the surface of placid, boring old consensual reality. Horror must be revolutionary, it must shock, or it is worthless. A horror movie dares you to see it. It's a test. Can you take it?

But does extreme film horror have value? Isn't it just, as the trend was termed at the turn of the twenty-first century, "torture porn"? Isn't it just sadistic gratification, taken to the extreme? So what is the attraction of watching the infliction of pain and splatterings of gore?

There's the challenge of it, usually spurred by peer pressure—especially if you are in the free-spending and suggestible eighteen-to-twenty-five-year-old male demographic. There's the reflexive gut-grab thrill of it. Part of it is catharsis—the vicarious experience of violent or defensive impulses. There's defiance as well—the impulse to cross whatever line of acceptability society draws in the sand is eternal. Curious and headstrong members of mankind can often be accused of not leaving well enough alone, not unlike the mad scientists they watch onscreen.

And there are people who just get off on it. Sadism and misogyny are found in every culture. This extreme category of horror films is just another manifestation of that. Women are disproportionately the victims in these films, as they have been throughout horror's history. The slow erosion of resistance to taboo topics and images, made more vivid by improved special effects and, finally, the no-holds-barred freedoms of CGI around 2000, led to a rushing tide of unnerving movies the visuals of which rivaled Hieronymus Bosch's fifteenth-century visions of Hell.

The early specialists in these repulsive endeavors were the Italians, and the pioneer and prime transgressor was Lucio Fulci. Starting out as a screenwriter, he moved from comedies and other genres into *giallo*, striving for hyperrealism. His production of *A Lizard in a Woman's Skin* (1971), which featured disemboweled dogs,

caused him to be hauled into court on charges of animal cruelty, until his special-effects expert, the great Carlo Rambaldi, brought the dog puppets constructed for the film into the courtroom to prove that no animal abuse occurred.

Fulci's *Zombi 2* (1979) was so over-the-top graphic it had to be cut significantly to achieve less than an "X" and equivalent ratings in English-language markets. It had the same appeal of the "mondo" pseudo-documentary films of the 1960s and the "cannibal" films of the 1970s, the latter launched by Umberto Lenzi's *Man from Deep River* (1972). The key to all these films is that they purport to be "the real thing," revealing forbidden and violent acts such as rape, torture, murder, and cannibalism. They transmit the bedrock shock of the body's inescapable animalness, its vulnerability and mortality, its helplessness in the face of pain, bodily dissolution, and death.

From the beginning, Fulci's scripts were cynical and pointedly anti-religious. As he told more graphic stories, his tone darkened as well, becoming absolutely despairing and full

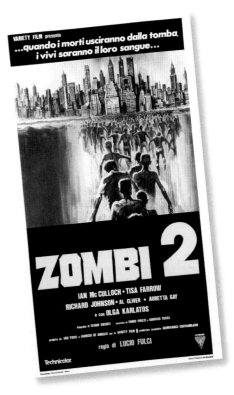

OPPOSITE: Detail from *The Garden of Earthly Delights* by Hieronymus Bosch.

Zombi 2 (1979) poster.

Man Bites Dog
(1992) poster.

The complete uncut version

A film by

**Remy Belvaux
Andre Bonzel
Benoit Poelvoorde**

Man Bites Dog

Winner Cannes 1992 Prix de la Critique Internationale

Cannes 1992 Prix de la Critique Française

Cannes 1992 Prix Spécial du Jury Prix de Jeunesse
Toronto Critics Award

Starring

Benoit Poelvoorde

Remy Belvaux

Andre Bonzel

18

*"Makes Reservoir Dogs
look like muzzled
mongrels".*
THE GUARDIAN

of sadism. His unofficial "Gates of Hell" trilogy, comprising *The City of the Dead* (1980), *The Beyond*, and *The House by the Cemetery* (both 1981), gradually abandon narrative altogether, compiling a series of bloody outrages before trailing off into incoherence, darkness, and despair. Working briskly, he completed many similar films until his death in 1996.

Contemporaries of Fulci, such as Lenzi, Ruggero Deodato, and the prolific Joe D'Amato, the last of whom made more than 200 films using more than four dozen aliases, all followed Fulci's lead, stimulating others in turn. In West Germany, Jorg Buttgereit's *Nekromantik* (1987) marked the beginning of graphic, government-banned "underground horror" by directors such as Andreas Schnaas, Olaf Ittenbach, and Timo Rose.

By 1984, British prosecutors developed a seventy-two-film list of "video nasties" deemed obscene, citing some of the work of the directors cited above, as well as films by Bava, Argento, Craven, Raimi, Hooper, and others. These films were variously banned, prosecuted, seized, destroyed, and/or restricted in a censorious effort that lasted until the early 2000s (and, of

course, this only increased their forbidden appeal worldwide).

The trend continued. Non-exploitation horror films upped their amounts of viscera as well. Remember, David Lynch's first feature film *Eraserhead* was initially notable for being almost unwatchably gruesome, but his surrealist, embryonic statement of the horror-tinged themes he was to pursue across his career seem pretty tame today (except for his thing-baby— never going to get over seeing that). Noted avant-garde filmmaker Alejandro Jodorowsky made *Santa Sangre* (1989), a heavy-handed horror story that plays like Fellini on crystal meth. Its circus-centered plot is heavily reminiscent of Browning's *Freaks*, but it's more graphic and perverse than even that act of transgression.

Andrzej Zulawski's brutal and fascinating 1981 *Possession* is a movie about the disintegration of a relationship couched in graphic style, as a murderous wife replaces her husband by constructing a doppelganger out of parts of her murder victims. This is a perfect nightmare of a film about the end of a relationship. Everything that can go wrong for the protagonist (Sam Neill) does as his unfaithful wife destroys him.

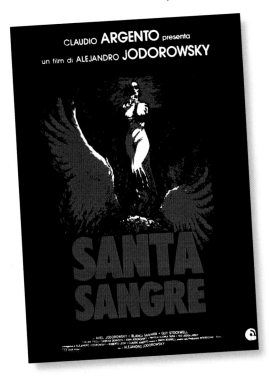

CLAUDIO **ARGENTO** presenta
un film di ALEJANDRO **JODOROWSKY**

SANTA SANGRE

AXEL JODOROWSKY • BLANCA GUERRA • GUY STOCKWELL

Santa Sangre
(1989) poster.

The aforementioned Rambaldi created a disturbing tentacled being whose lovemaking scene with Isabelle Adjani, who won Best Actress at Cannes that year for the role, is grimly unforgettable. It's the only film I can think of that was both honored at Cannes and banned in Britain.

Man Bites Dog (1992), from Belgium, is a fake documentary about a serial killer and the film crew tailing him who just can't help lending a hand. It's horribly graphic, and also the best film ever made about the mutually enabling symbiosis between criminal pathology and the media. The protagonist's camera-friendliness can't disguise his pseudo-intellectual self-satisfaction, misogyny, and racism. The quest to get the story means that killing and being killed become "occupational hazards."

Michele Soavi's *Cemetery Man* (1994) is ostensibly a zombie film, but is really an engaging delirium salad of sex and death. Rupert Everett plays the hero, who has to kill the dead who keep coming back to life, even as he pursues an ideal love in various guises, most of them corpses. Oliver Stone's hyper-stylized serial-killer black comedy romance *Natural Born Killers* (1994) upped the ante and stoked controversy. Adding elements of the romance, comedy, and action film to a gorefest was a way of making satirical points about America's violent culture, but many thought it hammered its points home way too hard.

Tarsem Singh's *The Cell* (2000), about a psychic investigator entering the dangerous subconscious of a serial killer, is terrifying and absolutely brilliant. A psychologist (Jennifer Lopez) must invade the mind of a schizophrenic, comatose killer in order to save the life of his latest victim. The representation of the psychic contents of an evil being have never been delineated as vividly as this, and it's unbearably

gruesome. Singh's dazzling visual style is unmatched, and the casting is perfect.

Mary Harron's *American Psycho* (2000) turns Bret Easton Ellis's 1991 novel about a yuppie serial killer into a comic parable about the dark impulses of the affluent and entitled. What do you get for the man who has everything? Victims for him to slaughter. A vain, trendy, and vapid investment banker (Christian Bale) is at its center. His life is so empty that he takes up serial killing as a hobby. Or does he? Harron's direction calls the narrator's reliability into account, so that even the killer's most resolute efforts aren't believed or even noticed.

Jennifer Lopez in a scene from *The Cell* (2000).

A copy of Bret Easton Ellis' novel *American Psycho*.

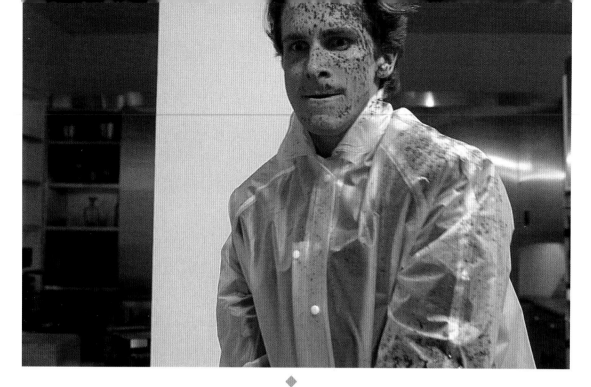

Christian Bale in *American Psycho* (2000).

All of these films had at least some artistic merit. Care had gone into their conception and execution, and they were all "serious" efforts, when compared to exploitation fare.

Given the financial success of more graphic fare and the evidence shown that it could be wielded in the service of a legitimate artistic effort, it was only logical that the practice would spread.

In Claire Denis's *Trouble Every Day* (2001), the impulse to rend flesh, to bite and to kill, takes over ordinary people. It makes no sense, and there is little narrative arc, but Denis's clear ideas make this is a chillingly cold examination of the animal roots of human behavior. This is the birth of the New French Extremity, a movement which despite its euphonious designation was largely torture porn Francais. Nonetheless, the trend produced some thoughtful films.

In Marina de Van's *In My Skin* (2002), self-mutilation becomes a metaphor for addiction. A seemingly fulfilled woman injures her leg by accident—and then begins cutting herself. A genuine psychological problem becomes a metaphor for our cult of physical perfectibility. In Fabrice du Welz's *Calvaire* (2004), a young man is put into the unenviable position of being the sexual object of an entire deranged village. Marc, a traveling performer, pulls into a small town, looking for a place to spend the night. Unfortunately, he's wandered into a village full

Director James Wan (left) and actor Cary Elwes on the set of *Saw* (2004).

of maniacs, all of whom want him as their "wife." *Calvaire* means "calvary," and crucifixion turns out to be Marc's least challenging problem.

The American family of *Dead End* (2003) is trapped in a gory comedy of manners. Arthouse favorite Gaspar Noé began his career with two highly transgressive films: *I Stand Alone* (1998) is about the dead-end life of a released killer, while *Irréversible* (2002) is a time-in-reverse study of violence and revenge. By and large, though, New French Extremity films such as *Frontiers* and *Inside* (both 2007) and *Martyrs* (2008) seemed to want to do little more than test the audience's intestinal fortitude.

The phenomenal success of James Wan's *Saw* franchise, beginning in 2004, cemented

a nice guy—save for the fact that he likes to kill women using his car. The larger *Grindhouse* film is punctuated with five very funny faux trailers for coming exploitation attractions such as *Werewolf Women of the SS*.

By 2009, torture porn's day in the sun was pretty much over, supplanted by a new wave of horror remakes and reboots, the reinstitution of another cycle of familiarity. Torture porn continued to be made and consumed, but it found its audiences via more discreet platforms such as DVDs and online streaming—much like sexual pornography itself.

So there are examples of extremely graphic horror films that possess quality, and many, many more that don't—about the same percentage as in any other subgenre of film or other art. Is it worth it? To the extent that it has a soul-destroying effect on the less-aware, the mentally vulnerable, and the sadistically inclined—no, not really.

the mainstream public's taste for graphic sadism. *Saw* is a throwback to the depiction of the Puritan punishments of transgressors as dramatized in the "moral fiction" of earlier times. Jigsaw, Wan's evil mastermind, plays moral games with his victims, torturing and killing them to fulfill his own unique code of justice. Eli Roth's *Hostel* (2005) went further, postulating a torture chamber that's a private club, kept for the enjoyment of its paying members, and stocked with unwitting, annoying exchange students traveling on Eurail passes.

Outrage greeted each new release in the subgenre. Finally, Quentin Tarantino and Robert Rodriguez's epic double-feature tribute *Grindhouse* seemed to wrap public interest in the phenomena, tying the trend back to its cheap exploitation-film roots.

This gaudy, greasy, grimy salute to the vulgar horror films of yesteryear is a three-hours-plus double feature, designed to resemble the program of the typical cheap movie house of the 1970s. (After it failed in theaters, the studio broke it into two films and redistributed it that way.)

Rodriguez scores first with the zombie fest *Planet Terror* (2007), featuring a heroine with a machine gun for a leg. Meanwhile, Tarantino's part of the double feature, *Death Proof*, concerns Stuntman Mike (Kurt Russell), who's a heck of

20

ZOMBIES!

SHE WAS NOT
ALIVE . . . NOR
DEAD . . . Just a

WHITE ZOMBIE

*Performing
his every*

Zombies are the slogging foot soldiers of horror film. Generic, anonymous, shedding parts hither and thither, they first shambled slowly and stiffly toward us, then picked up the pace as the decades progressed. We are currently up to our necks in zombies. How did they become so popular?

Perhaps it's because, given that zombies have no souls, we can project whatever we want onto them. The zombie film, scorned as the cheapest, grossest, and most amateurish of horror subgenres, proved to be one of the most durable and flexible out there. It's especially potent as black comedy: we have zombie rom-coms, zombie musicals, zombie Westerns, zombie martial-arts epics . . .

The first zombies on film were enchanted slaves, then the undead; now they're the infected. Precisely because it is such a generic concept, the zombie is a horror archetype that, like no other except, perhaps, the slasher, can mutate at will to meet the needs of succeeding generations.

The concept of the animated corpse in literature is ancient, stretching back to the Sumerian epic of Gilgamesh. It didn't really catch on as a coherent cultural concept, however, until 1929, when occultist and explorer William Seabrook published his book *The Magic Island*, about Haitian voodoo and witchcraft. Seabrook gave us the original definition of a zombie: a dead person brought back to life and controlled by a magician, made into a soulless slave. In this sense, the zombie is close in spirit (or rather spiritlessness) to the Golem, or Cesare the somnambulist in *The Cabinet of Dr. Caligari.*

The official debut of the zombie in horror film came in Victor Halperin's *White Zombie* (1932), in which evil voodoo master "Murder" Legendre (Bela Lugosi) enslaves souls for work on a sugar cane plantation. Here, zombies are a metaphor for the victims of colonialism. Legendre turns the native workers into perfect employees. They are docile, silent, and uncomplaining. They need no food or rest. In an offhand moment of horror early in the film, one of the zombies trips and falls silently into a vat where enormous

Santo vs. the Zombies (1962) poster.

blades turned by the workers churn the sugar cane to pulp. Without a pause, without a sound other than the ominous ongoing creaking of the machinery, the work continues as the victim is silently sliced to pieces.

The time wasn't right, though, for zombies to take center stage. Unlike marquee monsters such as Dracula and Frankenstein, zombies had nothing distinctive going for them. As the phrase "living dead" implies, they were not exactly the life of the party. They began to pop up here and there in horror films, especially horror-comedies.

Zombies made great henchmen (*Santo vs. the Zombies*, 1962) and random sources of menace (*Revolt of the Zombies*, 1936); in 1940's *The Ghost Breakers*, the token zombie is played by that wonderful and prolific African-American character actor Noble Johnson, the boyhood pal of Lon Chaney Sr. The notable exceptions were Jacques Tourneur's astonishing, melancholy beauty *I Walked with A Zombie* (1943), discussed earlier, and the charming *Plague of the Zombies* (1966), directed by John Gilling for Hammer Studios, concerning the solution to a daunting labor problem in a Cornish tin mine.

It took the inspiration of budding independent Pittsburgh filmmakers George A. Romero, John Russo, and Russell Streiner to

OPPOSITE: *White Zombie* (1932) poster.

I Walked with a Zombie (1943) poster.

dread of being preyed upon is still all-powerful within us, lurking below the surface. In zombies, we find the most intimidating predators of all. They are soulless, remorseless, relentless. Like the shark in Spielberg's *Jaws*, they are nearly unstoppable killing machines. (This lack of characterization is shared by the slasher film, embodied in its search-and-kill, video-game-like framework.)

Though they may resemble, or in fact be, our beloved family and friends, the as-yet-unbitten protagonists of the zombie film can "kill" them indiscriminately, reflexively, en masse and individually, using bullets, bombs, blades, what have you. Zombies are an inexhaustible source of menace, and an easy target for guilt-free violence and mayhem. This encouragement of vigilante-style violence merged with other trends to feed a surge in sadistic, callous horror cinema.

The zombie subgenre put forth rotting blossoms. In Spain, it produced Amando de Ossorio's *Tombs of the Blind Dead* four-film series (1972–1975) and Jorge Grau's wonderful *Let Sleeping Corpses Lie*, aka *The Living Dead at the Manchester Morgue* (1974). It also inspired no fewer than three Paul Naschy films in 1973: *Return of the Zombies* (he plays Igor, the grave robber), *Horror Rises from the Tomb* (he plays a warlock), and *Vengeance of the Zombies* (he plays a zombie and Satan).

George A. Romero found that a zombie-film franchise could carry a lot of metaphorical freight. His *Dawn of the Dead* (1978) goofed on

craft the game-changing *Night of the Living Dead* (1968). Russo and Romero's screenplay gives zombies a new origin story, motivation, and a set of "rules" that would come to redefine the zombie film. Now the menace came specifically from the reanimated dead.

The cause of their resurrection in *Living Dead* is vaguely attributed to a satellite spreading radiation on its return to Earth's atmosphere. What were originally termed "ghouls" and "flesh eaters" in the *Living Dead* script were now carnivores, with a definite preference for consuming living human flesh. Vulnerabilities? Well, they moved very slowly, and could be stopped altogether if their brains were destroyed.

This reconfiguration fueled an exponential burst of zombie movies. Why? First, they were cheap to make. As Romero and company had shown, zombie movies could be made for very little, and could gross an insane amount of money. The subgenre asked for little in the way of special effects or makeup; in Argentina's *Plaga zombie* (1997), the primary makeup ingredient was cake mix, and the feature-length zombie film *Colin* (2008) had a budget of $70.

Next, they reduced everything to a simple formula: hunted vs. hunters. Mankind has been the Earth's apex predator for a long time, but the

Best Horror Movies for Date Night
Candidates for flicks that will make you clutch each other.
Carrie (1976)

Scream (1996)

Sleepy Hollow (1999)

You're Next (2011)

Warm Bodies (2013)

consumer culture. In that film, Romero returned to his breakthrough modern zombie concept, staying with his homegrown aesthetic and turning horror into a potent source of social satire. Four survivors of the zombie plague hole up at a shopping mall, where the walking dead return out of habit. Throw in a feral pack of bikers and plenty of ammo, and you've got yourself a funny, self-aware classic.

Lucio Fulci's *The Beyond* (1981) was a depressing meditation on zombiehood as pain and nothingness. As Glenn Kay eloquently summarizes in *Zombie Movies: The Ultimate Guide*, "Life itself is a nightmare but our only sanctuary is to remain in this world, because what is beyond is worse."[1]

The prolific and inventive Dan O'Bannon expanded and codified the living-dead template with his now-disowned but still gripping *Dead & Buried* (1981), as well as the more distinctive and funny (check out the antics of horror regulars James Karen, Don Calfa, and Clu Gulager) *The Return of the Living Dead*, from 1985, in which it's established in zombie canon that zombies prefer brains, the consumption of which helps ease the pain of being undead. Natch.

A sea change in the behavior of zombies would take place with the premiere of *The Evil Dead* in 1981. Its director, Sam Raimi, possessed by the need to make movies, quit college and, with his friend, future character actor Bruce Campbell, and others, spent $90,000 to make *The Evil Dead*. In it, five college kids find the Necronomicon, a fictional Lovecraftian book of dark magic, in an old cabin, and possession and

dismemberment hijinks proceed apace. This bargain-basement effort is meticulously crafted, with tons of disturbing effects and lots of fresh, inventive camerawork.

Through pluck and luck, Raimi and company got the film shown at Cannes and picked up a positive blurb from, of all people, Stephen King. *The Evil Dead* quickly became a cult favorite. Raimi would make it a trilogy with the follow-ups, *Evil Dead II* (1987) and *Army of Darkness* (1992).

Raimi's horror has energy, a kind of mad exuberance that owes not a little to the Three Stooges. Those movies would pile on corny humor and gross effects that added up to a kind of "splatstick" comedy-horror hybrid. The protagonist, Ash Williams (Campbell), is a wisenheimer with a chainsaw arm, a cynic whose sense of humor is definitely the darkest of all the action heroes of the 1980s. "Good. Bad. I'm the guy with the gun," he muses at one point after

Bruce Campbell in a promotional image for T*he Evil Dead* (1981).

INSET: *The Evil Dead* (1981) poster.

Braindead (1992) poster.

blowing away his evil medieval twin, one of the "deadites." Both Campbell and Raimi would move on to more mainstream work. (As though on a dare, though, Raimi returned to the genre with the delightful *Drag Me to Hell* in 2009, proving that the old master still had his horror chops. Campbell, in turn, has a healthy sense of humor about his place in the horror pantheon.)

It definitely pushed zombie movies toward horror-comedy (China's hopping-vampire horror comedies were initiated by Sammo Hung around the same time). It also moved filmmakers into Lovecraftian horror. Raimi's horror is a jolting hybrid of both. It turns out that Lovecraft's twisted version of reality, in which everyday life was only a rude patch over an insane, brutal universe ruled by dark deities with unpronounceable names . . . needed some jokes.

Then came Stuart Gordon and Brian Yuzna's Lovecraft adaptation, *Re-Animator*, in 1985. In it, the mad scientist role goes to the arrogant Herbert West (an iconic performance by Jeffrey Combs), who has invented a serum that brings the dead back to life. Unfortunately, it brings them back in a psychotic, frenzied, and violent state. Under the sway of his beheaded nemesis (a deliciously villainous performance from David Gale), the dead attack the living with abandon.

At the other end of the spectrum, Wes Craven made the beautiful, low-key film fictionalization of ethnobotanist Wade Davis's book on Haitian voodoo, *The Serpent and the Rainbow* (1988). Here the creation of zombies is linked to the maintenance of political power, part of a terroristic grip maintained on a superstitious populace.

An essential director who got a leg up thanks to his use of zombies was Peter Jackson, who, prior to making his *Lord of the Rings* movies, directed the DIY alien-invasion horror comedy *Bad Taste* (1987). He followed it with the splatstick *Braindead*, aka *Dead Alive*, in 1992. Both exhibit the influence of Raimi and other American horror directors of the '80s. Jackson's *Heavenly Creatures* (1994), ostensibly a true-crime story, is really about two teenage girls falling into an alternate universe of delusion that leads to murder, the most subtly horrifying film Jackson has made yet. (His *The Frighteners*, 1996, an attempt to create a Bob Zemeckis-style romp, was a bit of a damp squib.)

As the zombie film grew in popularity, it became more schematic. The idea of slaughtering your way through a universe of the undead made perfect sense for a

Jeffrey Combs as Dr. Herbert West in *Re-Animator* (1985).

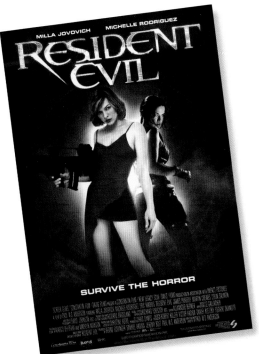

Resident Evil
(2002) poster.

video game. Beginning with *Resident Evil* (1996), other digital zombie-killing games such as *House of the Dead* (1997), *Left 4 Dead* (2008), *Red Dead Redemption: Undead Nightmares* (2010), and even *Plants vs. Zombies* (2009) made millions of fans. *Resident Evil* the movie (directed by Paul W. S. Anderson, 2002; Anderson helmed the graphic sci-fi/horror gem *Event Horizon* in 1997) spawned no fewer than five sequels.

As the steam ran out of the subgenre, zombie films got cheesier, including such recurring elements as Nazis and strippers. (Both represent notable transgressive absolutes—death and sex—and as such appeal directly to that ideal nineteen-year-old male customer.) One outstanding example is grimly satirical *Uncle Sam* (1996), in which a dead soldier comes back to life on the Fourth of July and starts slaughtering everyone in town— the inimitable indie filmmaker Larry Cohen wrote the script.

But what if a zombie movie was treated seriously, with strong production values and convincing performances? The innovative, Oscar-winning director Danny Boyle took a shot at it with *28 Days Later* (2002), in the process fundamentally changing the zombie movie a second time.

Just as *Night of the Living Dead* did, *28 Days Later* revived the zombie genre, combining it in this instance with a post-apocalyptic scenario. An easily spread "rage virus" turns the dead into superhuman manic killers, hastening the collapse of society. Boyle's ability to capture character and relationships on screen make this far more interesting than most films about the undead. Plus, he makes his zombies move at full speed and beyond, making them much more dangerous and terrifying.

Eli Roth, a master of body-horror, began his string of hits with virus-caused zombie-style mayhem in *Cabin Fever* the same year, as did

Cillian Murphy
in *28 Days Later*
(2002).

Film still from *House of 1000 Corpses* (2003).

the now-prominent Zack Snyder's first directorial outing.

In Bruce McDonald's *Pontypool* (2008), a shock-jock's morning radio show is interrupted by an outbreak of zombies. This time, however, the virus that triggers the plague is language itself. It's a fascinating examination of the relation between meaning and menace. In Spain, Jaume Balagueró and Paco Plaza crafted a pair of great found-footage zombie films in *[REC]* (2007) and *[REC 2]* (2009). The zombie film went to Africa in *The Dead* (2010) and to Cuba in the hilarious *Juan of the Dead* (2011).

Danny Boyle produced a zombie sequel, the equally intriguing *28 Weeks Later* (2007). *World War Z* (2013), based on the bestselling novel by Max Brooks, was a big-budget hit starring Brad Pitt. There were more "zom-coms" such as *Warm Bodies* (2013) and *Life After Beth* (2014). There's even a Christmas-themed zombie musical comedy, *Anna and the Apocalypse* (2017).

Today, the term zombie can mean anything from a live soul under the control of another's

heavy metal musician Rob Zombie (aka Bob Cummings), who directed *House of 1000 Corpses* a year later. Zombies were hot again.

Ironically, the word "zombie" is rarely heard in a zombie movie—euphemisms such as "infected," "biters," and "walkers" are used. In Edgar Wright's zombie comedy *Shaun of the Dead* (2004), the lead character refuses to use the term because it's "ridiculous!" *Shaun of the Dead* gives us a wimpy protagonist who can barely tell the difference between the living and the dead to begin with, and plays with the subgenre, turning it into a redemptive saga.

The hits just kept on coming. Romero continued his zombie chronicles with *Land of the Dead* (2005), the found-footage *Diary of the Dead* (2007), and *Survival of the Dead* (2009). *Night of the Living Dead* was remade for copyright purposes in 1990 (a simple error in the original print made it part of the public domain; this meant that Romero lost millions), and a *Dawn of the Dead* remake (2004) marked

(from left to right) Dylan Moran, Kate Ashfield, Simon Pegg, and Lucy Davis in *Shaun of the Dead* (2004).

This tribute to man's baser proclivities is what stands for a concept of strength now, in a time when the United States has chosen to break off with the world, to indulge its most deep-set prejudices, to openly hate and discriminate, to live in a simmering state of fear. Fast decisions and brutal actions are the answer. Kill them before they kill you. Worst-case thinking in a cynical time.

Who knows? Maybe fighting zombies is just a psychologically useful phase for society right now . . . and not a rehearsal for the end times.

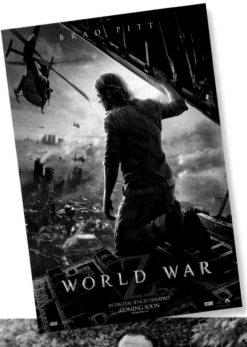

World War Z (2013) poster.

Andrew Lincoln in a scene from *The Walking Dead* (2010–2022).

will, to an infected maniac, to a corpse reanimated via voodoo, virus, and/or radiation. The twenty-first century has seen an exponential increase in zombie films and TV shows, exemplified by the long-running TV drama *The Walking Dead* (2010–2022).

Why do we seem to need zombies now? Zombies make great antagonists; soulless, they can be destroyed easily and without any moral qualms. As metaphors, they easily stand for whatever undesirable people the viewer might fantasize about killing without remorse—immigrants, unbelievers, the damned, the diseased. In other words, the superfluous. These designated monsters of America's psyche are numerous, and constantly shifting toward us.

Zombies also allow us to indulge in the cultural fatalism that usually accompanies the end of empires—America's, in this instance. What if the end times are here? What would we do in the face of the zombie apocalypse?

And how would we do it? America's macho, paranoid, survivalist mentality is on full display in the actions of the heroes and heroines of zombie films. In these films, problems aren't solved by scientists or the government; they are solved by resourceful rednecks with baseball bats, hatchets, and shotguns.

THERE'S USUALLY
A GORILLA

HORROR-COMEDIES

STIFFEN YOU WITH
LAUGHTER!

Comedy and horror naturally go together. Each one provides a primal release, one that short-circuits common sense. Comedy and horror share certain traits. Both disciplines demand timing, nuance, and surprise in order to deliver immediate, quantifiable results. You either laugh, or you don't. You scream, or you don't.

Comedy and horror work together intricately. When the point-of-view camera moves up behind the victim, we grow apprehensive, holding our breath—but then another shot reveals that it's only the pizza-delivery guy. What do we do? We laugh, of course, discharging that fight-or-flight impulse pleasantly. (Then, while we're relaxed for a second, that's when the good horror director goes for the scare.)

The horror-comedy subgenre is intertwined chronologically with the "serious" horror genre. These movies run parallel to, slightly behind, and in the perpetual shadow of the movies they mirror and mock. Always popular, they form a substantial body of commentary on, and criticism of, the horror genre as it has developed. Sometimes they even introduced new ideas, techniques, and archetypes.

Comedy has been used to mitigate horror in Western culture since the plays of the ancient Greeks. A gory tragedy would be followed by a satyr-play, a bawdy and nonsensical burlesque that served as comic relief from the heavy drama going down all day in Greek theatrical festivals. This kind of "dancing out" of forbidden impulses frames the serious action, transitioning the audience comfortably away from it as well (a traditional end-of-play dance at Shakespeare performances in today's Globe Theatre in London performs a similar function, breaking the tragic spell). Satyr-plays were seen as cruder fare than more literate traditional "comedy." They were the ancient equivalent of Three Stooges films, creating mayhem much as monsters did—comic mayhem. Like horror, comedy was an anarchic outpouring that provided communal catharsis.

By 1803, Jane Austen was already mocking the Gothic thriller in her parody novel *Northanger Abbey*—history's first horror-comedy. The heroine of this juvenile effort, Catherine Morland, is a kind of female Don Quixote, who is disabused of her genre-based illusions; less than forty years into the modern era of the horror genre, its conventions were already so universally familiar that the general reader got the jokes.

In silent film, scary situations were naturally built into comedy structures, situations, and gags. The first horror-comedy starred the stock "rube" character Uncle Josh, haunted thanks to a stop-motion ghost in *Uncle Josh in a Spooky Hotel* (1900). Silent comedy star Harold Lloyd made *Haunted Spooks* in 1920, and Buster Keaton made *The Haunted House* in 1921.

Before teaming with Oliver Hardy, Stan Laurel made the parody *Dr. Pyckle and Mr. Pryde* (1925); Laurel and Hardy's 1927 *Do Detectives Think?* contains a classic sequence in which the timid duo attempt to retrieve their hats from a graveyard on a windy night. In 1929's *Movie Night*, Charley Chase attempts to scare away his daughter's hiccups. The kid takes one look at him clad as a ghost and passes out. The Three Stooges made regular use of spooks in

OPPOSITE: *Bela Lugosi Meets a Brooklyn Gorilla* (1952) poster.

Laurel and Hardy face ghosts and killers in *Do Detectives Think?* (1927).

films such as *If a Body Meets a Body* (1945) and *The Ghost Talks* (1949).

The transition from silent horror to sound was aided greatly by the horror-comedy "old dark house" movie, a blend of mystery, horror, melodrama, and comedy. What writer Mark Vieira terms the "mystery/farce"[1] was adapted from a spate of popular stage plays of the period, including Paul Dickey and Charles Goddard's *Ghost Breaker* in 1909, Mary Roberts Rinehart and Avery Hopgood's *The Bat* in 1920, and John Willard's *The Cat and the Canary* in 1922. Each provoked numerous film adaptations through the years. *Ghost Breaker* spawned film versions in 1914, 1922, 1940, and, lastly, in 1953 with *Scared Stiff*, the basis for a Dean Martin/Jerry Lewis musical comedy.

Hollywood, with its voracious appetite for pre-tested crowd-pleasing material, snatched up the rights to these plays. The "old dark house" films worked twice over. The visual elements carried the silent versions, and the sound remakes had stage-tested dialogue on which to build. Both versions featured murderers in disguise, endangered heirs, a multitude of suspects, high-contrast lighting, and grotesque performances.

The best and most emblematic of these is Paul Leni's 1927 *The Cat and the Canary*. Leni mixed humor and scares with masterful judiciousness, using a freewheeling camera and advanced techniques such as underlighting, dissolves, and superimpositions.

In the "old dark house" story, there is always a logical explanation for the supernatural goings-on. Justice, either legal or rough, is served at the end. (The horror-comedy lives in perpetuity, most recently in the universe of TV's animated *Scooby-Doo* series, about a quartet of mystery-

solving teens and the hound of the title.) The supernatural aspect is debunked.

In the same way, Leni took the unsettling avant-garde techniques of Expressionism and tamed them, turned them to tricks that were equally capable of serving a silly horror-comedy as they were a stark, weighty, experimental film. Leni's attention to ambiance and detail, and his invigorating freeness with film as a medium, percolated into the sensibilities of American filmmakers in every genre. And Universal had another horror hit on its hands.

Variations on the theme issued forth from all the studios—*The Monster* (1925), *The Thirteenth Guest* (1932), *The Monster Walks* (1932), *The Ghost Walks* (1934), *One Frightened Night* (1935), *The Rogues' Tavern* (1936), *The Gorilla* (1939)—and finally spoofs, starting with James Whale's witty 1932 deconstruction *The Old Dark House*. In it, a dark and stormy night traps a house full of travelers and eccentrics together, leading to deadly dangers. It features Whale regulars Karloff and Ernest Thesiger; tongue firmly in cheek, Melvyn Douglas goes up against Charles Laughton in the latter's first American film.

And there was usually a gorilla. This is one of those seemingly inexplicable Hollywood tropes.

Why, over and over, did gorillas menace our heroes and heroines? The idea of a frightening, deadly anthropoid is as old as Poe's 1841 story "The Murders in the Rue Morgue" (to be fair, that was actually a rather large orangutan). Gorillas weren't even observed in the wild until the relatively recent date of 1856. Their novelty, their human resemblance, and their relation to the evolution debate of the late nineteenth century put them in the public's mind as a paradigm of frightening, dangerous, subhuman ferociousness.

Ralph Spence's hit 1925 play *The Gorilla* introduced the idea of a killer in an ape suit. *The Gorilla* wound up being made into films in 1927, 1930, and 1939 (and there's a version in which an octopus takes the place of a gorilla, the prosaically titled *Sh! The Octopus*, in 1937). A few actors made donning a gorilla suit their specialty—the first was Charles Gemora, followed by others such as Ray "Crash" Corrigan, George Barrows, Steve Calvert, and Emil van Horn. It was a fast and cheap way to throw some scares into a horror movie (much like zombies), and a good comic could milk an array of frightened takes, double-takes, and triple-takes in the presence of a big, threatening monkey.

The worst of these was probably *Bela Lugosi Meets a Brooklyn Gorilla*, filmed in one week in 1952 by prolific cheapie director William "One-Shot" Beaudine, starring the sadly decayed Lugosi alongside a Jerry Lewis imitator, seventeen-year-old adenoidal pest Sammy Petrillo. The silly tradition continued. The first movie made by comedy-horror expert John Landis was the parody *Schlock* (1973), in which he also starred as the prehistoric ape-man of the title—in a gorilla suit.

A couple of horror-comedy classics were made during the 1940s, including Frank Capra's *Arsenic and Old Lace* (1944) and Chuck Jones's *Hair-Raising Hare* (1946). *Arsenic* is still one of the most popular plays produced in America, and the film is an adaptation of Joseph Kesselring's 1941 Broadway hit, filmed in the same year but not released until 1944, when the play's long Broadway run had finally ended.

It's the story of two sweet spinsters from a prominent old American family in Brooklyn who happen to be benevolent and circumspect homicidal maniacs. Their nephew Mortimer (Cary Grant), a hapless drama critic who hates the theatre, attempts to commit them to an institution while dealing with his equally deadly older brother Jonathan, on the lam and disguised badly by plastic surgery. "He said I looked like Boris Karloff!" exclaims Jonathan, excusing his latest murder. That Karloff himself originated the role of Jonathan on Broadway was a self-referential treat for audiences and the actor as well. (Ironically, Karloff was replaced in the film by Raymond Massey, precisely because Karloff was still playing to packed Arsenic houses on Broadway and couldn't get out of his stage contract.)

Arsenic combined the gruesome, the whimsical, and the farcical in perfect proportion. The animated short *Hair-Raising Hare* injects stock horror characters into the Bugs Bunny template, in which the offended mammal destroys those who scheme against him. In this outing, Bugs is lured by a sexy bunny robot to a castle that is helpfully adorned with a flashing neon sign that discreetly reads "EVIL SCIENTIST." As usual, someone wants to eat

(Clockwise from bottom left) Priscilla Lane, Jean Adair, Cary Grant, and Josephine Hull in *Arsenic and Old Lace* (1944).

him. Once inside, Bugs goes into combat mode with the mad doctor (a Peter Lorre lookalike) and his giant hungry hairy orange monster, clad in sneakers. The usual slapstick mayhem culminates with Bugs frightening the monster away by breaking the fourth wall and pointing out the audience to him. "PEE-PUL!" it screams, and dashes away from the camera to the vanishing point, tearing monster-shaped holes in the scenery as he goes. We are by far the scariest thing at the horror movie.

The comedy duo of thin, exasperated straight man Bud Abbott and short, fat gagster and designated 'fraidy-cat Lou Costello had been together for a decade, but their popularity was slipping. They had already done their variation on the haunted-house film with *Hold That Ghost* in 1941.

Then Universal paired them with Frankenstein, Dracula, and the Wolf Man in *Abbott and Costello Meet Frankenstein* (1948). "The laughs are MONSTERous! Bud and Lou are in a stew when they tangle with the titans of TERROR!" declared one poster for the film. The potent combination of the monsters' attacks and the comics' fright takes was incredibly popular, leading to four more horror-related, ever-worsening *Abbott and Costello Meets . . .* efforts.

However, Hollywood took note again. Scares plus laughs equaled big box office.

Roger Corman and his gang at American International Pictures didn't just turn out classy Technicolor horror product, based on Poe and Lovecraft. They churned out horror-comedies such as *Invasion of the Saucer Men* (1957), *A Bucket of Blood* (1959), *Little Shop of Horrors* (1960), *Creature from the Haunted Sea* (1961), *The Raven* (1963), and *The Comedy of Terrors* (1964).

Little Shop of Horrors was shot in two days at a cost of $30,000. It was a so-bad-it's-good cult classic for many years. The story is strong, however. A nebbishy flower-shop clerk, Seymour, breeds a wonderful plant that makes his fortune. The problem: it thrives on human blood. The film sparked an Off-Broadway musical comedy adaptation in 1982, which launched the careers of Disney musical greats Alan Menken and Howard Ashman. The film version of the Menken/Ashman production was made in 1986, given an imposed happy ending and a slightly larger budget: $25 million.

The Comedy of Terrors is a superior black farce written by Richard Matheson, directed by the ever-dependable Jacques Tourneur in 1963. AIP was good at corny humor (these were the days of *Beach Party* and Eric von Zipper), but this comedy is actually funny, with a well-diagrammed farcical plot, featuring most of the rogue's gallery of Karloff, Rathbone, Price, and, as the romantic lead, Peter Lorre, appropriately enough. It's the story of an unscrupulous undertaker (Price) who has to make some killings in order to make a living.

Mel Brooks's *Young Frankenstein* (1974) is one of the funniest film comedies in history, taking the familiar mad doctor premise and running it through the wringer. Brooks was a television comedy writer, who burst into popularity with his Western parody *Blazing Saddles*, released earlier the same year. *Young Frankenstein* plays with the structure and content of the original series of Universal Studios' *Frankenstein* movies, banking on the audience's familiarity with their characters and incidents.

This parody of Universal's *Frankenstein* cycle works due to a brilliant ensemble cast and a sardonic affection for the original films. The respect for the original production design is enormous: Brooks even found and used Ken Strickfaden's laboratory apparatus created for the 1932 original. In this version, Frankenstein's embarrassed grandson (Gene Wilder) reluctantly goes back to Transylvania to claim his inheritance. Of course, he begins "vollowing in hiss grantfadda's FOOTSHTEPS!"

Young Frankenstein plays in a series of scenes much like a connected burst of short TV comedy sketches, and the style is broad and full of shtick, even breaking the fourth wall to address the viewer. Brooks kept up his line of parodies, ending in 1995 with *Dracula: Dead and Loving It*, which tried to capture the Young Frankenstein vibe but failed.

In an extremely different way, Jim Sharman's 1975 *The Rocky Horror Picture Show* leaned hard on the same kind of audience familiarity. It's a "midnight movie" that married the musical comedy to the classic horror film—and to glitter rock and a drag-queen festival. Co-creators Richard O'Brien (who also plays Riff Raff, the skeevy, cadaverous butler) and Sharman turned the Mad Doctor/Creature story into a farce about the lure of alternative sexualities, in which Dr. Frank N. Furter (Tim Curry, in full makeup, corset, and stockings) creates his perfect mate, a beefy blond surfer boy in gold lame trunks, Rocky.

The intrusion of a naïve young straight couple, Brad and Janet, leads to bizarre complications. All of this is set to rock songs and framed as a kind of EC Comics horror tale narrated by the criminologist, played by Charles Gray (a nice reference as Gray was a Hammer horror regular).

These two films proved that the archetypes of the horror film were thoroughly understood by the average filmgoer. They also demonstrated that horror characters and stories were flexible. Old horror premises could be reworked, made fresh and relevant again.

A bumper crop of successful horror-comedies were released during the 1980s. Hong Kong filmmakers

Marty Feldman as Igor in *Young Frankenstein* (1974).

Rick Moranis (left) and the ghost Slimer, voiced by Ivan Reitman, in *Ghostbusters* (1984).

came up with a comedy/horror/action hybrid formula, beginning with Sammo Hung's entertaining *Encounters of the Spooky Kind* in 1980. Mixing horror, martial arts, and comedy, it sparked numerous *jiangshi*—zombie-vampires, reanimated corpses that steal the qi, or life energy, of their victims—movies. Ricky Lau's *Mr. Vampire* (1985) sparked four sequels, and even an affectionate remake/tribute in 2013, *Rigor Mortis*. Actor Lam Ching-Ying played Taoist priest "One-Brow" Master Gau, an Asian Van Helsing equivalent, in *Mr. Vampire*, a role he would reprise in many other films before his death at forty-four in 1997.

The tone of most Hollywood horror was humorous in the 1980s, especially after the record-breaking success of Ivan Reitman's *Ghostbusters* (1984).

Ghostbusters is a perfect blend of haunted-house tale, buddy comedy, adventure film, and special-effects extravaganza. A trio of eccentric, devil-may-care paranormal researchers start their own ghost-extraction service, and their exuberant, hipper-than-thou, smart-alecky approach calls to mind the tone of the Crosby-Hope "road" movies.

A horror movie was now the feel-good movie of the decade. In fact, a hallmark of mainstream 1980s horror is its cheery, cute, kid-friendly,

Gizmo in *Gremlins* (1984).

upbeat tone—much closer in tone to the likes of funhouse fantasy, such as that found in the Joe Dante's 1984 hit *Gremlins.*

Joe Dante was the premier horror-comedy director of the day, rivaled only by his friend John Landis. "People forget that comedy and horror are the two genres that get the least respect and are by far the most difficult," said Landis.[2]

Both directors openly adore and celebrate the cheesy delights of 1950s sci-fi/horror, and their films are crammed with references to that period. Their films have the wacky, exuberant energy of cartoons, punctuated with very gripping, state-of-the-visual-effect horror sequences. Both directors have also done good non-genre films, in up-and-down careers typical of Hollywood. Landis's *An American Werewolf in London* (1981) had the same dark humor and snappy banter found in his previous film, the huge comedy hit *Animal House* (1978), and added Oscar-winning special-effects transformations by Rick Baker.

In *An American Werewolf in London*, an exchange student is bitten on the English moors; his murdered buddy comes back from the dead,

nagging him to kill himself so that he won't victimize others when he transforms. Our hero is reluctant to face the truth. Landis undercuts Rick Baker's shattering and revolutionary makeup and prosthetic transformations (it hurts to become a werewolf) with droll humor and genre gags.

Joe Dante couldn't put a foot wrong. In his *The Howling* (1981), he turns the werewolf movie inside out, making them creatures who go into therapy in an effort to stop changing into monsters and killing people. Dante loves to cast horror vets, and here can be seen such horror stalwarts as actors John Carradine, Kevin McCarthy, Kenneth Tobey, Dick Miller, and even, in cameo roles, director Roger Corman and Forrest J. Ackerman.

Dante distorts, inverts, and otherwise plays with every Wolfman-movie convention there is. Both *American Werewolf* and *Howling* are full of references to the Golden Age horror taken in by the Baby Boomer generation on late-night TV.

The same is true for Dante's biggest hit, *Gremlins*—which opened the same weekend as *Ghostbusters*. A cautionary tale about responsibility, it unleashes cute little creatures called mogwai that easily multiply and become murderous devils, all in a wintry Christmas setting. There was even a merchandising angle, as there was for *Ghostbusters*—a new development for horror film, but one that would become increasingly common.

Dante would continue with upbeat, jokey, special-effects-rich hits such as *Innerspace* (1987)

and the inevitable *Gremlins 2: The New Batch* (1990). Dante's delirious memory piece *Matinee* (1993) centers on an early 1960s movie promoter, much like the gimmicky William Castle, who wows his kiddie audiences with his B-epic sci-fi/horror film *Mant!* ("Half-man, half-ant!!").

This tongue-in-cheek approach worked for other films such as *Fright Night* (1985), *Chopping Mall* (1986), *Killer Klowns from Outer Space* (1988), and the like. A variant of this, gross-outs mixed with belly laughs and dubbed "splatstick," started up. Notable examples include Stuart Gordon and Brian Yuzna's *Re-Animator*, which used twenty-four gallons of fake blood during filming, Sam Raimi's *Evil Dead 2: Dead by Dawn*, and Peter Jackson's first two features, *Bad Taste* and *Braindead*. They are a delight for the non-squeamish.

Feminist author Rita Mae Brown wrote a parody of a slasher-film screenplay, which morphed into *The Slumber Party Massacre* (1982). It spawned two funny sequels and is still the only horror series made exclusively by women.

In the 1990s, Joe Dante's torch was taken up by directors such as Barry Sonnenfeld and Robert Zemeckis. They began using CGI to create

The Slumber Party Massacre (1982) poster.

The Cabin in the Woods (2011) poster.

elaborate imaginary worlds, opening a huge range of possibilities and enabling the lensing of frights that before seemed too difficult or cost-prohibitive to stage.

Sonnenfeld's *Addams Family* and *Addams Family Values* films (1991 and 1993) were worthy elaborations of the original dark, sardonic Charles Addams cartoons (1938–1988) and the TV series they inspired (1964–1965). Sonnenfeld also created a mammoth franchise with his *Men in Black* trilogy (1997, 2002, and 2012), concerning a secret law force that polices alien refugees on Earth. The idea was adapted from the independent comic-book series by Lowell Cunningham and Sandy Carruthers (1990–1991), an early example of a film adaptation of a graphic novel.

Zemeckis, an Oscar-winning director and screenwriter, has proved adept at many movie genres, but he has a soft spot for horror. His *Death Becomes Her* (1992) is a slapstick horror-comedy about the desire for eternal youth, and its unintended consequences. *What Lies Beneath*

You think you know the story.

THE
CABIN
IN THE WOODS

APRIL 13

(2000) is an effective thriller. Zemeckis also created some episodes for TV series such as *Amazing Stories* and *Tales from the Crypt*. It is as a producer and master of cutting-edge special effects that Zemeckis has most profoundly affected the horror film.

One of the great overlooked horror-comedy directors is Spanish director Alex de la Iglesia. His hilarious and blasphemous horror-comedy *The Day of the Beast* (1995) is just one high point in his eclectic career. He burst onto the screen with a frantic, Pedro Almodóvar-produced science-fiction black comedy *Acción Mutante* (1993), in which the ugly are rebels in a world tyrannized by the attractive. In *Beast*, a mild-mannered priest must sell his soul to the Devil in order to stop the birth of the Antichrist—which leads him to commit as many sins as possible, of course.

Iglesia's films are filled with action, highly kinetic, and flamboyantly designed. They contain lots of eccentric characters, black humor, and a very dim view of the human race's potential. He has rung the changes through genres throughout his career—spaghetti Western, crime film, action, thriller—but his horror, including the Hitchcockian *The Oxford Murders* (2008) and the horror-comedy *Witching & Bitching* (2013), is unique and highly entertaining.

(from left) Judith Malina, Christina Ricci, Raul Julia, Carel Struycken, Angelica Huston, Christopher Lloyd, and Jimmy Workman in *The Addams Family* (1991).

Familiarity bred contempt, and parodies, whether fun or foul, multiplied, such as the five-installment *Scary Movie* series (2000–2013), *The Cabin in the Woods* (2011), and the mellifluously titled *Hey, Stop Stabbing Me!* (2003).

The horror-comedy-musical banner was held aloft by the creators of the long-running *South Park* animated TV series, Trey Parker and Matt Stone. While students at the University of Colorado, they made the hilarious *Cannibal! The Musical* (1993), based extremely loosely on the true story of nineteenth-century cannibal Alferd Packer. It was distributed three years later by Troma Entertainment. Troma is an independent film company in New York founded by Lloyd Kaufman and Michael Herz in 1974, noted for its string of gruesome, campy, no-budget horror-comedies such as *The Toxic Avenger* (1984) and *Class of Nuke 'em High* (1986).

Don Coscarelli of *Phantasm* fame turned out to be one of the wittiest horror-comedy directors. His *Bubba Ho-Tep* (2002) stars horror icon Bruce Campbell as Elvis Presley, anonymous and in hiding in a retirement home. With the help of a wheelchair-bound man who claims to be John F. Kennedy (Black acting great Ossie Davis), he sets out to destroy a soul-sucking mummy. The film ends up being a moving meditation on choices and regrets, and features one of Campbell's best performances.

Coscarelli's bizarre interdimensional epic, *John Dies at the End* (2012), is a particularly assured hallucinogenic romp, *Naked Lunch* crossed with *Bill & Ted's Excellent Adventure*. A being from another dimension uses a sentient drug dubbed "the Soy Sauce" to create a beachhead in our reality, resulting in a kind of buddy comedy set during Armageddon. Chase Williamson, as protagonist and narrator David Wong, proves capable of looking quietly freaked out longer and in more ways than any actor in film history.

Excellent horror-comedies continue to pop up all the time. Mitchell Lichtenstein takes the legend of the vagina dentata and makes it come to life in *Teeth* (2007), about a chaste young woman who finds herself the target of sexual assault, leading her to discover her power to bite off offending penises. Sean Byrne's *The Loved Ones* (2009) turns the teen queen and her doting dad into monsters who kidnap young men and force them to recreate Prom Night over and over again, never quite getting it right . . .

New hybrids spring up as well. Adam Wingard's *You're Next* (2011) combines the barbed, confessional family dramedy with the slasher film to hilarious effect, and features *Re-Animator* heroine Barbara Crampton. Jemaine Clement and Taika Waititi's *What We Do in the Shadows* (2014) is a great mockumentary on the problems of contemporary vampires ("I go for a look which I call dead but delicious").

Happy Death Day (2017) is, in essence, the 1993 time-loop comedy *Groundhog Day* cross-pollinated with the slasher film, and the I-must-identify-my-killer whodunit D.O.A. provoked a sequel, *Happy Death Day 2U*, in 2019.

Even the horror-comedy-musical tradition continues, with entries such as Shawn Ku's short *Pretty Dead Girl* (2004), about a morgue attendant who just isn't into dating the living, and John McPhail's *Anna and the Apocalypse*, which may be the ultimate genre mashup—a zombie horror comedy musical set at a high school during Christmas. Something for everyone!

Taika Waititi in *What We Do in the Shadows* (2014).

MASTERS FOR
A NEW
MILLENNIUM

22

Horror film since the turn of the twenty-first century has sprouted, slithered, and taken many turns, like an untethered fire hose at full blast.

With the rise of the Digital Age, the means of film production and distribution were now in everyone's hands, and any place in the world was now capable of being an origin point for new horror films. Countries never before heard from were producing horror films, including unlikely candidates such as Cuba, Israel, and even the Republic of Maldives (*E Re'ah Fahu*, 2016). It has become standard procedure to adapt successful horror films made in foreign countries in America, fare such as *The Ring* (2002), *Dark Water* (2005), *The Eye* (2008), and *Let Me In* (2010).

As new media platforms proliferated and evolved, horror became available in an unprecedented number of ways. For decades, film fans had to check their newspaper listings and circle their calendars to make sure to see both beloved and unseen horror films, either at whatever mainstream and arthouse cinemas they could, or by tuning in at a predetermined time to one of the few broadcast television stations within the viewer's primitive electronic range.

The heyday of the VHS tape (1977–1997) ended this limitation and spawned the video rental store, which always seemed to accumulate a wide variety of obscure horror titles. Blank tapes and programmable video cassette recorders also made it possible to watch, for instance, a rerun of *Vampire Circus* at a more convenient time, freeing the viewers from the tyranny of the TV schedule. VHS was killed by the adoption of the DVD release in 1997. (I still have *The Flesh and the Fiends* on VHS. Just in case.) Video stores persisted until Netflix subverted the business model by physically mailing requested DVDs to subscribers, starting in 1998.

In 2007, Netflix and many other internet content-providing entertainment companies went further, solving the problems of computer streaming and on-demand services, converting the film market to one in which viewers subscribe to the desired channel or request service, or order films digitally à la carte.

The creation of a huge digital social network during the same period, capable of spanning the globe and uniting people instantaneously and simultaneously, led to a profound increase in the sharing of information. You could see, read, hear all—films, critiques, parodies, podcasts, and chat rooms, dedicated sites curated by everyone from the sloppiest of fanboys to the most meticulous of film historians.

It's a paradox. There have never been more ways to see movies, from around the world and from 1895 to the present, on demand. But the audience is dependent on the provider-curator. And what if the owner of the rights to a particular film doesn't "program" it by allowing it to be placed on an online menu?

Currently, it is not even necessary for a film ever to be contained, or ever to exist, as a physical artifact. And some films don't make the jump from one outmoded medium to another, more current one, leaving pieces of horror history locked away from viewing. (Yes, I have all my horror DVDs stowed away as well. Just in case!)

Overlooked Gems

Island of Lost Souls (1932)

The Black Cat (1934)

Mad Love (1935)

Kwaidan (1964)

Quatermass and the Pit (1967)

Let Sleeping Corpses Lie (1974)

Near Dark (1987)

Lady in White (1988)

Society (1989)

Day of the Beast (1995)

May (2002)

Bubba Ho-tep (2002)

Tideland (2005)

The Woman in Black (2011)

OPPOSITE: Chloe Grace Moretz in *Let Me In* (2010).

American Horror Story (2011–) poster.

As easily as nitrate prints can deteriorate, digital files can get lost, deleted, or corrupted, become outmoded in turn. I fear that horror and other film historians may have already had the best opportunity to see all the films in a given canon. Meanwhile, historians maintain their obsolete playback systems and hope old media someday has a resurgence, as vinyl did.

The power of choice is supreme, and the market is bigger (and more segmented) than ever. The new digital-provider competitors generated a huge upswing in demand. Old-school broadcast networks had to appeal to everyone, provide public service, observe a moderate amount of censorship, and create family-friendly content. Cable TV channels, pioneered by HBO in the early 1990s, could ignore those restrictions, tailoring their content to the demands of their niche audiences. (The first dedicated all-horror channel launched in 2004; currently there are six on air, delivering shocks 24/7.) Content brokers

eventually became content producers, forming their own studios much as the first-generation movie moguls like Universal's Carl Laemmle did.

Horror television entered a third classic phase. Joss Whedon's *Buffy the Vampire Slayer* (1997–2003) was a vast improvement on its 1992 origin film, combining a teen heroine in an everyday-USA high-school setting with horror, action, and wit, resulting in popular and critical success. In its wake came other outstanding TV series, including the demon-hunting *Supernatural* (2005–2020), the serial-killer story *Dexter* (2006–2013), the vampire saga *True Blood* (2008–2014), the zombie epic *The Walking Dead* (2010–2022), the period horror drama *Penny Dreadful* (2014–2016), and the brilliant anthologies *American Horror Story* (2011–present) and *Black Mirror* (2011–present).

Director Frank Darabont, who created *The Walking Dead*, taken from the Robert Kirkman/Tony Moore comic book (2003–2019), has enjoyed the closest and most fruitful collaborations with horror master Stephen King (*The Shawshank Redemption*, 1994; *The Green Mile*, 1999) to date. Darabont made the best King horror-film adaptation to date with his ruthless, brilliant *The Mist* in 2007.

The Mist contains sci-fi/horror paranoia, vivid Lovecraftian monsters, and graphic gore, but its genius lies in its examination of people in shock in the face of terror and despair. The back-and-forth between neighbors trapped in a grocery

Promotional image of the cast of *Buffy the Vampire Slayer* (1997–2003).

store as bloodthirsty creatures from another dimension devour them is compelling and true to life. It's chilling to watch a father, trying to protect his small son, find out what people are capable of.

A brilliant Marcia Gay Harden plays a fundamentalist who gradually takes control of the crowd, providing an argument in miniature for the abolishment of organized religion. (The TV pop phenomenon *Stranger Things* [2016–present] went all-in on the recreation of a 1980s-era, Stephen King-style horror story, filmed in imitation of Spielberg's signature camerawork. Its use of alternate-dimension monsters owes an enormous debt to *The Mist*.)

Anything could be adapted into filmed horror. Not only did *Resident Evil* make its way from the game console to the big screen, but *Silent Hill* (2006) was a rare example of an effective adaptation of a video game, breaking up the sequential "chapters" of predictable violent gaming-like action with actual storytelling and effective performances.

Graphic novels exploded into popularity with Art Spiegelman's horrifying Holocaust tale *Maus* (1980–1991), which proved that the "comic book" medium could contain serious, complex, and affecting material. Writers and illustrators, and many writer/illustrators, began to explore the medium's potential. Soon superhero and other genre comics were hauled back into the light and reexamined and given new legitimacy, often in a darker tone.

The rise of CGI meant that previously unfilmable ideas could be executed, leading to a vast release of fantasy, science fiction, and horror in cinemas, all spearheaded by the amazing

growth of the superhero film. Film adaptations of graphic horror novels, such as the *Blade* vampire-hunting trilogy (1998–2004), *From Hell* (2001), Guillermo del Toro's *Hellboy* (2004), and David Slade's *30 Days of Night* (2007), all did well at the box office.

Horror connoisseurs were also a factor in the multiplication of horror film festivals over the last forty years. These concentrated, days-long screenings of movies, combined with talkbacks, interviews, and symposia, were crammed with eager fans. They served as a boost to local economies, and to the cinematic IQ of the attendees.

They provided plenty of opportunities for up-and-coming auteurs, and allowed space for retrospectives of both important and neglected filmmakers, and spotlights on specific themes and topics. Many times, these get-togethers allowed filmmakers to network and find collaborators and investors. Some became famous as "marketplace" festivals, at which films would be optioned for distribution and future productions would be bankrolled.

At most recent count, there are no fewer than twenty-eight annual film festivals

Hellboy (2004)
poster.

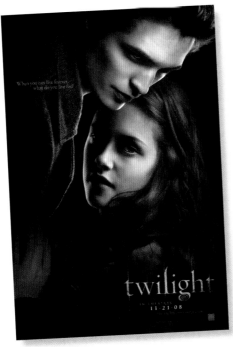

Twilight (2008) poster.

worldwide dedicated specifically to horror film. Furthermore, there has been a proliferation of various massive, yearly, internationally attended, themed "cons"—that is, conventions, filled with participating artists and performers, as well as adoring fans, the latter often in full and elaborate costume. These "cons" celebrate fantasy, sci-fi, and horror, in the process increasing the last's ubiquity and acceptability. The culture of horror fandom has never been stronger.

Meanwhile, horror content waxed and waned. A slew of remakes and reboots flooded the market in the latter half of the 2000s: new versions of *The Amityville Horror* (2005), *Halloween* (2007, and again in 2018), *The Crazies* (2010), *A Nightmare on Elm Street* (2010), and many more.

New franchises were launched, and new names were rising to recognition. Horror merged with action/adventure. What's more, female protagonists were starting to crop up more frequently. *Resident Evil*, starring actress Milla Jovovich, has spawned five sequels to date. Up-and-coming English actress Kate Beckinsale took the lead role in *Underworld* (2003), a vampires-versus-werewolves saga that made her a popular lead player in action and horror films.

The Blair Witch Project (1999) poster.

Underworld has generated four more films in the series. And in the *Twilight* quintet (2008–2010), based on Stephanie Meyer's young-adult vampire novels, Kristen Stewart is a kind of soap-opera heroine in love with a bloodsucker.

James Wan's *Saw* octet of films (2004–2017) came along following the creation of James Wong's *Final Destination* and its descendants (2000–2011), all concerning the cheating of fate. These, along with the six-film *Wrong Turn* set (2003–2014), centering on a marauding band of cannibals, rotated in and out of the multiplexes.

The success of the low-budget pseudo-documentary *The Blair Witch Project* in 1999 gave birth to a legion of "found-footage" horror films that mimicked documentary and amateur techniques, the most successful of which, *Paranormal Activity* (2007), has given birth to five sequels to date. Prolific genre directors such as Alex Chandon, David DeCoteau, William Lustig, and Charles Band kept cranking out films in the standard categories (zombie, slasher, etc.) with breathtaking rapidity.

And there were innovators. Lucky McKee's 2002 film *May*, about a murderously insane but

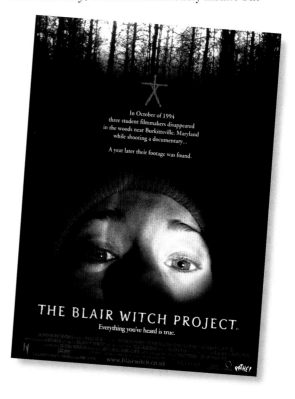

pitiable protagonist who creates a new friend in a unique way, has been followed by intriguing horror entries from him such as *The Woods* (2006), *The Woman* (2011), and *All Cheerleaders Die* (2013). Vincenzo Natali's visually cold horror pieces such as *Cube* (1997) and *Splice* (2011) reveal human emotion in the ragged extreme. (His *Nothing*, 2003, supposedly a comedy, is one of the most terrifying things I've ever seen.) Bryan Bertino's masterful and thought-provoking *The Strangers* (2008) gives us the ultimate home-invasion horror film—whose victims are targeted only because "you answered the door."

The last two decades have produced a number of individual films that deserve attention. Bill Paxton, known as an actor, made his directorial debut in 2001 with *Frailty*, a tense and thought-provoking story about a man who believes he is a divinely appointed killer on a mission. British filmmaker Edgar Wright launched his "Three Flavours Cornetto" film trilogy with his *Shaun of the Dead*, a shambling, shaggy-dog zombie epic that made a star of actor and writer Simon Pegg.

The Spanish New Cinema's founder, the outrageous and perceptive Pedro Almodóvar, spearheaded Hispanic filmmaking's resurgence. Almodóvar made a terrifying and thoughtful body-horror film, *The Skin I Live In*, in 2011. Antonio Banderas plays a mad plastic surgeon who changes a male suspect in the death of his daughter into his ideal woman, the image of his dead wife. It's *Bride of Frankenstein* reconsidered, laced with Almodóvar's quirks and flair for melodrama.

Following Almodóvar was a wave of versatile Spanish filmmakers with strong commercial sensibilities, who didn't mind working in genre, directors such as Bigas Luna, Vicente Aranda, Fernando Trueba, Julio Medem, Alex de la Iglesia, and Alejandro Amenábar. Amenábar's *The Others*

(2001) is a perfect little Victorian ghost story à la *The Turn of the Screw*, and Juan Antonio Bayona's beautiful, dark *The Orphanage* (2007) is a success in the same vein.

Swede Tomas Alfredson's melancholy, low-key vampire tale *Let the Right One In* (2008) was quickly remade in English. It's an extraordinary vampire tale, in which a boy befriends a young female blood-drinker, adapted by John Ajvide Lindqvist from his 2004 novel. The film's careful and realistic delineation of character turns what might have been a typical horror story into a moving and melancholy meditation on love and risk.

Then, with films such as the zombie drama *Wake Wood* (2009) and the solid Victorian ghost story *The Woman in Black* (2012), England's Hammer Studios returned to life. Irish director Neil Jordan made the highly anticipated, profitable but critically unregarded *Interview with the Vampire* (1994). This was adapted from the bestselling 1976 Gothic horror novel of the same name by Anne Rice. Rice's sensuous, convoluted works stirred some interest and spurred a trend toward gloomy supernatural romances, but did not inspire Stephen King-level waves of film adaptations.

New variants on familiar patterns continue to be made. Neil Jordan's original effort, *Byzantium*

Actor Elena Anaya (left) and director Pedro Almodovar film *The Skin I Live In* (2011).

The Babadook (2014) poster.

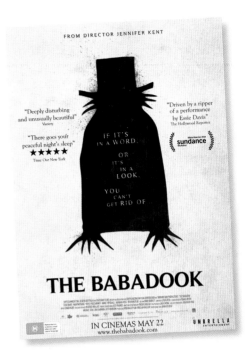

(2012), is a contemporary and much more powerful vampire movie than his *Interview*. Even avant-garde director Jim Jarmusch created a pair of brooding, melancholy, erudite bloodsuckers for his *Only Lovers Left Alive* in 2013, while the director's zombie comedy, *The Dead Don't Die*, hit the screen in 2019.

David Robert Mitchell's *It Follows* (2014) did a number on sex-breeds-consequences horror. The same year, Jennifer Kent's *The Babadook*, about a child's nightmare come to life, failed to impress in Australia where it was made, but became a big hit overseas. It's an interrogation of parenthood, as a young boy becomes obsessed with a mysterious monster, and his increasingly unhinged behavior starts to affect his single mother as well. It's a movie that deals with the idea of accommodating evil rather than eliminating it.

Fabrice du Welz, who made one of the few thoughtful French Extreme films, *Calvaire*, made the best yet of four film examinations of the Fernandez/Beck "Lonely Hearts" murders of 1949, *Alleluia*, in 2014. Sion Sono's *Tag* from 2015 is gruesome but deeply affecting. A high-school girl finds herself trapped inside the deadly and sexist machinations of a video game. The result

is one of the most compelling recent horror films out there, an eloquent postmodern commentary on the victimization of women in media.

Karyn Kusama's *The Invitation* (2015) is deliciously restrained, an apt metaphor for the placid politeness that veneers collective contemporary madnesses. A woman invites her ex-husband to a dinner party, where he and a collection of their friends are told about a new spiritual group called "The Invitation." Gradually, it becomes apparent that the group is a doomsday cult. The slow descent into murderous chaos is paced exquisitely, and the ensemble cast is top-notch.

Most Prolific Horror Directors

Terence Fisher (20 films)

Wes Craven (18)

Tobe Hooper (14)

George Romero (13)

Lucio Fulci (11)

Mario Bava (11)

Dario Argento (11)

John Carpenter (10)

James Wan (7)

Steve Miner (7)

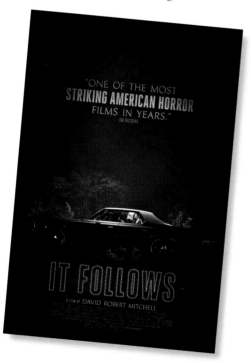

It Follows (2014) poster.

Jeremy Saulnier's *Green Room* (2015) is a perfect little locked-room puzzle of a horror-thriller. A band is trapped in a backstage "green room" by a bunch of neo-Nazis after witnessing a murder. It features Shakespearean and *Star Trek* star Patrick Stewart in a gripping turn as the cold-blooded leader of the skinheads.

Some horror directors moved on to bigger things. Sam Raimi went from his *Evil Dead* films to the first *Spider-Man* trilogy (2002–2007), a wider variety of films, and projects on which he served as a producer. He even brought his signature body horror flair (and a Bruce Campbell cameo) to 2022's *Dr. Strange in the Multiverse of Madness*, a big-budget part of the Marvel Cinematic Universe. Peter Jackson proceeded to remake *King Kong* (2005), and embarked on a decade-plus process of bringing Tolkien's *The Lord of the Rings* and *The Hobbit* to the big screen. Another New Zealander, Taika Waititi, co-crafter of the vampire comedy *What We Do in the Shadows*, directed *Thor: Ragnarok* (2017), the most deliberately funny Marvel superhero movie to date, as well as the Oscar-nominated *Jojo Rabbit* (2019). James Wan, after the runaway success of the *Saw* franchise and other horror outings such as

Insidious (2010) and *The Conjuring* (2013), graduated to the big-budget superhero movie with *Aquaman* (2018).

The biggest change in recent horror film is the increase in directors who neither remain specialists in "straight" horror nor use horror as a stepping-stone to mainstream films. More and more, their horror-permeated projects edged closer to mainstream fare, gaining critical acclaim and begging the question: has horror gone legit?

Patrick Stewart (center) leads a gang of neo-Nazis in *Green Room* (2015).

23

IS HORROR LEGIT?

The year 2018 was a banner one for horror. For the first time, two movies anchored in the horror genre were nominated for Best Picture at the Oscars in a single year. Jordan Peele's *Get Out* used the tropes of mad science and possession to craft a powerful fable about the relations between Black and white people in America, while Guillermo del Toro's *The Shape of Water* took the most inarticulate Universal monster, the Creature from the Black Lagoon, and made him into a romantic hero. (*Get Out* won for Best Original Screenplay; *The Shape of Water* took home four statuettes, including Best Picture.)

As always, mainstream culture has a hard time categorizing superior horror. For instance, *Get Out* was nominated for two Golden Globes, where it was slotted into the unhelpful "musical or comedy" category. Likewise, *The Shape of Water* was thought of as a fantasy, though its roots are firmly in horror. These developments underscore the ongoing struggle of horror to break out of its genre ghetto. In fact, a unique subgroup of recent filmmakers incorporate horror as the primary element in dramas of larger scope, maintaining a steady undercurrent of uncertainty and dread. One might best call these films horror-inflected, -integrated, or -permeated.

Guillermo del Toro with his Oscars for *The Shape of Water* (2017) at the 90th Academy Awards.

The prime example of this is America's own Cocteau on steroids, David Lynch. The cult success of *Eraserhead* started a career that has contained many dark masterpieces—*Blue Velvet* (1986), TV's *Twin Peaks* (1990–1991, 2017), *Lost Highway* (1997), and *Mulholland Drive* (2001), to name a few—that can all be read as horror texts. You might say Lynch's vision of America, and everyday reality, is essentially a horrific one.

Veteran fantasist Terry Gilliam, the American-born animator of *Monty Python* fame, always includes elements of horror and the grotesque in his movies, especially in such films as *Brazil* (1985), *The Fisher King* (1991), and the criminally under-regarded *Tideland* (2005). It's *Alice in Wonderland* crossed with Cronenberg as Gilliam's freakish imagination gives life and heart to this dark fairy tale of a young girl trapped on the Texas prairie with her

Personal Best

Guillermo del Toro

Cronos (1993)

The Devil's Backbone (2001)

Pan's Labyrinth (2006)

Crimson Peak (2015)

The Shape of Water (2017)

OPPOSITE: Jordan Peele with his Oscar at the 90th Academy Awards.

Get Out (2017) poster.

Director M. Night Shyamalan (left) and actor James McAvoy on the set of *Split* (2016).

RIGHT: The poster for Shyamalan's *The Sixth Sense* (1999).

father's corpse, exposed only to a couple of local eccentrics.

M. Night Shyamalan burst onto the scene with the success of his ghost drama *The Sixth Sense* (1999), and although his gimmicky Hitchockian movies tend toward sci-fi, he has skirted closer to horror in his *The Village* (2004), *The Visit* (2015), and *Split* (2016).

As horror gains critical acceptance, it is often reclassified as something "above" the genre. Yet another group of directors—Lars von Trier, Darren Aronofsky, and Michael Haneke—are more assertive. Each directed at least one outright horror film, and their other films sport massive amounts of terrifying concepts and imagery, subordinated to imaginations that conceive mankind as a failure in progress, victim to its inherent moral bankruptcy.

Von Trier sees life as "evil and soulless," and his films are a testament to that. His second film, *Epidemic* (1987), uses a plague as a metaphor. His later films contain much violence, disturbing imagery, and a pronounced streak of misogyny. His *Antichrist* (2009), filled with sadomasochism, is an indictment of womanhood. Von Trier's latest film, *The House That Jack Built* (2018), the saga of a serial killer, was quickly dismissed as torture porn.

Darren Aronofsky, creator of films of hallucinatory intensity, is the most prominent horror-inflected American director of the day. His first feature, *Pi* (1998), is a horror film about a mathematical savant who is pursued by many violent interests after he manifests a "perfect number" that can change the world. His anti-drug fable *Requiem for a Dream* (2000), based on Hubert Selby Jr.'s 1978 novel, plays like a horror film. *Black Swan* (2010) chronicles a ballerina's descent into madness, and *mother!* (2017) features a tortured female protagonist, a metaphor for Earth itself, dragged through insanity, torture, and death.

Austrian Michael Haneke, whose works are thought of as disturbing thrillers or dramas, has a connection to horror that is unmistakable. In almost every one of his films, he ruthlessly interrogates mankind—its morals, its hypocrisy, its sadism. In *Benny's Video* (1992), parents must

casually and leisurely torture and kill the family, all the while breaking the fourth wall, cracking jokes, and even replaying a scene to do it over if it doesn't work out to their liking. The victims are doomed, and we viewers are forced to ask what our part in this is.

In contrast to this book's original definition of the nature of horror—that it is either something external or something latent, hidden within us—Haneke, von Trier, and Aronofsky seem to propose that the horror simply is us, the daylight, everyday life, each of us containing what Hannah Arendt referred to in regard to the perpetrators of the Holocaust as "the banality of evil." They give us no cheap resolution, and no easy out—no way out at all.

Haneke is a behavioral theorist whose equations are terrifying. For him, the mundane doings of humanity are horror enough. Uncovering the subtle, granular horrors that push mankind into savagery is part and parcel of his *The White Ribbon* (2009), in which pre-World War I German society is seen as a breeding ground for fascism, peppered with everyday horrors no one seems to really notice.

The current premier auteur of traditional horror is Mexico's Guillermo del Toro, an exciting and playful filmmaker who grew up on his own country's first-generation horror gems, as well as the standard *Shock Theater* package and plenty of Hammer horror as well. His love for almost every manifestation of nineteenth- and twentieth-century horror and fantasy makes his work a compelling compendium of subjects and styles. Above all, del Toro understands the connection of horror to mythic feeling.

His *Cronos* (1993) is an elegant reworking of vampire myth. An ancient device grants eternal life and youth

deal with the actions of their conscienceless, murderous teen.

Funny Games (2007) concerns two polite serial killers who torment a family at length—killers who implicate the viewer in the carnage. Two nice young men knock on the door of a rich family at their summer home. Can they borrow some eggs? What follows is a bold indictment of the horror audience's expectations. The two

Arno Frisch (right) and Frank Giering (left) torment Stefan Clapczynski in Michael Haneke's *Funny Games* (1997).

but demands unholy sacrifices. Del Toro's inventive, deeply observed combination of old horror ideas and new emotional content would be a hallmark of all his later work.

He came to America to make the bug-monster flick *Mimic* (1997), a terrible experience for the filmmaker (and an inferior effort). He went to Spain to make the brilliant ghost story *The Devil's Backbone* (2001). He garnered acclaim for his direction of *Blade II* (2002), about a vampire hunter, and finally indulged his steampunk design ethos fully in the baroque graphic-novel adaptation *Hellboy* (2004), in which the monster is an amiable, wisecracking action hero.

Pan's Labyrinth (2006) is a masterful dark vision that unfolds seamlessly. In the midst of the Spanish Civil War, a young girl goes on a quest to the underworld, in a story intertwined with her opposition to her new stepfather, a fascist military man.

Del Toro's success with reviving these dormant styles and forms stems from his intelligence about how the genre works and his deep love for it. Since then, del Toro has done his take on the *kaiju* giant-monster subgenre (*Pacific Rim*, 2013), Hammer horror (*Crimson Peak*, 2015), and the aforementioned Creature from the Black Lagoon (*The Shape of Water*, 2017).

Pan's Labyrinth and *The Shape of Water* feature actor Doug Jones, a frequent collaborator with del Toro, as various mythical creatures; Jones's balletic, mime-like physicality and clarity of expression make him nearly a throwback to the silent era. In *The Shape of Water*, the clumsy and inarticulate Creature from the Black Lagoon is reconceived as a positive and powerful being. The Amphibian Man played by Jones is a captured Amazonian "god," imprisoned by the American government during the Cold War and thought of as a specimen to be dissected. His romance with a mute cleaning lady turns the horror premise on its head, revealing a dynamic similar to the romantic fantasy of Cocteau's *Beauty and the Beast* (1946).

Another unique performer in horror and fantasy today is Andy Serkis. A frequent player in Peter Jackson films, Serkis created a unique niche as the go-to motion-capture artist in film, a sort of digital Lon Chaney. Using technology, directors can now record a performance and craft a CGI character on top of it, retaining the heart and immediacy of the human actor while allowing him or her to be transformed into any onscreen creature (or menace) desired. Serkis has incarnated characters such as Jackson's King Kong and Gollum, as well as Caesar in the popular 2011–2017 reboot of the *Planet of the Apes* sci-fi film series.

This long list of successes stands in sharp contrast to the recent efforts of Universal Studios, which recently abandoned a dismal attempt to relaunch its "Dark Universe" classic monsters in a series of new films—Frankenstein, Dracula, Wolfman, and so on—retooling them for another era. A *Wolfman* reboot in 2010 was a failure. (Its lead actor, Benicio del Toro, ironically made his film debut as Duke, the Dog-Faced Boy, in *Big Top Pee-wee*, 1988). Universal's dismal *The Mummy* (2017) turned into a Tom Cruise vanity project and wound up a poorly CGI'd bomb. Universal put its ambitious plans on the back burner. It crept back into the

A scene from *Pan's Labyrinth* (2006).

Horror at the Oscars

Typically, horror doesn't rank high on the lists generated by the Academy of Motion Picture Arts and Sciences, but there are some notable exceptions:

1931 – Best Actor, Fredric March, *Dr. Jekyll and Mr. Hyde*

1943 – Best Art Direction, Best Cinematography, *The Phantom of the Opera*

1945 – Best Cinematography, *The Picture of Dorian Gray*

1962 – Best Costume Design, *What Ever Happened to Baby Jane?*

1968 – Best Supporting Actress, Ruth Gordon, *Rosemary's Baby*

1973 – Best Adapted Screenplay, Best Sound, *The Exorcist*

1976 – Best Original Score, *The Omen*

1979 – Best Visual Effects, *Alien*

Anthony Hopkins (left) and Jodie Foster with their Oscars at the 64th Academy Awards.

1981 – Best Makeup, *An American Werewolf in London*

1986 – Best Makeup, *The Fly*
Best Sound Editing, Best Visual Effects, *Aliens*

1990 – Best Actress, Kathy Bates, *Misery*

1991 – Best Picture; Best Director, Jonathan Demme; Best Actor, Anthony Hopkins; Best Actress, Jodie Foster; Best Adapted Screenplay, *The Silence of the Lambs*

1992 – Best Makeup, Best Costume Design, Best Sound Effects Editing, *Bram Stoker's Dracula*

1999 – Best Art Direction, *Sleepy Hollow*

2007 – Best Art Direction, *Sweeney Todd: The Demon Barber of Fleet Street*

2010 – Best Actress, Natalie Portman, *Black Swan*

2017 – Best Original Screenplay, *Get Out*
Best Picture; Best Director, Guillermo del Toro; Best Production Design, Best Original Score, *The Shape of Water*

Kathy Bates with her Best Actress Oscar at the 63rd Academy Awards.

The Invisible Man
(2020) poster.

fray with an interesting take on *The Invisible Man* (Leigh Whannell, 2020).

Meanwhile, quality horror films just keep springing up in odd places. French director Julia Ducournau's *Raw* (2016) is a wry, fresh take on cannibal compulsion, while Romanian filmmaker Adrian Tofei's goofy *Be My Cat: A Film for Anne* (2015) is his purported love letter to American actress Anne Hathaway, which somehow results in him slaughtering several nice young aspiring actresses. Uruguayan Fede Alvarez turned out the heart-stopping *Don't Breathe* in 2016.

Danish director Nicolas Winding Refn's *The Neon Demon* (2016), while critically scorned and unattended in theaters, is still a fascinating take on vampirism. Gore Verbinski, known for his *Pirates of the Caribbean* films, attempted medical horror in *A Cure for Wellness* (2017) with intriguing but largely unwatched results.

Even remakes could be enthralling. Jim Mickle's 2013 *We Are What We Are* takes a premise established by Spanish director Jorge Michel Grau (not to be confused with *Let Sleeping Corpses Lie* director Jorge Grau) in 2010 and completely transforms it. In Mickle's update, an isolated family practices cannibalism as a kind of sacrament, replacing Grau's social satire with a dense, serious, thought-provoking, darkly

The Neon Demon
(2016) poster.

beautiful drama that takes religious feeling and rigorously interrogates it.

The most successful recent horror film is fortunately also one of the best: Jordan Peele's *Get Out* is a classic horror story, but also a penetrating satirical take on America's Black-white relations. The discomfort of interracial dating is taken to its logical extreme when a young Black man is brought home to meet his white girlfriend's family, and finds that to them he is merely a subject in an ongoing experiment that seeks to prolong the lives of affluent liberal white people by placing their brains in the bodies of Black "guinea pigs."

Get Out asserts that majority culture co-opts and commodifies difference, if it finds any value in it. The symbolism is heavy-handed, but Peele's long experience as a comedian helps him to tease out the full humorous potential with his script. His expertise in his rookie outing as a director allows him to pace the scares effectively and keep the action fresh. Peele's 2019 movie *Us* is a classic doppelganger story adapted for modern

(from left to right)
Daniel Kaluuya,
Keke Palmer, and
Brandon Perea in
Nope (2022).

times (with a bit of a nod to Shimizu's *Marebito* thrown in).

Peele's film, *Nope* (2022), is another hybrid—part horror movie, part Western, part disquisition on Black identity, and a sly satire of capitalism as well. The protagonists are modern African-American cowboys who work with the film industry. A mysterious object hovers in the sky near their ranch and soon they and others try to capture, record, and monetize it.

The film's many tonal shifts are harmonized by Peele's intellectually insatiable approach. He explodes myths, and in the process of doing so pulls the rug out from under the audience, again and again. The movies he crafts are literal thrill rides.

And horror can still prophesy. James DeMonaco's dystopian *Purge* series, which began in 2013, could be said to be a harbinger of America in the era of Trump. In it, a future totalitarian American government institutes a once-a-year event, "The Purge": twelve hours in which all crime is legal, and the slaughter is general. The idea that the nation needs nothing more than to blow off steam with a little armed chaos and bloodletting, vigilantism as sport, is a chilling one that's popular enough to have prompted three sequels to date.

The most affecting recent horror film uses no special effects. Trey Edward Shults's 2017 *It Comes at Night* is set at an archetypical lonely cabin in the woods. This one is occupied by a father, mother, and son, who are heavily armed and locked in against the chaos and violence resulting from a plague that has wiped out most of mankind. They capture an intruder, a man scavenging supplies for himself, his wife, and son. The first family takes them in, but their uneasy alliance is extremely fragile.

Every character is delineated slowly and carefully through expert performances. As they slowly reveal themselves to each other, the audience warms to them and dares to invest some hopeful energy into seeing that things turn out right. But—it becomes excruciatingly clear that everyone is acting with the best of intentions, and that they are all doomed nonetheless. There is no unsympathetic character in the film, which makes what happens intensely affecting, with a tragic dimension. It's horror as directed by filmmaker Jean Renoir, who famously stated in character in one of his films: "The awful thing about life is this: everyone has their reasons."[1]

This is a horror film in which, ultimately, no one is the monster. Horror often plays out as a bargain-basement form of tragedy, and *It Comes at Night* is close to a pure example of that. As historian Will Durant wrote, "As in all great tragedies, every participant fought for what seemed to him right, and can claim a portion of our sympathy."[2]

POST-HORROR
AND BEYOND

LET THE

FESTIVITIES

BEGIN

JULY 3

As with other genres, horror films run in waves and in cycles, from the Gothic impulses of the 1930s to the sci-fi-centric '50s, through the slasher films of the 1980s, and so on. Success in a particular subgenre breeds imitation. Sometimes, too, something in the zeitgeist seeps into the creative work of a particular era, something that later comes into focus through the lens of critical examination.

Such is the case with post-horror. The last decade has seen a proliferation of horror films that utilize the rhythms and techniques of the serious, modern art drama to enhance (or not) their frights. In the previous chapter, I characterized this kind of film, then still emerging, as horror-inflected or horror-permeated. Examples: Karyn Kusama's creepy dining-room tale *The Invitation* (2015) and Trey Edward Shults' plague-obsessed *It Comes at Night* (2017).

Since that writing, these tendencies have solidified into the hallmarks of a subgenre, dubbed post-horror by film critic Steve Rose in July 2017, and codified in David Church's masterful exegesis, 2021's *Post-Horror: Art, Genre, and Cultural Elevation*. The subgenre has also been referred to as art-horror, smart horror, elevated horror, and prestige horror.

(A previous spurt of prestige horror, prompted by the success of *The Silence of the Lambs,* 1991, led to films such as Francis Ford Coppola's *Bram Stoker's Dracula,* 1992; Robert De Niro as the monster in *Mary Shelley's Frankenstein*, 1994; Mike Nichols' *Wolf*, 1994; and the Julia Roberts Jekyll/Hyde misfire *Mary Reilly*, 1996.)

In his book, Church works with critic David Bordwell's description of art cinema as containing "drifting, circular, and open-ended narratives; ambiguous and psychologically complex characters; and various forms of spatial and temporal manipulation," and adds the qualities of "visual restraint and stylistic minimalism." Church identifies dozens of films from the period of 2009 through the present that commingle horror with these more elite aesthetic values, dwelling in atmosphere and ambiguity rather than the graphic shock and jump scares of more traditional horror fare.

Enough with definitions: what does a post-horror film feel like? Well, for one thing, it takes its time. Unlike the efficient, machine-like pace and overdeveloped emotions of traditional horror, post-horror can both meander and quietly mull over details, asking much patience of its audience.

Sometimes this creates a gently-paced gem such as Olivier Assayas' *Personal Shopper*, about a psychic seeking contact with her dead brother, or Liam Gavin's plaintive *A Dark Song*, about a mother seeking revenge through magic (both 2016), and sometimes more problematic works such as the over-the-top symbolic *mother!*, the enigmatic mysteries of *The Killing of a Sacred Deer* (both 2017), and the seeming aimlessness of the contagion drama *She Dies Tomorrow* (2020).

OPPOSITE:
Midsommar
(2019) poster.

Personal Shopper
(2016) poster.

Berberian Sound
Studio (2012)
poster.

Post-horror is subtle. *A Ghost Story* (2017) places its dead protagonist drolly under a sheet with two eyeholes, and with gentle humor shows him haunting the site of his death through the ages. *Swallow* (2019) is a feminist fable couched in the story of a pregnant woman who feels compelled to swallow small objects. In *Berberian Sound Studio* (2012), is a technician (a brilliant Toby Jones) losing his mind or succumbing to evil impulses? Is *The Lighthouse* (2019) a horror story or a meditation on melancholy and menace?

It depends on who you talk to. The gap between the critic and the horror fan has never been wider. Church writes, "Often heralded for possessing an aesthetically 'higher' tone than the average multiplex horror movie, these films have received disproportionate critical acclaim for catering to more rarified tastes, even as viewers with more populist tastes have proved ambivalent or even hostile toward the films'

A spectral scene
from *A Ghost
Story* (2017).

aesthetic strategies, and dedicated horror fans have decried the critical conversation around these works."

This is the crux of the post-horror dilemma. The more a horror film conforms to the style of the art film, the fewer typical horror "moves" it makes, the more it appeals to the traditional cultural gatekeepers that look down on horror and the less scary it tends to be. Traditional fans can feel cheated and angered by films that don't deliver the horror goods, the fast-moving, gory, graphic goodness they've grown to expect from the genre. Thus critical and popular "scores" for post-horror films wind up in sharp disagreement with each other.

But are these post-horror films scary, or just mopey and pretentious? The designation of a film as post-horror doesn't denote its inherent superiority or inferiority. As with all artistic products, these films must be judged on an individual basis. It is important as well to remember that the individual filmmakers are working as independent agents, unaware of or uncaring about their films' future critical designations. They are trying to make compelling entertainments.

The most interesting development in the present period is not the development of post-horror, but since then the ascent and achievement of several young, horror-centric directors who are making a name for

themselves in the genre. Though they may use post-horror elements, their films subsume these techniques for the sake of the effectiveness of their films as a whole. Most important, these directors are without genre shame. They are happy to make horror movies.

Robert Eggers began his career as a feature film director with the folk horror tale *The Witch* (folk horror dealing in a return to pre-Christian and Satanic practices). In it, a family in colonial New England is forced out into the wilderness due to its patriarch's religious pride. There, they encounter increasing evidence that dark forces are thwarting them.

The film takes its period details very seriously, and the film has a meditative pace. It evokes the wildness, danger, and mystery of the untamed forest the family finds itself in, and slowly chips

Anya Taylor-Joy in *The Witch* (2015).

away at the individuals' will to resist evil. This can be understood as an anti-religious film, for here Eggers posits a Deity that is as terrifying as its antithesis. The director himself characterized the shoot as "miserable and self-serious."

But by grounding the plot developments in a bare-bones, almost documentary style, Eggers makes the horrors much more convincing. This could be a fever dream, or an unacknowledged reality. The same thing is true of his next film, *The Lighthouse* (2019), which has been characterized not only as a horror film, but as a thriller, a mood piece, and a dark fantasy.

Appropriately, the movie takes its inspiration from an unfinished Poe story. In it, two men (Willem Dafoe, Robert Pattinson) work at a lonely lighthouse in 1890s New England. Dogged by ill luck (and perhaps a seagull's curse), they spiral into madness as a storm bears down on them and their supplies run out. Shot in a black-and-white style that leans heavily into a blue-gray sheen, like that of old daguerreotypes, the film is crammed with ideas and influences, from symbolism, surrealism, Melville, Lovecraft, and Stevenson. Eggers takes the horror template and enriches it with fertile bursts of dark imagery.

Julia Ducournau is a director firmly ensconced in the making of body-horror films. She has been identified with the "New French

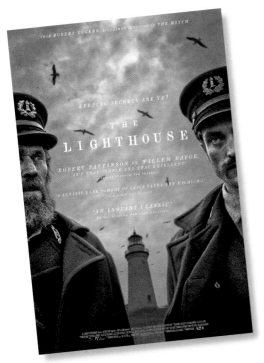

The Lighthouse (2019) poster.

Director Julia Ducournau poses with the Palme d'Or Best Movie Award for *Titane* (2021) during the 74th Annual Cannes Film Festival.

Extreme," identified in 2004 as a spate of disturbing and explicit films that deal with violence, death, "sexual ugliness," and psychosis. Films such as *In My Skin* (2002), *Frontier(s)* (2007), *Inside* (2007), and *Martyrs* (2008) exemplify this jarring trend, and could be easily lumped under the designation of torture porn.

During this period, there was a rise in graphic horror films in America as well. This led to the recognition of a so-called "Splat Pack" of directors who favored bloody, visceral horror. These directors included Eli Roth (*Cabin Fever*, 2002; *Hostel*, 2005; *The Green Inferno*, 2013), Greg McLean (*Wolf Creek*, 2005; *Rogue*, 2007), James Wan (*Saw*, 2004; *Dead Silence*, 2007; *Insidious*, 2010; *The Conjuring*, 2013), Rob Zombie (*House of 1000 Corpses*, 2003; *The Devil's Rejects*, 2005), and Darren Lynn Bousman (*Repo! The Genetic Opera*, 2008; *Mother's Day*, 2010; *11-11-11*, 2011).

Ducournau's first feature *Raw* (2016) bears some resemblance to Claire Denis' *Trouble Every Day* (2001). In it, a young woman discovers a taste for raw flesh and goes to more and more extreme lengths to get it. The cannibalism is shocking, but the director foregrounds the emotional and social aspects of the compulsion with restrained naturalism. Her second film, *Titane* (2021) is a much more flamboyant outing, concerning a serial killer who has sex with motor vehicles. For her efforts on this film, Ducournau was given the Palme d'Or at the Cannes Film Festival, its highest award.

Director and screenwriter Ari Aster struck a chord with his first two feature films, *Hereditary* (2018) and *Midsommar* (2019). Both are folk-horror movies, and both are deeply impressive. Both were also phenomenally successful.

Hereditary takes the nuclear family and explodes it from the inside. A secretive grandmother dies, and her family begins to fracture. Generational conflicts lead to tragedy and despair, and soon it seems that demonic conspiracies underlie everything. By grounding his narrative strongly in family drama for the first half of the film, the filmmaker captures

Agathe Rousselle as Alexia in Julia Ducournau's *Titane* (2021).

our attention to and identification with the characters, making their later transformations and fates all the more terrifying.

He uses the same strategy in *Midsommar*, beginning his story with the dilemma of and awkwardness around a dying relationship. The characters are well-delineated, once again luring the viewer (like the protagonists) into identification with them, heightening the nightmare part of the scenario. A story about an isolated group of Scandinavian pagans and their visitors, Aster's ingenious plotting raises the tension slowly but inexorably to a shattering climax. In his films, he finds a balance between floating complicated ideas and keeping the story moving forward, making him the most commercially successful of his contemporaries.

One new director has an impeccable horror pedigree. Osgood "Oz" Perkins is the oldest son of *Psycho* star Anthony Perkins. He has made a career of horror films, starting with *The Blackcoat's Daughter* in 2015, a dark tale of murder and madness completed using a fractured time scheme. *I Am the Pretty Thing That Lives in the House* (2016) is a ghost story that moves with slow and subtle surety to its melancholy conclusion. *Gretel & Hansel* (2020) is an imaginative and meditative take on the

Grimms' fairy tale, visually sumptuous and featuring a stunning performance by Alice Krige as the Witch.

The most prolific purveyor of horror currently is Mike Flanagan. The director is the most traditional in approach compared to his contemporaries, but his calling card is his ability to tackle so many different forms of horror. He started with *Absentia* (2011), an excellent low-budget horror debut about a haunted tunnel and missing persons; Flanagan has a gift for writing dialogue and the characters here bounce off each other in toxic ways, further manifesting the doom that awaits them all.

He followed that with the creepy *Oculus* (2013), about a haunted mirror and a traumatized pair that try to fight it, then hit the trifecta in 2016 when three films of his were released. *Hush* takes on the home-invasion movie, giving us a disabled heroine much as in films like *The Spiral Staircase* (1946), *Lady in*

Milly Shapiro (left) and Toni Collette in *Hereditary* (2018).

Poster for *Gretel & Hansel* (2020), directed by Oz Perkins, son of Anthony Perkins.

a Cage (1964), and *Wait Until Dark* (1967). The film features an excellent central performance from Kate Siegel, who co-wrote the script with Flanagan. *Before I Wake* (2016) moves more in the realm of dark fantasy; it is a story about what happens when dreams literally come true. *Ouija: Origin of Evil* (2016) is a prequel to a cursed-object horror film, and it's rated much more highly than the original.

Flanagan has spent his recent years dealing with the master, writer Stephen King. He directed the adaptation of King's *Gerald's Game* (2017), previously thought to be unfilmable; his *Doctor Sleep* (2019) is a King-approved sequel to *The Shining*. Of late, Flanagan has been engaged with creating horror content for streaming television, including an adaptation of Shirley Jackson's *The Haunting of Hill House* for Netflix.

The most interesting of all the newbies is Ti West. Beginning with *The Roost* in 2005, West has built a body of solid horror work. His *Trigger Man* (2007) is a hunter-becomes-the-hunted story. He is fond of the look of the horror films of the '70s and '80s, and he replicates it in *The House of the Devil* (2009), about satanic possession. West disowned his next outing, *Cabin Fever 2: Spring*

M3GAN (2023)
poster.

Best Post-Horror Films

Under the Skin (2013),
dir. Jonathan Glazer

A Girl Walks Home Alone at Night (2014),
dir. Ana Lily Amirpour

Goodnight Mommy (2014),
dir. Severin Fiala, Veronika Franz

The Invitation (2015),
dir. Karyn Kusama

Green Room (2015),
dir. Jeremy Saulnier

The Witch (2015),
dir. Robert Eggers

Personal Shopper (2016),
dir. Olivier Assayas

A Dark Song (2016),
dir. Liam Gavin

A Ghost Story (2017),
dir. David Lowery

It Comes at Night (2017),
dir. Trey Edward Shults

Fever (2009), but his *The Innkeepers* (2011) is a classic post-horror film, slowly paced and filled with ambiguous characters. His found-footage film, *The Sacrament* (2013), about a cult similar to Jim Jones' infamous Peoples Temple, followed.

West's most interesting work to date is his ongoing trilogy, the first two films of which have already been released as of the time of this writing. *X* (2022) goes back again to the 1970s, giving us an isolated farm and a heedless group of porn filmmakers who go there to make one of their movies. The conservative old couple who live there, Howard and Pearl, take exception to the group's licentiousness, and the slaughter begins. *Pearl* (2022), a prequel, gives us the villains' backstories, filmed in a jarringly wholesome manner, as though we were watching an MGM musical during a bad acid trip. (The third film in the series, *MaXXXine*, has yet to obtain a release date.)

Two film production companies have recently become synonymous with horror output. Blumhouse, formed in 2000, has given us such franchise-launching films as *Paranormal Activity* (2007), *Insidious* (2010), *Sinister* (2012), and *The Purge* (2013). A24 is another production company that began to lean heavily on horror content, beginning with films such as 2014's *Enemy* and *Under the Skin*. Since then, they've released horror fare as varied as *The Witch*, *Green Room*, *It Comes at Night*, and *Midsommar*.

That specific companies are looked to as a good bet for quality horror content is remindful of the similar status of other film studios in decades past—Universal in the 1930s, RKO in the 1940s, and Hammer Films in the 1950s. The stepping-up of horror output bodes well for the future of the genre. We may be at the beginning of another golden age.

And so it continues, big-budget and DIY, on film and digital, with or without cutting-edge effects. Horror is an irreplaceable genre in world culture. It's based in our biology, the fight-or-flight impulse. We seem to need it, for a variety of reasons. To artificially recreate the feeling of being reduced to predator or prey. To quench suppressed impulses. To articulate and defuse dread. To express awe and dismay in the face of the incomprehensible universe. To feel the giddy thrill of terror.

We still need darknesses to overcome, and monsters to defeat.

(from left) Owen Campbell, Brittany Snow, Mia Goth, Scott Mescudi (aka Kid Cudi), and Jenna Ortega in *X* (2022).

Glossary
Subgenres of Horror

The horror film genre can easily be subdivided into a stable and extensive system of subgenres. Some directors elect to specialize in a single subgenre; other, more versatile creators (like Hitchcock and del Toro) try their hand at many different subgenres.

Here is a glossary of the macabre to aid you on your journey.

▶ **ANTHOLOGY:** A number of smaller horror stories within a larger "frame" story.
Examples: *Dead of Night* (1945), *Dr. Terror's House of Horrors* (1965), *Creepshow* (1982)

▶ **B-MOVIE HORROR:** With lo-fi special effects, cheesy acting, and inane scripts, B-movie horrors are an acquired taste.
Examples: *It Conquered the World* (1956), *Plan 9 from Outer Space* (1957), *Chopping Mall* (1988)

▶ **BODY HORROR:** Deals with the alteration or bizarre evolution of the human body.
Examples: *Eraserhead* (1979), *Videodrome* (1983), *Tetsuo: The Iron Man* (1989)

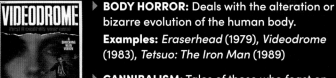

▶ **CANNIBALISM:** Tales of those who feast on forbidden flesh.
Examples: *Cannibal Girls* (1973), *Cannibal Holocaust* (1980), *Raw* (2016)

▶ **CLASSIC:** Horror films made during the Golden Age of Hollywood.
Examples: *Dracula* (1931), *Bride of Frankenstein* (1935), *The Wolf Man* (1941)

▶ **CREATURE FEATURES:** Monsters, both man-made and natural.
Examples: *King Kong* (1933), *Godzilla* (1954), *Alien* (1979)

▶ **DEMONIC POSSESSION:** The Devil is real, and he's coming after you.
Examples: *The Exorcist* (1973), *Insidious* (2013), *Hereditary* (2018)

▶ **EROTIC:** Horror with a healthy side of sex.
Examples: *Daughters of Darkness* (1971), *Crash* (1996), *Under the Skin* (2013)

▶ **FOLK HORROR:** Set primarily in rural areas, folk horror uses elements of folklore and myth to terrify.
Examples: *The Blood on Satan's Claw* (1971), *The Wicker Man* (1973), *The Witch* (2015)

▶ **FOUND FOOTAGE:** Resembling amateur video footage, it seeks to imitate the documentary style.
Examples: *The Blair Witch Project* (1999), *Paranormal Activity* (2007), *[Rec]* (2007)

▶ **GHOST STORY:** The dear departed interfere with the land of the living.
Examples: *The Haunting* (1963), *Poltergeist* (1982), *A Ghost Story* (2017)

▶ **GIALLO:** The word means yellow in Italian, and refers to the yellow-backed mystery and thriller novels of that country, many of which were adapted into films swarming with mysterious killers.
Examples: *Blood and Black Lace* (1964), *A Bay of Blood* (1971), *Deep Red* (1975)

▶ **GOTHIC:** Quasi-historical settings, isolated and oppressive, where battles with evil take place.
Examples: *The Innocents* (1961), *The Others* (2001), *Crimson Peak* (2015)

▶ **HAGSPLOITATION:** Known also as the "psycho-biddy" subgenre, it features older actresses in demented and criminal roles.
Examples: *What Ever Happened to Baby Jane?* (1962), *Hush . . . Hush, Sweet Charlotte* (1964), *What Ever Happened to Aunt Alice?* (1969)

HORROR COMEDY: A bundling together of laughs and gasps.
Examples: *Abbott and Costello Meet Frankenstein* (1948), *Ghostbusters* (1984), *Cabin in the Woods* (2011)

KAIJU: A Japanese word meaning "strange beast" is also the name for that country's giant monster movies.
Examples: *Godzilla* (1954), *Mothra* (1961), *Destroy All Monsters* (1968)

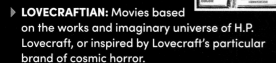

LOVECRAFTIAN: Movies based on the works and imaginary universe of H.P. Lovecraft, or inspired by Lovecraft's particular brand of cosmic horror.
Examples: *The Haunted Palace* (1963), *Re-Animator* (1985), *From Beyond* (1986)

MAD SCIENTISTS: Tampering with secrets which man was never meant to know.
Examples: *Dr. Jekyll and Mr. Hyde* (1931), *The Invisible Man* (1933), *Eyes Without a Face* (1960)

NATURAL HORROR: Flora and fauna turn against mankind.
Examples: *The Birds* (1963), *Genocide* (1968), *Willard* (1971)

PARANORMAL: Bumps in the night and otherworldly visitations.
Examples: *The Changeling* (1980), *Lady in White* (1988), *Personal Shopper* (2016)

POST-HORROR: Scary films that take on the rhythms and seriousness of mainstream adult dramas.
Examples: *The Witch* (2015), *Personal Shopper* (2016), *It Comes at Night* (2017)

PSYCHOLOGICAL HORROR: Dealing entirely with purely mental aspects of horror.
Examples: *Diabolique* (1955), *The Innocents* (1961), *Repulsion* (1965)

SCI-FI/HORROR: Scares meet science fiction.
Examples: *Scanners* (1981), *Aliens* (1986), *Event Horizon* (1997)

SERIAL KILLER: Murders that go on and on . . .
Examples: *Peeping Tom* (1960), *The Silence of the Lambs* (1991), *Se7en* (1995)

SLASHER: A killer with a knife or other implement stalks his victims.
Examples: *Halloween* (1979), *Scream* (1996), *You're Next* (2013)

SPLATSTICK: A mixture of extreme graphic horror and slapstick comedy.
Examples: *Evil Dead 2: Dead by Dawn* (1987), *Dead Alive* (1992), *Cemetery Man* (1994)

TEEN: The adults are clueless. It's up to the kids to set things straight.
Examples: *A Nightmare on Elm Street* (1984), *I Know What You Did Last Summer* (1997), *The Faculty* (1998)

TORTURE PORN/ SPLATTER/GORE: Movies with extremely graphic violence and gore.
Examples: *Blood Feast* (1963), *Bad Taste* (1987), *Saw* (2004)

VAMPIRE: Stories of legendary bloodsuckers.
Examples: *Nosferatu* (1922), *The Hunger* (1983), *The Lost Boys* (1987)

WEREWOLF: Transformational stories, but not in a good way.
Examples: *The Wolf Man* (1941), *The Howling* (1981), *An American Werewolf in London* (1981)

WITCHCRAFT: Dealing with practitioners of dark magic.
Examples: *The Seventh Victim* (1943), *Black Sunday* (1960), *The Witch* (2015)

ZOMBIE: The undead come after the living.
Examples: *Night of the Living Dead* (1968), *28 Days Later* (2002), *Shaun of the Dead* (2004)

Notes

CHAPTER ONE

1. Roy Kinnard, *Horror in Silent Films: A Filmography*, 1896–1929 (Jefferson, NC: McFarland & Company), 1999.
2. Jeffrey Vance, with Tony Maietta, *Douglas Fairbanks* (Berkeley: University of California Press, 2008), 169.

CHAPTER TWO

1. Michael F. Blake, *A Thousand Faces: Lon Chaney's Unique Artistry in Motion Pictures* (Vestal, NY: Vestal Press, 1990), 182.
2. Blake, *A Thousand Faces*, 150.
3. Blake, *A Thousand Faces*, 196.

CHAPTER THREE

1. "Boris Karloff Dies in London Hospital at 81," *Los Angeles Times*, February 4, 1969.

CHAPTER FOUR

1. "Curt Siodmak Dies at 98; Created Modern 'Wolf Man'," *New York Times*, November 19, 2000.
2. Gregory William Mank, *Hollywood Cauldron: Thirteen Horror Films from the Genre's Golden Age* (Jefferson, NC: McFarland & Company, 1994), 238–64, 324–50.

CHAPTER FIVE

1. Edmund G. Bansak, *Fearing the Dark: The Val Lewton Career* (Jefferson, NC: McFarland & Company, 1995), 128–29.
2. Dana Polan, "Cat People," *International Dictionary of Films and Filmmakers*, 4th edition, eds. Tom and Sara Pendergast (New York: St. James Press, 2000), 212–13.

CHAPTER SEVEN

1. Howard Maxford, *Hammer Complete: The Films, The Personnel, The Company* (Jefferson, NC: McFarland & Company, 2019), 274.

CHAPTER NINE

1. Victoria Price, Vincentprice.com, www.vincentprice.com/pages/about-vincent-price.
2. Internet Movie Database, imdb.com/name/nm0001637/quotes.

CHAPTER TEN

1. Lawrence McCallum, *Italian Horror Films of the 1960s: A Critical Catalog of 62 Chillers* (Jefferson, NC: McFarland & Company, 1998), 42.

CHAPTER ELEVEN

1. Internet Movie Database, imdb.com/name/nm0000472/quotes.

CHAPTER FOURTEEN

1. Salvador Murguía, ed., *The Encyclopedia of Japanese Horror Cinema* (Boulder, CO: Rowman & Littlefield, 2016).

CHAPTER SIXTEEN

1. John Wooley, *Wes Craven: The Man and His Nightmares* (Hoboken, NJ: John Wiley & Sons, 2011), 59.
2. Orrin Grey, "Cosmic Horror in John Carpenter's 'Apocalypse Trilogy,'" Stranger Horizons, October 24, 2011, strangehorizons.com/non-fiction/articles/cosmic-horror-in-john-carpenters-apocalypse-trilogy/.
3. Chris Rodley, ed., *Cronenberg on Cronenberg* (London: Faber and Faber, 1992), 59.

CHAPTER SEVENTEEN

1. https://en.wikipedia.org/wiki/List_of_horror_films_of_1987.
2. Peter Ackroyd, *London: The Biography* (New York: Doubleday, 2000), 268.
3. Daryl Jones, *Sleeping with the Lights On: The Unsettling History of Horror* (Oxford University Press, 2018), 113.

CHAPTER TWENTY

1. Glenn Kay, *Zombie Movies: The Ultimate Guide*, second edition (Chicago: Chicago Review Press, 2008), 113.

CHAPTER TWENTY-ONE

1. Mark Vieira, *Hollywood Horror: From Gothic to Cosmic* (New York: Harry N. Abrams, 2003), 19.
2. Brian Lloyd, "In Conversation with . . . John Landis," entertainment.ie., 2017.

CHAPTER TWENTY-THREE

1. *The Rules of the Game*, dir. Jean Renoir, 1939.
2. Will Durant, *The Age of Louis XIV* (New York: Simon and Schuster, 1963), 287.

Image Credits

GETTY: Cover yamonstro, Collection: iStock. **Page 8** Silver Screen Collection. **Page 9** Universal History Archive. **Page 9** Hulton Archive **Page 10** Universal Pictures/Moviepix. **Page 11** Catherine McGann/Archive Photos. **Page 13** Smith Collection/Gado/Archive Photos. **Page 14** Bettmann **Page 14** Universal Images Group. **Page 15** ullstein bild. **Page 15** Universal Images Group. **Page 16** Bettmann Collection **Page 18** Movie Poster Image Art/Moviepix. **Page 19** Buyenlarge/Archive Photos. **Page 19** Frederic Lewis/Archive Photos. **Page 20** Hulton Archive. **Page 22** Sunset Boulevard/Corbis Historical. **Page 23** Hulton Archive. **Page 24** Movie Poster Image Art/Moviepix. **Page 26** Bettmann. **Page 27** United Archives/Hulton Archive. **Page 30** FPG/Archive Photos. **Page 31** University of Southern California/Corbis Historical. **Page 32** Silver Screen Collection/ Moviepix. **Page 32** Movie Poster Image Ar/Moviepix. **Page 33** LMPC **Page 33** Transcendental Graphics/Archive Photos. **Page 34** Bettmann. **Page 34** Hulton Archive/Moviepix. **Page 35** Archive Photos/Moviepix. **Page 36** Archive Photos/Moviepix. **Page 37** Herbert Dorfman/Corbis Historical. **Page 38** Screen Archives/Moviepix. **Page 38** Henry Guttmann Collection,/Moviepix. **Page 39** John Springer Collection/Corbis Historical. **Page 40** Movie Poster Image Art/Moviepix. **Page 41** Bettmann. **Page 42** Archive Photos/Moviepix. **Page 43** LMPC. **Page 44** LMPC. **Page 45** Silver Screen Collection/Moviepix. **Page 46** George Rinhart/Corbis Historical. **Page 47** LMPC. **Page 48** Universal Pictures/Moviepix. **Page 49** LMPC. **Page 50** Hulton Archive. **Page 51** LMPC. **Page 52** Movie Poster Image Art/Moviepix. **Page 54** John Kobal Foundation/Moviepix. **Page 55** – LMPC. **Page 56** LMPC. **Page 56** LMPC, Collection. **Page 57** Ernest Bachrach/ Moviepix. **Page 58** LMPC. **Page 59** Movie Poster Image Art,/ Moviepix. **Page 60** Movie Poster Image Art/Moviepix. **Page 60** United Archives/Hulton Archive. **Page 61** Allied Artists/Moviepix. **Page 61** LMPC. **Page 62** (Before They Were Big sidebar) Archive Photos/Moviepix. **Page 63** LMPC. **Page 64** Bettmann. **Page 65** Silver Screen Collection/Moviepix. **Page 66** LMPC. **Page 67** PA Images. **Page 68** LMPC. **Page 69** Universal Pictures/ Moviepix. **Page 70** LMPC. **Page 71** Silver Screen Collection/Moviepix. **Page 72** Movie Poster Image Art/Moviepix. **Page 73** LMPC. **Page 73** LMPC. **Page 74** Hulton Archive/Archive Photos. **Page 75** Bettmann. **Page 76** Silver Screen Collection/Moviepix. **Page 78** Archive Photos/Moviepix. **Page 80** Buyenlarge/Archive Photos. **Page 80** LMPC. **Page 84** LMPC.**Page 87** LMPC. **Page 87** LMPC. **Page 88** LMPC. **Page 88** Archive Photos/Moviepix. **Page 89** LMPC. **Page 90** Mondadori Portfolio. **Page 91** LMPC. **Page 92** Movie Poster Image Art/Moviepix. **Page 93** Laura Cavanaugh, Collection/WireImage. **Page 94** Weegee (Arthur Fellig)/International Center of Photography. **Page 95** LMPC. **Page 96** Silver Screen Collection/Moviepix. **Page 96** Hulton Archive/Archive Photos. **Page 97** LMPC. **Page 98** Pictorial Parade/Moviepix. **Page 98** Herbert Dorfman/Corbis Historical. **Page 100** Movie Poster Image Art/Moviepix. **Page 100** Movie Poster Image Art/Moviepix. **Page 101** Movie Poster Image Art/Moviepix. **Page 101** Michael Ochs Archives/Moviepix. **Page 102** Movie Poster Image Art,/Moviepix. **Page 104** Michael Ochs Archives/Moviepix. **Page 105** LMPC. **Page 105** LMPC. **Page 106** LMPC. **Page 107** Silver Screen Collection/Moviepix. **Page 107** LMPC. **Page 108** LMPC. **Page 108** Archive Photos/ Moviepix. **Page 109** Archive Photos/Moviepix. **Page 110** Fine Art, Collection/Corbis Historical. **Page 112** LMPC. **Page 112** Michael Ochs Archives/Moviepix. **Page 118** LMPC. **Page 122** Movie Poster Image Art/Moviepix. **Page 123** Bettmann. **Page 124** Embassy Pictures/Moviepix. **Page 125** LMPC. **Page 125** Hulton Archive/Archive Photos. **Page 126** LMPC. **Page 128** LMPC. **Page 130** Movie Poster Image Art/Moviepix. **Page 131** Michael Ochs Archives/ Moviepix. **Page 132** J. Vespa, Collection/WireImage. **Page 132** LMPC. **Page 136** Evan Hurd Photography,/Sygma. **Page 137** LMPC. **Page 138** LMPC. **Page 139** Michael Ochs Archives / Stringer, Collection/Moviepix. **Page 140** Sunset Boulevard/Corbis Historical. **Page 141** ("Spotlight On" sidebar) Kevin Winter/Getty Images Entertainment. **Page 148** ("Spotlight On" sidebar) Xavier ROSSI/Gamma-Rapho. **Page 218** LMPC.

ALAMY: Pages 2-3 (title page) © BASARA PICTURES/Collection Christophel. **Page 5** Photo 12, Photographer/A7A Collection. **Pages 6-7** MARKA. **Page 8** Everett Collection. **Page 8** Compass International Pictures/ScreenProd /Photononstop **Page 8** Photo 12, Photographer/Archives du 7e Art collection. **Page 8** Universal Pictures/Album **Page 8** Photo 12, Photographer/A7A Collection. **Page 8** PictureLux/The Hollywood Archive. **Page 9** ICON FILM DISTRIBUTION/Maximum Film. **Page 9** TCD/Prod.DB. **Page 9** TOHO COMPANY/Ronald Grant Archive. **Page 9** CHEONGEORAM / Album. **Page 9** Moviestore Collection Ltd. **Page 9** Ralf Ramge. **Page 11** Retro AdArchives. **Page 12** Bill Waterson. **Page 20** (Most Valuable Monster sidebar) Production company: Hammer Films. Distributed by Warner-Pathé (UK) and Warner Bros. Pictures (US & Worldwide)/Atlaspix. **Page 23** JJs. **Page 24** © MGM Pictures/Collection Christophel. **Page 25** Historic Collection. **Page 28** Pictorial Press. **Page 29** © MGM/TCD/Prod.DB. **Page 29** Everett Collection. **Page 53** Everett Collection. **Page 62** (Before They Were Big sidebar) PARAMOUNT PICTURES/AJ Pics. **Page 68** Pictorial Press. **Page 74** FILMSONOR/ Album. **Page 77** © Anglo Amalgamated,/TCD/Prod.DB. **Page 79** Pictorial Press. **Page 81** Moviestore Collection. **Page 83** CINEMAN PRODUCTIONS/Cinematic Collection. **Page 85** Photo 12, Photographer/A7A Collection. **Page 86** © Galatea Film/Jolly Film/Collection Christophel. **Page 90** © Seda Spettacoli,/ TCD/Prod.DB. **Page 96** Everett Collection. **Page 103** © Amicus Productions/TCD/Prod.DB. **Page 104** © Tigon British Film Productions/TCD/Prod.DB. **Page 111** Ronald Grant Archive. **Page 113** TCD/Prod.DB. **Page 114** Everett Collection. **Page 115** SilverScreen. **Page 116** ALBATROS/Album. **Page 117** Mary Evans/STUDIOCANAL FILMS LTD **Page 117** CBW. **Page 119** Everett Collection. **Page 120** © Plata/TCD/Prod.DB. **Page 121** © Maxper Producciones/TCD/Prod.DB. **Page 129** ScreenProd/Photononstop. **Page 130** United Archives GmbH, Photographer: Impress. **Page 131** © Marianne Productions/TCD/Prod.DB. **Page 133** © Apolo/TCD/Prod.DB. **Page 134** Photo 12. **Page 135** LOBSTER ENTERPRISES/All Star Picture Library Ltd. **Page 137** ©New World Pictures/courtesy Everett Collection. **Page 139** Photo 12, Photographer: Archives du 7e Art. **Page 140** Pictorial Press. **Page 142** - Moviestore Collection. **Page 143** Film Plan Int./Album. **Page 144** PictureLux/The Hollywood Archive. **Page 144** BFA/New World Pictures. **Page 145** BFA/Dimension Films. **Page 146** Ronald Grant Archive. **Page 147** ©Columbia/ courtesy Everett Collection. **Page 149** Pictorial Press. **Page 150** HBO/20TH CENTURY FOX TELEVISION/AJ Pics. **Page 150** AIP/Maximum Film. **Page 151** Entertainment Pictures. **Page 152** POLYGRAM/Maximum Film. **Page 153** (From Scream Queens to Final Girls sidebar) LOBSTER ENTERPRISES/All Star Picture Library Ltd., Photographer: AA Film Archive. **Page 154** ©Paramount/courtesy Everett Collection. **Page 155** © New World Pictures/Courtesy: Everett Collection. **Page 156** CASTLE ROCK ENTERTAINMENT/Maximum Film. **Page 157** BFA/Warner Bros. **Page 158** WARNER BROS/Maximum Film. **Page 159** PictureLux/The Hollywood Archive. **Page 159** BFA/New Line Cinema. **Page 160** Photographer: Photo 12/7e Art/Asmik Ace Entertainment. **Page 161** ZUMA Press, Inc. **Page 161** TOHO COMPANY/All Star Picture Library Limited. **Page 162** 2018 TIFF/AFLO/Alamy Live News/Photographer: Nippon News. **Page 162** Moviestore Collection. **Page 163** RGR Collection. **Page 163** BFA / Toho. **Page 164** (Remakes and Reboots sidebar) Pictorial Press **Page 164** (Remakes and Reboots sidebar) Photo 12, Photographer: Photo12/7e Art/New Line Productions. **Page 165** Omega Project/AFDF/Album. **Page 165** Photo by Eric Vandeville/Abaca Press. **Page 166** ©Anchor Bay/courtesy Everett Collection. **Page 168** Contributor: RGR Collection. **Page 169** Production companies: Next Entertainment World and RedPeter Film. Distributed by Next Entertainment World/ Lifestyle Pictures. **Page 170** CBW. **Page 171** © Variety/TCD/Prod.DB. **Page 172** ©Republic Pictures/Courtesy Everett Collection. **Page 172** RGR Collection. **Page 173** NEW LINE/AJ Pics. **Page 173** CBW. **Page 174** PictureLux/The Hollywood Archive. **Page 174** UNIVERSAL PICTURES/AJ Pics. **Page 175** RGR Collection. **Page 175** RGR Collection. **Page 176** Pictorial Press. **Page 177** Everett Collection. **Page 178** RKO / Album. **Page 179** NEW LINE CINEMA/Allstar Picture Library Ltd, Photographer: AA Film Archive. **Page 179** PictureLux/The Hollywood Archive. **Page 180** Wingnut Films/Album. **Page 180** ANCHOR BAY/AJ Pics. **Page 181** Pictorial Press. **Page 181** PictureLux/The Hollywood Archive. **Page 182** Pictorial Press. **Page 182** Entertainment Pictures. **Page 183** Plan B Entertainment/Album. **Page 183** ©Filmax/Courtesy Everett Collection. **Page 183** DARKWOODS PRODUCTIONS/Album, Contributor: Album. **Page 184** Everett Collection. **Page 185** Entertainment Pictures. **Page 186** Ronald Grant Archive. **Page 187** PictureLux/The Hollywood Archive. **Page 188** World History Archive. **Page 188** Everett Collection. **Page 189** PictureLux/ The Hollywood Archive. **Page 190** Warner Bros. Pictures/Amblin E, Contributor: ScreenProd / Photononstop. **Page 190** Pictorial Press. **Page 191** © New World Pictures/courtesy Everett Collection. **Page 192** PARAMOUNT/AJ Pics. **Page 192** BFA/Lionsgate. **Page 193** UNISON FILMS/AJ Pics. **Page 194** Photo 12, Photographer: Archives du 7e Art. **Page 196** Pictorial Press. **Page 196** 20th Century Fox TV/Album. **Page 197** sjbooks. **Page 197** COLUMBIA PICTURES/Album. **Page 198** Ronald Grant Archive. **Page 198** Imprint Entertainment/Maverick Films/Summit Entertainment/Album. **Page 199** EL DESEO/Cinematic Collection. **Page 200** BFA / RADiUS-TWC. **Page 200** Photo 12. **Page 201** Production companies: Broad Green Pictures, FilmScience, distributed by A24/Atlaspix. **Page 202** AFF, Photographer: Janet Gough. **Page 203** PA Images, Photographer: Ian West. **Page 203** BFA/Universal Pictures. **Page 204** © Buena Vista/ courtesy Everett Collection. **Page 204** PictureLux/The Hollywood Archive, Photographer: PictureLux. **Page 205** WEGA FILM/Maximum Film. **Page 205** Moviestore Collection Ltd. **Page 206** WARNER BROS./AJ Pics. **Page 207** (Horror at the Oscars sidebar) Photo by Barry King/Alamy Stock Photo. **Page 207** (Horror at the Oscars sidebar) RGR Collection. **Page 208** Space Rocket Nation/Vendian Entertainment/Bold Films. **Page 208** Blumhouse Productions/Dark Universe/Universal Pictures/Album. **Page 209** Moviestore Collection Ltd. **Page 210** BFA /A24. **Page 211** CG CINEMA /Album. **Page 212** ARTIFICIAL EYE /Cinematic Collection. **Page 212** Pictorial Press Ltd. **Page 213** BFA / A24. **Page 213** UNIVERSAL PICTURES INTERNATIONAL/AJ Pics. **Page 214** BFA /Carole Bethuel/Diaphana Distribution. **Page 214** dpa picture alliance. **Page 215** BFA /United Artists Releasing. **Page 215** A24/Lifestyle Pictures. **Page 216** © Magnet Releasing, Contributor: Everett Collection, Inc. **Page 216** © Universal Pictures/Entertainment Pictures. **Page 217** Bron Studios/Album. **Page 218** Moviestore Collection Ltd. **Page 218** 20TH CENTURY FOX/Allstar Picture Library Ltd, Photographer: AA Film Archive. **Page 218** UNIVERSAL/AJ Pics. **Page 219** United Archives GmbH, Photographer: IFA Film **Page 219** Everett Collection. **Page 219** Pictorial Press Ltd. **Page 219** Everett Collection, Inc. **Page 232** ScreenProd/Photononstop.

Bibliography

Ackroyd, Peter. *London: The Biography* (New York: Doubleday, 2000).

Andersen, Hans Christian. *The Complete Fairy Tales and Stories*. Trans. Erik Christian Haugaard (New York: Anchor, 1974).

Anderson, Robert G. *Faces, Forms, Films: The Artistry of Lon Chaney* (New York: Castle Books, 1971).

Bansak, Edmund G. *Fearing the Dark: The Val Lewton Career* (Jefferson, NC: McFarland & Company, 1995).

Baudelaire, Charles. *Letters to His Mother*. Trans. Arthur Symons (New York: Haskell House Publishers, 1971).

Beard, William. *The Artist as Monster: The Cinema of David Cronenberg* (Toronto: University of Toronto Press, 2001).

Blake, Michael F. *Lon Chaney: The Man Behind the Thousand Faces* (Vestal, NY: Vestal Press, 1990).

Brunas, John, Michael Brunas, and Tom Weaver. *Universal Horrors: The Studio's Classic Films, 1931–1946* (Jefferson, NC: McFarland & Company, 1990).

Cherry, Brigid. *Horror* (New York: Routledge, 2009).

Church, David. *Post-Horror: Art, Genre, and Cultural Elevation* (Edinburgh: Edinburgh University Press, 2021).

Clarens, Carlos. *An Illustrated History of Horror and Science-Fiction Films* (New York: Da Capo Press, 1997).

Clark, Mark. *Smirk, Sneer, and Scream: Great Acting in Horror Cinema* (Jefferson, NC: McFarland & Company, 2011).

Conrich, Ian, and David Woods, eds. *The Cinema of John Carpenter: The Technique of Terror* (London: Wallflower Publishing, 2004).

Dante. *The Inferno*. Trans. John Ciardi (New York: Mentor, 1954).

Del Vecchio, Deborah, and Tom Johnson. *Hammer Films: An Exhaustive Filmography* (Jefferson, NC: McFarland & Company, 1996).

Derry, Charles. *Dark Dreams 2.0: A Psychological History of the Modern Horror Film from the 1950s to the 21st Century* (Jefferson, NC: McFarland & Company, 2009).

Dixon, Wheeler Winston. *A History of Horror* (Brunswick, NJ: Rutgers University Press, 2010).

Durant, Will. *The Age of Louis XIV* (New York: Simon and Schuster, 1963).

Eisner, Lotte H. *The Haunted Screen: Expressionism in the German Cinema and the Influence of Max Reinhardt* (Berkeley: University of California Press. 1973).

Enright, D. J., ed. *The Oxford Book of Death* (Oxford: Oxford University Press., 1983).

Euripides, *Medea*. Trans. Alistair Elliot (London: Oberon Books, 1993).

Everman, Welch. *Cult Horror Films* (New York: Citadel Press, 1993).

Goethe, Johann Wolfgang von. *Faust*. Trans. Walter Kaufmann (New York: Anchor Books, 1962).

Grant, Keith, ed. *Robin Wood on the Horror Film: Collected Essays and Reviews* (Detroit: Wayne State University Press, 2018).

Greene, Doyle. *Mexploitation Cinema* (Jefferson, NC: McFarland & Company, 2005).

Grimm, Jacob, and Wilhelm Grimm. *Grimm's Tales for Young and Old: The Complete Stories*. Trans. Ralph Mannheim (New York: Anchor, 1983).

Hallenbeck, Bruce G. *Comedy Horror Films: A Chronological History, 1914–2008* (Jefferson, NC: McFarland & Company, 2009).

Heffernan, Kevin. *Ghouls, Gimmicks, and Gold: Horror Films and the American Movie Business, 1953–1968* (Durham, NC: Duke University Press, 2004).

Herzogenrath, Bernd, ed. *The Films of Tod Browning* (London: Black Dog Publishing, 2006).

Humphries, Reynold. *The Hollywood Horror Film, 1931–1941: Madness in a Social Landscape* (Lanham, MD: Scarecrow Press, 2006).

Hutchings, Peter. *Hammer and Beyond: The British Horror Film* (Manchester: Manchester University Press, 1993).

Hutchings, Peter. *Historical Dictionary of Horror Cinema* (Lanham, MD: Scarecrow Press, 2008).

Jancovich, Mark. *Rational Fears: American Horror in the 1950s* (New York: St. Martin's Press, 1996).

Jensen, Paul M. *The Men Who Made the Monsters* (New York: Twayne, 1996).

Jones, Alan. *The Rough Guide to Horror Movies* (London: Rough Guide Reference, 2005).

Jones, Darryl. *Sleeping with the Lights On: The Unsettling History of Horror* (Oxford: Oxford University Press, 2018).

Kawin, Bruce F. *Horror and the Horror Film* (London: Anthem Press, 2012).

Kay, Glenn. *Zombie Movies: The Ultimate Guide*, second edition (Chicago: Chicago Review Press, 2008).

King, Stephen. *Danse Macabre* (New York: Everest House, 1981).

Kinnard, Roy. *Horror in Silent Films: A Filmography, 1896–1929* (Jefferson, NC: McFarland & Company, 1995).

Landis, John. *Monsters in the Movies: 100 Years of Cinematic Nightmares* (New York: DK, 2011).

Laws, Reverend Peter. *The Frighteners: A Journey Through Our Cultural Fascination with the Macabre* (New York: Skyhorse Publishing, 2018).

Lazaro-Reboll, Antonio. *Spanish Horror Film* (Edinburgh: Edinburgh University Press, 2012).

Maddrey, Joseph. *Nightmares in Red, White and Blue: The Evolution of the American Horror Film* (Jefferson, NC: McFarland & Company, 2004).

Magistrale, Tony. *Abject Terrors: Surveying the Modern and Postmodern Horror Film* (New York: Peter Lang, 2005).

Mank, Gregory William. *Hollywood Cauldron: Thirteen Horror Films from the Genre's Golden Age* (Jefferson, NC: McFarland & Company, 1994).

Marriott, James. *Horror Films* (London: Virgin Books, 2004).

Marriott, James, and Kim Newman. *Horror! 333 Films to Scare You to Death* (London: Carlton Books, 2010).

Martin, Daniel, and Alison Peirse, eds. *Korean Horror Cinema* (Edinburgh: Edinburgh University Press, 2013).

Matthews, Melvin E., Jr. *Fear Itself: Horror on Screen and in Reality During the Depression and World War II* (Jefferson, NC: McFarland & Company, 2009).

Maxford, Howard. *Hammer Complete: The Films, The Personnel, The Company* (Jefferson, NC: McFarland & Company, 2019).

McCallum, Lawrence. *Italian Horror Films of the 1960s: A Critical Catalog of 62 Chillers* (Jefferson, NC: McFarland & Company, 1998).

McRoy, Jay, ed. *Japanese Horror Cinema* (Edinburgh: Edinburgh University Press, 2005).

Meikle, Denis. *A History of Horrors: The Rise and Fall of the House of Hammer*, revised edition (Lanham, MD: Scarecrow Press, 2009).

Miller, Cynthia J., and Bowdoin A. Van Riper, eds. T*he Laughing Dead: The Horror-Comedy Film from Bride of Frankenstein to Zombieland* (Lanham, MD: Rowman & Littlefield, 2016).

Miller, Jeffrey S. *The Horror Spoofs of Abbott and Costello: A Critical Assessment of the Comedy Team's Monster Films* (Jefferson, NC: McFarland & Company, 2000).

Muir, John Kenneth. *Eaten Alive at a Chainsaw Massacre: The Films of Tobe Hooper* (Jefferson, NC: McFarland & Company, 2002).

Muir, John Kenneth. *The Films of John Carpenter* (Jefferson, NC: McFarland & Company, 2000).

Muir, John Kenneth. *The Unseen Force: The Films of Sam Raimi* (New York: Applause Theatre & Cinema Books, 2004).

Muir, John Kenneth. *Wes Craven: The Art of Horror* (Jefferson, NC: McFarland & Company, 1998).

Murguía, Salvador, ed. *The Encyclopedia of Japanese Horror Films* (Boulder, CO: Rowman & Littlefield, 2016).

Nemerov, Alexander. *Icons of Grief: Val Lewton's Home Front Pictures* (Berkeley: University of California Press, 2005).

Newman, Kim, ed. *The BFI Companion to Horror* (London: Cassell, 1997).

Nollen, Scott Allen. *Boris Karloff: A Critical Account of his Screen, Stage, Radio, Television, and Recording Work* (Jefferson, NC: McFarland & Company, 1991).

Paszylk, Bartlomiej. *The Pleasure and Pain of Cult Horror Films* (Jefferson, NC: McFarland & Company, 2009).

Paul, William. *Laughing Screaming: Modern Hollywood Horror & Comedy* (New York: Columbia University Press, 1994).

Phillips, Kendall R. *Dark Directions: Romero, Craven, Carpenter, and the Modern Horror Film* (Carbondale, IL: Southern Illinois University Press, 2012).

Pirie, David. *A New Heritage of Horror: The English Gothic Cinema* (London: I. B. Tauris & Co., 2008).

Pitts, Michael R. *Horror Film Stars* (Jefferson, NC: McFarland & Company, 1981).

Poe, Edgar Allan. *Tales of Edgar Allan Poe.* Ed. Hervey Allen (New York: Random House, 1944).

Price, Michael H., and George E. Turner. *Forgotten Horrors: Early Talkie Chillers from Poverty Row* (Hartford, CT: A. S. Barnes and Company, 1979).

Raw, Laurence. *Character Actors in Horror and Science Fiction Films, 1930–1960* (Jefferson, NC: McFarland & Company, 2012).

Rodley, Chris, ed. *Cronenberg on Cronenberg* (London: Faber and Faber, 1992).

Savada, Elias, and David J. Skal. *Dark Carnival: The Secret World of Tod Browning* (New York: Anchor Books, 1995).

Schlegel, Nicholas G. *Sex, Sadism, Spain, and Cinema* (Lanham, MD: Rowman & Littlefield, 2015).

Schneider, Steven Jay, ed. *100 European Horror Films* (London: British Film Institute, 2007).

Senn, Bryan. *Golden Horrors: An Illustrated Critical Filmography, 1931–1939* (Jefferson, NC: McFarland & Company, 1996).

Shelley, Mary. *Frankenstein: or, The Modern Prometheus* (New York: Signet Classic, 2000).

Shipka, Danny. *Perverse Titillation: The Exploitation Cinema of Italy, Spain, and France, 1960–1980* (Jefferson, NC: McFarland & Company, 2011).

Siegel, Joel E. *Val Lewton: The Reality of Terror* (New York: Viking Press. 1973).

Skal, David J. *The Monster Show: A Cultural History of Horror* (New York: Faber & Faber, 2001).

Skal, David J. *Screams of Reason: Mad Science and Modern Culture* (New York: W. W. Norton & Company, 1998).

Smith, Don G. *Lon Chaney, Jr.: Horror Film Star, 1906–1973* (Jefferson, NC: McFarland & Company, 1996).

Stoker, Bram. *Dracula* (London: Titan Books, 2014).

Telotte, J. C. *Dreams of Darkness: Fantasy and the Films of Val Lewton* (Chicago: University of Illinois Press, 1985).

Vance, Jeffrey, with Tony Maietta. *Douglas Fairbanks* (Berkeley: University of California Press, 2008).

Vieira, Mark. *Hollywood Horror: From Gothic to Cosmic* (New York: Harry N. Abrams, 2003).

Weaver, Tom. *Poverty Row Horrors! Monogram, PRC and Republic Horror Films of the Forties* (Jefferson, NC: McFarland & Company, 1993).

Wells, Paul. *The Horror Genre: From Beelzebub to Blair Witch* (London: Wallflower Publishing, 2000).

Wooley, John. *Wes Craven: The Man and His Nightmares* (Hoboken, NJ: John Wiley & Sons, 2011).

Worland, Rick. *The Horror Film: An Introduction* (Malden, MA: Blackwell Publishing, 2007).

Index

Page numbers in **bold** indicate illustrations

180, 191, 193
The Red Shoes (1948), 76
Red Dead Redemption: Undead Nightmares video game (2010), 181
Reefer Madness (1936), 149
The Reflecting Skin (1990), 158
The Reincarnation of Peter Proud (1975), 168
Repo! The Genetic Opera (2008), 214
Reptilicus (1961), 63
Repulsion (1965), **128**, 129, **129**
Requiem for a Dream (2000), 204
Resident Evil video game (1996), 181
Resident Evil (2002), 181, **181**, 197, 198
The Resurrected (1991), 156
Resurrection (1999), 154
The Resuscitated Monster (1953), 112
The Return of Chandu (1934), 33
The Return of the Living Dead (1985), 151, 153, 156, 179
Return of the Zombies (1973), 178
Revenge of the Creature (1955), 62, 63
Revolt of the Zombies (1936), 31, 177
Rhinestone (1984), 137
Rigor Mortis (2013), 190
The Ring (2002), 164, 167, 195
Ringu (1998), 151, **160**, 163, **163**, 164, 165
Rip van Winkle (1903), 13
The Rocky Horror Picture Show (1975), 149, 189
Rogue (2007), 214
The Rogues' Tavern (1936), 186
The Roost (2005), 216
Rosemary's Baby (1968), 77, 94, 98, 129, 130, **130**, 207
R-Point (2004), 167

S
The Sacrament (2013), 217
Sadako vs. Kayako (2016), 167
The Sadistic Baron Von Klaus (1962), 116–117, **116**
Salem's Lot miniseries (1979), 144, 153
Santa Sangre (1989), 172, **172**
Santa's Slay (2005), 138
Santo contra los mujeres vampiros (1962), 113
Santo vs. the Zombies (1962), 177, **177**
Satyricon (1969), 149
Saw series (2004–2017), 149, 174–175, **174**, 198, 214
Scanners (1981), **134**, 143, **143**, 152
Scared Stiff (1953), 186
The Scarlet Claw (1944), 50
Scary Movie series (2000–2013), 193
Schlock (1973), 187
Science Fiction Theatre television series (1955–1957), 95
The Sorcerers (1967), 106
Scream series (1996, 1997, 2011), 138,

145, **145**, 152, 158, 159, 178
Scream and Scream Again (1970), 106, **107**
Se7en (1995), 152, 159, **159**
Seconds (1966), 98
Seoul Station (2016), 168
The Serpent and the Rainbow (1988), 145, 180
Seven Days in May (1964), 98
The Seventh Victim (1943), 48, 53, 55–56, **56**, 130
Sex Maniac (1934), 29
Shake, Rattle, and Roll series (1984–present), 169
The Shape of Water (2017), 201, 203, **203**, 206, 207
Shaun of the Dead (2004), 152, 167, 182, **182**
The Shawshank Redemption (1994), 196
She Dies Tomorrow (2020), 211
The She-Wolf (1965), 112
The Shining (1980), 155, 158, 159
Shivers (1975), 143
Shock Theater, 95–96
Short Night of the Glass Dolls (1971), 89
The Shout (1978), 157
Sh! The Octopus (1937), 187
Shutter (2004), 169
Sigaw (2004), 169
The Sign of Death (1939), 112
The Silence of the Lambs (1991), 158, 159, **159**, 207, **207**, 211
Silent Hill (2006), 197
Silent Night, Bloody Night (1972), 138, 154
Silent Night, Evil Night (1974), 137–138, **137**
Sinister (2012), 217
The Sixth Sense (1999), 204, **204**
The Skin I Live In (2011), 199, **199**
Sleepy Hollow (1999), 152, 178, 207
The Slumber Party Massacre (1982), 191, **191**
The Snake King's Child (2001), 169
Society (1989), 151, 152, 155, 195
Song at Midnight (1937), 127
Son of Dracula (1943), 44, 46
Son of Frankenstein (1939), 33, 37, **40**, 41–43, **41**
Son of Kong (1933), 41
Sorority Babes in the Slimeball Bowl-O-Rama (1988), 151–152
The Sound of Music (1964), 57
Species (1995), 62
The Spiders (1919–1920), 18
The Spiral Staircase (1946), 50, 215
Spirits of the Dead (1968), 88
Splice (2011), 199
Split (2016), 204, **204**

Star Wars (1977), 135, 147
Stories to Keep You Awake television series, 118
Strange Circus (2005), 166
Strange Confession (1945), 46
The Strangers (2008), 199
Stranger Things television series (2016–present), 197
The Student of Prague (1913, 1926), 14, 15, 19
Student Bodies (1981), 150
The Stuff (1985), 62, 136, 137
Sugar Hill (1974), 97
Suicide Club (2001), 166
Sukob (2006), 169
Supernatural (1933), 31
Supernatural television series (2005–2020), 196
Survival of the Dead (2009), 182
Suspiria (1977, 2018), 89, **90**, 91, **91**, 145, 164, **164**
Svengali (1927), 15
Swallow (2019), 212
Sweeney Todd: The Demon Barber of Fleet Street (2007), 152, 207
Sweet Home (1989), 162
Le systeme du docteur Goudron et du professeur Plume (1913), 14

T
Tag (2015), 200
A Tale of Two Sisters (2003), 167
Tales from the Crypt (1972), 138, 191
Tales from the Crypt comic book, 96
Tales from the Crypt television series (1989–1996), 150, **150**, 192
Tales from the Darkside television series (1983–1988), 150
Tales from the Hood (1995), 155
Tales of Terror (1962), 63, 82, 148
Tales of the Unexpected television series (1979–1988), 150
Tarantula (1955), 62, 63
Target Earth (1954), 61
Targets (1968), 100
Taste the Blood of Dracula (1970), **20**, 70
Teenagers from Outer Space (1959), 61
Teeth (2007), 193
The Tenant (1976), 129, 130, 131, **131**
Tenebrae (1982), 89
Teorema (1968), 104
Terror Is a Man (1959), 132
Terror Train, 141
Tetsuo: The Iron Man (1989), 161–162, **162**
The Texas Chain Saw Massacre (1974), 100–101, **100**, 133, 135, 136, 145, 150, 153, 164
The Texas Chain Saw Massacre (2003), 164

About the
Author

Brad Weismann is an award-winning writer and editor. His work has appeared in such publications as *Senses of Cinema, Film International, Backstage, Muso, Parterre, 5280,* and *Boulder Magazine*. His first book, *Lost in the Dark: A World History of Horror Film*, was recently published by the University Press of Mississippi. He contributed to the critical collection *100 Years of Soviet Cinema*, and he was chosen by the Library of Congress to contribute explanatory essays to its National Recording Registry.

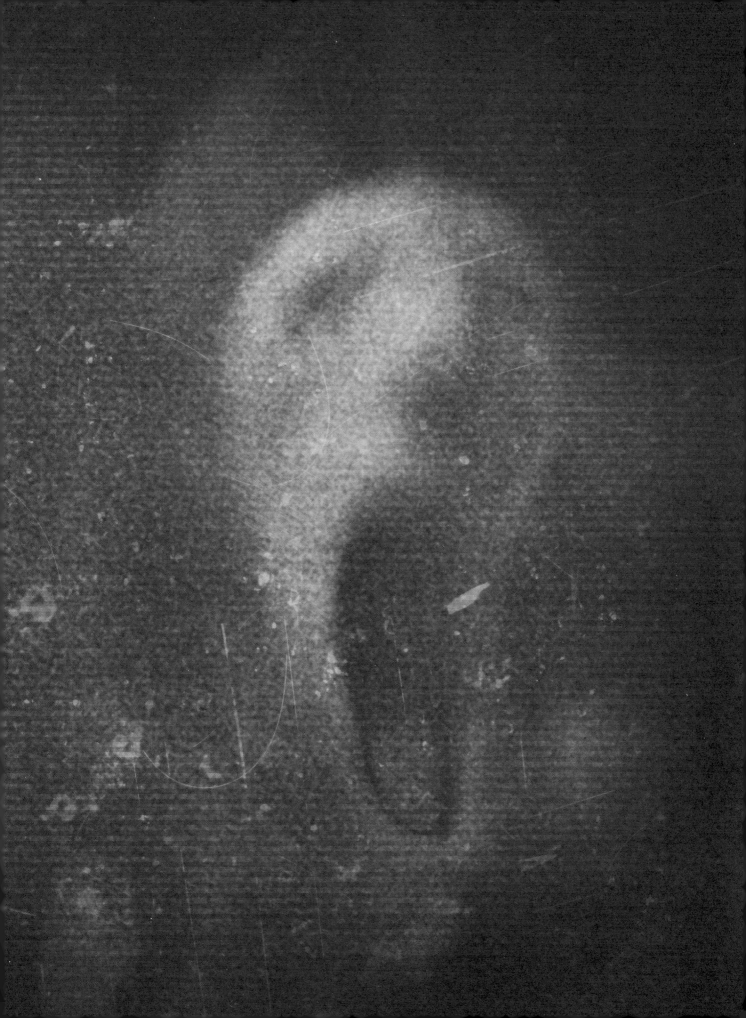